BANNOCKBURN
HIGH SCHOOL
MODERN STUDIES

# Politics in a Democratic Society

*by Alan MacDermid, Jim McGregor, Harry Blee, Graham Dalglish, Sandy McCann and John McGuire*

imprint
publishing systems

Imprint Publishing Systems,
Glasgow G62 6DJ.

Published by Imprint Publishing 1998

Copyright © Imprint Publishing Systems 1998

Written by Alan MacDermid, Jim McGregor, Harry Blee, Graham Dalglish,
Sandy McCann and John McGuire.

ISBN 1 872 035 54 X

Editors Harry Blee, Graham Dalglish and Jim McGregor.
Designed by Kenneth Maskrey.

Printed by J. S. Burns & Sons, Glasgow.

# Contents

## The Electoral System, Voting and Political Attitudes

*Study Topic 1:* What are the main factors
which influence voters? .................................................................. 5
*Study Topic 2:* Electoral systems –
what effects do they have upon the distribution of power? .......... 29
*Study Topic 3:* How does the media shape political attitudes? .... 42

## Political Parties and their Policies

*Study Topic 1:* What function do political
parties play in a democracy? ........................................................ 61
*Study Topic 2:* In what ways do the ideologies
of the main parties differ? ............................................................ 73
*Study Topic 3:* How is party policy framed? .............................. 79
*Study Topic 4:* What are the policies of the
main political parties? .................................................................. 83
*Study Topic 5:* Have the major parties
changed in recent years? .............................................................. 88
*Study Topic 6:* To what extent have the Liberal Democrats
and SNP challenged the major parties in recent years? .............. 102

## Decision Making in Central Government

*Study Topic 1:* To what extent can pressure groups
and public opinion influence decision making? .......................... 107
*Study Topic 2:* How effective is Parliament? ............................ 120
*Study Topic 3:* What is the executive and
how does it function? .................................................................. 137

## Central and Local Government in Scotland

*Study Topic 1:* What is the place of Scotland
within the United Kingdom? ...................................................... 155
*Study Topic 2:* How is Scotland governed at present? .............. 160
*Study Topic 3:* Why was there a demand for change? .............. 165
*Study Topic 4:* How is Scottish local government organised? .... 175

# Acknowledgement

Contributions by Alan Grieve and Michèle Etherson Scott.

# The Electoral System, Voting and Political Attitudes

STUDY TOPIC 1

## What are the main factors which influence voters?

### Introduction

Voters make their final choice of candidate and political party in the privacy of a polling booth. To ensure that elections are fair and to protect against corrupt or illegal electoral practices, it is a secret ballot and voters are not required to disclose how they voted nor to give the reasons for their decision.

Indeed, available evidence from exit polls conducted during the 1992 General Election campaign suggests that some voters may choose to mislead those who make enquiries as to how they have cast their vote. Despite the fact that exit polls involve voters being questioned as they leave the polling station, they still significantly underestimated the Conservative vote in 1992.

Furthermore, the decision to vote for a particular party is often based on a number of considerations and, even when voters are willing to cooperate fully, they may find it difficult to provide a detailed explanation of the various factors which led to their decision.

Accordingly, it should be stated that voting behaviour is a complex issue.

Nevertheless, exhaustive research undertaken by psephologists (those who make a statistical study of elections and electoral choice) has made it possible to identify a range of factors which influence voters to a greater or lesser extent.

In order to make sense of the factors which affect voting behaviour, it is important to distinguish between long-term and short-term influences. Long-term influences are those which operate over a considerable period of time. Although gradual change does take place, such factors tend to stabilise voting behaviour by ensuring that each political party can count on a 'hard vote' which is made up of voters who identify strongly with the party of their choice. In contrast, short-term influences add to electoral volatility by encouraging voters to transfer their support from one party to another.

# Long-Term Influences

The experiences of individuals living in Britain vary according to social factors. These factors help to develop a sense of identity which influences voting behaviour. There are many social factors which are considered to affect electoral choice. These include age, ethnicity, family, gender, religion and region. However, a substantial number of studies of voting behaviour focus on social class as the most important influence.

## Social Class

Social class can be defined in a number of ways. The elements which can be included within a working definition encompass occupation, education, income, wealth and patterns of consumption. However, the most widely recognised definitions are those of the Registrar General and the IPA (Institute of Practitioners in Advertising) which are represented in the diagram below.

**DIAGRAM 1**

| Definition of Registrar General / IPA Definition | |
| --- | --- |
| Class | Example |
| **I or A**<br>Higher managerial, administrative or professional | accountant, bank manager, dentist, doctor, solicitor |
| **II or B**<br>Lower managerial, administrative or professional | farmer, librarian, sales manager, teacher |
| **III or C1 (Non-Manual)**<br>Clerical and minor supervisory | clerk, police officer, shop assistant |
| **III or C2 (Skilled Manual)**<br>Clerical and minor supervisory | electrician, mechanic, plumber |
| **IV or D**<br>Semi-skilled manual | assembly line worker, builder, lorry driver, postal worker |
| **V or E**<br>Unskilled | cleaner, labourer |

# Political Socialisation

Social class is believed to influence voting behaviour through the effects of political socialisation. It is argued that the majority of people retain party preferences and voting habits which are formed when they first become politically aware. According to Butler and Stokes (1974), family background plays an important part in the formation of political attitudes. They found that there was a strong link between the political views of parents and those adopted by their children. On the basis of surveys that were conducted during the 1960s, Butler and Stokes established that more than 75% of voters interviewed had voted or intended to vote the same way as their parents.

However, family background is not the only influence at work. A further factor affecting voting behaviour is the locality or neighbourhood effect. Working class neighbourhoods are predominantly Labour and condition those who live within them to become Labour voters. Middle class districts have, in contrast, a number of characteristics which tend to develop support for the Conservative Party.

As one observer put it:

*"if almost everyone whom a voter meets at work, in shops, in pubs and clubs, at church or on the housing estate appears to support the same party then there is strong pressure on the individual to support that party too." (Denver, 1993, Page 66).*

Throughout the 1950s, approximately two thirds of the working class voted Labour and four fifths of the middle class voted Conservative. It was this which led Peter Pulzer (1967) to comment, *"class is the basis of British party politics; all else is embellishment and detail."*

During the post-war period 1945-70, the great majority of voters considered themselves to be either working or middle class with the result that both of the major parties could depend on a 'hard vote' which would remain loyal regardless of party performance. This strong party allegiance was based on the fact that such voters identified with their party in terms of social class. The extent of this social class identification is shown in Diagram 2 below.

However, despite the fact that social class was the dominant factor in any explanation of voting behaviour through to the 1970s, not all voters voted for their class party.

The existence of working class Conservatives and middle class radicals has been a long standing feature of British politics. Indeed, due to the fact that working class voters in the C2–E range predominate, it would not be possible for the Conservative Party to be elected if it failed to gain a significant percentage of the working class vote.

DIAGRAM 2

## Class Percentages Voting Conservative and Labour 1945-58

|  |  | AB | C1 | C2 | DE |
|---|---|---|---|---|---|
|  | Conservative | 85 | 70 | 35 | 30 |
|  | Labour | 10 | 25 | 60 | 65 |

# Working Class Conservatives

At general elections since the Second World War, the Conservative Party has normally managed to attract more than one third of the total working class vote. The main explanations for working class Conservative support are as follows:

## ■ Social and Political Deference

The belief that, by virtue of their 'superior' social and educational background, Conservative politicians deliver more competent government.

## ■ Social Advancement

Some working class voters may associate support for the Conservative Party with improved social status. If they view themselves as, or aspire to be, middle class they are more likely to vote Conservative.

## ■ Policies

Opinion surveys have shown that a significant proportion of working class voters are attracted by policies which are perceived to represent strong responses to important issues such as law and order and defence. It is argued that Conservative Party policies have held more appeal in this regard than those of the other parties.

## ■ Value Systems

A number of commentators believe that a middle class view of society is promoted by the media and other important British institutions. It is argued that this influences some members of the working class to vote Conservative.

## ■ Improving Living Standards

According to this view, improving living standards have led to a significant advancement in the lifestyle of skilled workers. It is claimed that this makes them more prepared to adopt middle class values including Conservative Party support.

## ■ Neighbourhood or Locality Effect

As has already been noted, many observers take the view that political socialisation leads people to adopt the dominant values existent in their locality and it has been established that working class people living in middle class areas are more likely to vote Conservative than those who remain in working class neighbourhoods.

However, another possible interpretation of this finding is that such people strive to reside in those areas because they already aspire to be middle class.

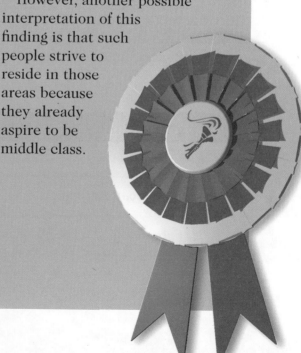

DIAGRAM 3

## 1992 General Election

**Class Percentages Voting Conservative, Labour and Liberal Democrat**

|  |  | AB | C1 | C2 | DE |
|---|---|---|---|---|---|
| | Conservative | 56 | 52 | 38 | 30 |
| | Labour | 20 | 25 | 41 | 50 |
| Liberal Democrats | Liberal Democrat | 22 | 19 | 17 | 15 |

## 1997 General Election

**Class Percentages Voting Conservative, Labour and Liberal Democrat**

|  |  | AB | C1 | C2 | DE |
|---|---|---|---|---|---|
| | Conservative | 42 | 26 | 25 | 21 |
| | Labour | 31 | 47 | 54 | 61 |
| Liberal Democrats | Liberal Democrat | 21 | 19 | 14 | 13 |

*Source: BBC/NOP exit poll*

# Middle Class Radicals

It can be noted from Diagram 3 that Labour is able to attract a significant proportion of middle class support. The 1992 General Election was fairly typical in that 20 per cent of middle class voters, as represented by the AB occupational classification, chose to vote Labour. In 1997, the surge to Labour was such that fully 31 per cent of the AB group offered their support.

A number of explanations have been advanced to account for the phenomenon of the middle class Labour vote:

## ■ Public Sector Employees

The public sector contains a large number of middle class employees including teachers, health service workers and social workers. Such employees are often attracted to Labour Party policies on social welfare spending.

The strong Conservative Party commitment to reduce public sector spending has proved unpopular with this substantial section of the middle class and may help to explain why middle class Labour support has held up well despite the fact that the Labour Party has suffered significant reverses at recent general elections.

## ■ Intellectual Influences

It is claimed that certain middle class voters, as a result of educational influences and relative economic security, take a less self-interested view of politics with the result that socialist policies are more attractive to them.

## ■ Residual Class Loyalty

Due to increasing opportunities for social mobility developed since the Second World War, a significant proportion of the middle class vote is comprised of first generation professionals. Some of this group will choose to retain the values developed by their working class backgrounds.

## ■ Policy Realignment

Some commentators have claimed that since the Labour Party modernised its policies and structure, some voters may have found it difficult to distinguish between the policies of Tony Blair's 'New Labour' and those of the Conservatives under John Major.

# Recent Changes in Voting Behaviour

Since the 1970s, there has been a noted decline in commitment to the main political parties. Between 1945 and 1970, the Conservative and Labour Parties each enjoyed the support of approximately 45 per cent of the electorate.

However, during the period 1970-87, this aggregate share of the vote fell to 75 per cent although it increased slightly to 76 per cent at the 1992 General Election.

The Labour Party was particularly disadvantaged by this development. At the 1983 General Election, its vote plummeted to 27.6 per cent but recovered from this low at both the 1987 and 1992 General Elections. The 1997 General Election produced a Labour resurgence which resulted in the party being supported by 44.4 per cent of voters.

However, it is significant that Labour's electoral revival in 1997 was largely at the expense of the Conservative Party. The Conservatives managed to attract only 31.2 per cent of the total vote, their lowest share of the vote since 1832. Of the 3.2 million people who switched their allegiance from the Conservative Party, it is estimated that 1.4 million moved directly to Labour.

Consequently, the 1997 General Election continued the trend whereby the two main parties have been noted to attract approximately three quarters of the total vote. Its unusual feature was the collapse of the Conservative vote.

DIAGRAM 4

| Percentage Support for the Labour and Conservative Parties at Selected General Elections | | | | | | | |
|---|---|---|---|---|---|---|---|
| | 1959 | 1964 | 1974 | 1979 | 1983 | 1992 | 1997 |
| Labour | 43.8 | 44.1 | 39.2 | 36.9 | 27.6 | 34.4 | 44.4 |
| Conservative | 49.4 | 43.4 | 35.8 | 43.9 | 42.4 | 41.9 | 31.2 |
| Total | 93.2 | 87.5 | 75.0 | 80.8 | 70.0 | 76.3 | 75.6 |

# Partisan Dealignment

The term partisan dealignment describes a complex process which has resulted in a decline in support for the two major parties. The declining commitment to the main political parties as represented in Diagram 4 is the direct consequence of a number of factors operating together to bring about a significant change in voting behaviour.

## Third Party Influence

The fall in the share of the vote attracted by the two major parties can be explained, in part, by the rise of the Liberal Party and the increased popularity of the nationalist parties.

The share of the vote achieved by the Liberal Party rose rapidly from 7.5 per cent in 1970 to 19.3 per cent in February 1974. Since then, the Liberal Party (in its reincarnations as the Liberal/SDP Alliance and, thereafter, Liberal Democrats) has been able to attract approximately one fifth of the total number of votes although its totals for 1987, 1992 and 1997 represent a retreat from the peak of 25.4 per cent reached by the Liberal/SDP Alliance at the 1983 General Election.

The main strength of the Liberal Party has been its image as a moderate voice operating in the centre of the British political spectrum. As a result, it has attracted a fairly even distribution of voters drawn from all social classes. In many South of England constituencies, the Liberals have been the main challengers to the Conservative Party at the 1983, 1987, 1992 and 1997 General Elections.

However, as the Labour Party has moved to regain the middle ground of British politics the Liberal Democrats have suffered declining support. The Liberal Democrats' 17.2 per cent share of the vote at the 1997 General Election represented a slight fall from its total of 17.8 per cent in 1992 and the 18.3 per cent share it enjoyed in October 1974. Nevertheless, in terms of seats won, the 1997 General Election constituted a remarkable breakthrough for the Liberal Democrats. By winning 46 seats, they achieved their best election result for nearly 70 years.

In Scotland, the rise of nationalism has been significant with the Scottish National Party (SNP) becoming Scotland's second party. In October 1974, the SNP gained one third of all Scottish votes and it is currently supported by approximately one in five Scottish voters. However, in terms of the 1997 General Election, the SNP threat to Labour did not materialise. The SNP doubled its representation to six seats but its share of the national vote rose by less than one per cent to 21.9 per cent. This was due, in part, to continuing advances made by Labour in Scotland. In 1997, Labour registered its highest share of the vote since 1966 and the largest number of MPs in its history.

## Tactical Voting

The emergence of a significant third force in British politics has led to an element of tactical voting. Tactical voters do not vote for their preferred party but instead choose another party which they believe has a real chance of defeating the party that they most dislike. There has been some evidence of this in recent general elections. Butler and Kavanagh (1992) argued that tactical voting had a greater impact in the 1992 General Election than at any previous general election. They provided evidence of tactical voting on the part of Liberal Democrat supporters based on the fact that the swing to Labour was significantly greater in marginal seats.

Further evidence of tactical voting was provided by the 1994 English local election results. In these elections, the Liberal Democrats were able to secure a large increase in the number of seats that they held despite the fact that their share of the vote rose only slightly.

The 1997 General Election offered some further evidence of tactical voting. In the constituency of Crosby, the Liberal Democrat vote collapsed to Labour's advantage. Whereas, the constituencies of Sheffield Hallam, Knaresborough and Harrogate went against the national trend – with the Labour vote falling – to allow the Liberal Democrats to secure victory.

Nevertheless, the key feature of the 1997 General Election was the anti-Conservative swing which involved 1.4 million former Conservative voters switching to Labour and 1.2 million transferring their support to the Liberal Democrats. In the South West, where Liberal Democrat support is concentrated, support for both the Liberal Democrats and Labour tended to increase and this helped the Liberal Democrats to secure victory in a number of key seats. For example, increased support for Labour in the Isle of Wight, Portsmouth South and Torbay allowed the Liberal Democrats to win despite the fact that their support in those constituencies actually fell below 1992 levels.

At the 1997 General Election, voters showed a remarkable propensity to switch directly from Conservative to Labour and, in this respect, this election is without recent precedent.

# Class Dealignment

## Social Change

Many commentators take the view that the reduction in support for the two major parties has been caused by changes in Britain's social structure and a weakening of social class identification with the Conservative and Labour Parties.

Since 1979, there has been considerable deindustrialisation with the result that traditional industries such as engineering, mining, shipbuilding and steel production have shed significant amounts of labour power.

During the same period of time, the information technology revolution and the further development of the service sector have created new sources of employment which have tended to be white collar in nature. Consequently, the working class has declined in size while middle class employment opportunities have increased.

The percentage of employees who can be classified as manual workers has fallen from 47 per cent in the early 1970s to 34 per cent at present. A parallel development has been the growth in managerial employment from 18 per cent to 27 per cent.

The impact of such extensive social change on the Labour Party has been recognised. It is generally accepted that the decline in the size of the working class has been a significant factor in explaining reduced electoral support for Labour. One set of commentators (Heath, Jowell and Curtice 1987) has estimated that the smaller size of the working class explains about half of the decline in Labour's vote since 1964.

## The Changing Nature of the Working Class

However, it is argued that it is not simply the reduced size of the working class which is important in explaining the electoral difficulties experienced by the Labour Party throughout the 1980s and early 1990s but also the changing characteristics of working class voters.

Significant changes have affected the British working class. For example, in 1979, 13.3 million people (53 per cent of the workforce at that time) were trade union members. By 1990, this had fallen to 10.2 million or 38 per cent of the workforce. In view of the traditionally close links between the trade union movement and the Labour Party, this has potentially important implications for electoral choice.

Ivor Crewe, in analysing recent developments affecting the working class which have included a declining proportion of manual workers and council house tenants, concluded that a new working class could be identified which encompasses those living in the South who own their own homes, work in the private sector and are not trade union members. This new working class is considered important because it is claimed that it exhibits very different voting behaviour to that of the shrinking, traditional working class.

The statistics which Crewe provided relating to the 1987 and 1992 General Elections indicated that the working class had become fragmented and that there was a weakening relationship between a significant element of the working class and the Labour Party. It was noted that strong support for Labour within the traditional working class contrasted sharply with its position in terms of the new skilled working class.

To an important extent, the activities of the Labour leadership in preparing for recent elections reveals the extent to which it has been accepted by the Party hierarchy that Labour must evolve to accommodate social change. Policies have been developed to ensure that the Labour Party has broad-based appeal across social classes and age groups.

DIAGRAM 5

## The Traditional and the New Working Class

### 1987 General Election

| The New Working Class | | | | |
|---|---|---|---|---|
| Party | Lives in South | Home owner | Non-union member | Private sector worker |
| Con | 46 | 44 | 40 | 38 |
| Lab | 28 | 32 | 38 | 39 |
| Lib/SDP | 26 | 24 | 22 | 23 |

| Traditional Working Class | | | | |
|---|---|---|---|---|
| Party | Lives in Scotland or North | Council tenant | Union member | Public sector worker |
| Con | 29 | 25 | 30 | 32 |
| Lab | 57 | 57 | 48 | 49 |
| Lib/SDP | 15 | 18 | 22 | 19 |

### 1992 General Election

| The New Working Class | | | | |
|---|---|---|---|---|
| Party | Lives in South | Home owner | Non-union member | Private sector worker |
| Con | 40 | 40 | 37 | 32 |
| Lab | 38 | 41 | 46 | 50 |
| Lib/SDP | 23 | 19 | 17 | 18 |

| Traditional Working Class | | | | |
|---|---|---|---|---|
| Party | Lives in Scotland or North | Council tenant | Union member | Public sector worker |
| Con | 26 | 22 | 29 | 36 |
| Lab | 59 | 64 | 55 | 48 |
| Lib/SDP | 15 | 13 | 16 | 16 |

*These tables show how different groups of people voted in the 1987 and 1992 General Elections. Some columns do not add up to 100% since the figures have been rounded up. (Adapted from Crewe 1987 and Crewe 1992.)*

This approach met with limited success at the 1987 and 1992 General Elections. Whereas, Labour's share of the skilled working class vote fell from 45 per cent in 1979 to 32 per cent in 1983, there has been a noted improvement since. At the 1987 General Election, 36 per cent of skilled workers voted for Labour and, in 1992, Labour attracted the support of 41 per cent of skilled workers.

However, the 1997 General Election provided startling evidence of the extent to which New Labour's policies had allowed the Party to recapture the middle ground in British politics. Labour support among C1 voters increased from 25 per cent to 47 per cent. In contrast, Conservative support within this group fell from 52 per cent to 26 per cent. Similarly, during the same period, support for the Conservatives among C2 voters declined from 38 per cent to 25 per cent whereas Labour support more than doubled from 25 per cent to 54 per cent.

The results of the general elections held in 1987 and 1992 led a number of commentators to conclude that Labour had become a minority party due to the fact that British society had developed more middle class features. However, the extraordinary swing to Labour which was a feature of the 1997 General Election has necessitated a reappraisal of the situation. The Labour Party appears to have been successful in developing broad-based appeal to the extent that long established social class based voting trends seem to have been undermined. For example, at the 1997 General Election, the Conservatives led Labour in terms of the support of AB voters by only 11 per cent. This was in contrast to the 36 per cent gap which existed at the 1992 General Election.

This has provided additional evidence of the existence of class dealignment whereby a reducing percentage of voters provide consistent support for their 'natural class' party. Crewe established that whereas two thirds of all voters voted for their class party during the period 1945–70, since 1983 this proportion has reduced to less than half (44–47 per cent).

However, it must be remembered that despite the existence of class dealignment, social class remains the single most important factor influencing voting behaviour.

DIAGRAM 6

# Party Support by Region  (1997 General Election)

### Adapted from May '97 Special Edition Page 12, New Statesman

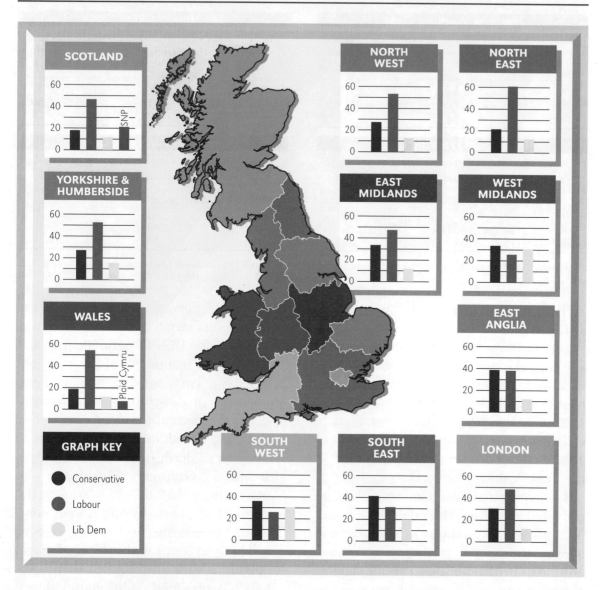

DIAGRAM 7

## Skilled Manual Working Class (C2): Trends in Political Party Support

| General Election | Conservative | Labour | Liberal Democrats |
| --- | --- | --- | --- |
| 1983 | 40 | 32 | 26 |
| 1987 | 40 | 36 | 22 |
| 1992 | 38 | 41 | 17 |
| 1997 | 25 | 54 | 14 |

# Geographical Influences

Some of the changes in Britain's social structure are reflected in regional voting variations. Scotland, the North of England and Wales have become predominantly Labour while the South is a stronghold of Conservative support. The extent to which a geographical divide exists is shown in the diagram opposite.

The existence of a geographical divide was most graphically illustrated by the fact that the 1997 General Election resulted in a complete wipeout of Conservative MPs in Scotland and Wales. The Conservative Party gained 17.5 per cent of the total vote in Scotland and 20 per cent in Wales but their support was not sufficiently concentrated within any constituency to secure the election of a single MP.

In the North of England, a traditional Labour stronghold, Labour secured 60 per cent of the total vote and reduced the number of Conservative seats from six to three. The 1997 General Election also resulted in the North West having the largest number of Labour MPs of any region in Britain. These results represented further indications of a trend which has been developing since 1979. In attempting to explain the reasons, the following factors are relevant.

Scotland, the North of England and Wales were particularly affected by the decline in traditional industries (deindustrialisation) which intensified after 1979. It seems clear that this has resulted in an erosion in Conservative Party support and consolidation of the Labour vote in those areas.

Until the 1997 General Election, it was noted that the Conservative Party benefited considerably in terms of support from the fact that the South of England contains a higher concentration of middle class and new working class voters. However, New Labour's broad-based appeal and anti-Conservative sentiment combined to erode the traditional electoral strength of the Conservative Party in the Midlands and in the South of England. In the South East of England, the Conservatives lost 39 seats and Labour won 31 of them. In London, the Conservatives lost 30 seats of which Labour took 25.

Therefore, while the North-South divide still exists in terms of electoral support, it is evident that the South of England can no longer be viewed as barren territory for the Labour Party.

# The Ideology Gap

As has been noted, from the late 1970s onwards, the forces of social change generated a degree of fragmentation within the working class. It is claimed by many observers that a sizeable proportion of the new working class rejected certain Labour Party policies as they seemed in conflict with their ambitions and inclinations. The policies which caused most concern in this regard were Labour's commitment to higher direct taxation in order to fund its public spending programme, its resistance to trade union reform and its support for unilateral nuclear disarmament.

This contention appears to have been accepted by the Labour leadership as successive party leaders, Neil Kinnock 1983-92, John Smith 1992-94 and Tony Blair 1994-present have all worked with some success to ensure that Labour is viewed by the electorate as a modern party with broad-based policy appeal. Labour's success in the 1997 General Election was largely due to its capacity to enlist the support of C1 (white collar) workers and C2 (skilled) workers. Part of the Labour campaign strategy designed to achieve this was to develop policies which indicated that society could be improved without the need for new public spending pledges which would lead to increased taxation.

# The Production-Consumption Divide

According to this view, a clear divide exists between public and private sector employees. Those who earn their living within the public sector are considered to be more likely to vote Labour than those who are employed by privately owned businesses.

Similarly, it is claimed that those who depend on public services such as transport and council houses have a greater propensity to vote Labour than those who own a private car and have bought their home.

This analysis relates directly to the concepts of middle class radicals and the new working class which have been examined previously. Indeed, some observers take the view that the voting behaviour of professionals working in the public sector (e.g. teachers, health workers and social workers) is such that they cannot be viewed as part of the traditional middle class.

Diagrams 5 and 8 illustrate that voting behaviour is influenced by such factors as public sector employment, home ownership and trade union membership.

DIAGRAM 8

| Middle Class Occupations and Party Identification (1994) | | | |
|---|---|---|---|
| Occupation | Conservative | Labour | Others |
| Security Forces | 91 | 3 | 6 |
| Airline Pilots | 81 | 6 | 13 |
| Accountants | 65 | 13 | 22 |
| Judges/Lawyers | 61 | 20 | 19 |
| Health Professionals | 53 | 21 | 26 |
| Teachers | 43 | 28 | 29 |
| Scientists | 42 | 27 | 31 |
| Social Workers | 35 | 45 | 20 |

*Source: R. Jowell, J. Curtice, L. Brook, D. Ahrendt (1994)*

DIAGRAM 9

## 1997 General Election (Voting Behaviour)

| Category | Conservative | Labour | Liberal Democrats |
| --- | --- | --- | --- |
| Home Owner | 39 | 37 | 17 |
| Mortgage Payer | 29 | 46 | 19 |
| Council Tenant | 12 | 66 | 16 |
| Trade Unionist | 16 | 59 | 20 |

*Source: NOP/BBC Exit Poll*

## Education and Television

A further possible explanation of the changes in voting behaviour in recent times which have resulted in reduced support for the two major parties (partisan dealignment) is the influence of television. According to this view, the electorate is better educated and therefore more able to take into account a range of factors, not simply social class background, in deciding how to cast their vote.

Linked to this argument is the contention that television has a strong educational influence on the electorate. It is claimed that the high quality of television coverage of political issues has meant that voters have more information than ever before on which to base their voting decision.

# Other Social Factors Influencing Voting Behaviour

## Gender

The evidence suggests that, until recently, some element of gender gap existed in British politics with women being more likely than men to vote Conservative. However, the extent of this gap has varied considerably in recent elections and it appears to have been closed by Labour at the 1997 General Election.

DIAGRAM 10

| Gender and Party Support at the 1992 General Election | | | |
|---|---|---|---|
| | Conservative | Labour | Liberal Democrats |
| Men | 41 | 37 | 18 |
| Women | 44 | 34 | 18 |

| Gender and Party Support at the 1997 General Election | | | |
|---|---|---|---|
| | Conservative | Labour | Liberal Democrats |
| Men | 29 | 47 | 18 |
| Women | 29 | 47 | 18 |

In the 1992 General Election, the Conservative Party had the lead over the Labour Party in every category of female vote except the 18-24 age group. Overall, 44 per cent of women voted Conservative against 41 per cent of men; this contrasted with 37 per cent of men voting Labour as opposed to 34 per cent of women.

However, the 1997 General Election suggests that Labour has eliminated the gender gap. In attempting to advance explanations for this, it is worthy of note that New Labour has sought to ensure that its policies are appealing to women and that Labour selected a significant number of women as party candidates with the result that 101 Labour MPs are women. This represents approximately one quarter of all Labour MPs.

# Age

DIAGRAM 11

| Age and Party Support at the 1992 General Election | | | |
|---|---|---|---|
| | Conservative | Labour | Liberal Democrats |
| 18–24 | 35 | 39 | 19 |
| 25–34 | 40 | 38 | 18 |
| 35–54 | 43 | 34 | 19 |
| 55+ | 46 | 34 | 17 |
| Pensioner | 48 | 34 | 16 |

| Age and Party Support at the 1997 General Election | | | |
|---|---|---|---|
| | Conservative | Labour | Liberal Democrats |
| 18–24 | 18 | 59 | 19 |
| 25–29 | 21 | 58 | 17 |
| 30–44 | 24 | 51 | 18 |
| 45–64 | 31 | 45 | 19 |
| 65+ | 41 | 35 | 17 |

The view is often taken that younger people are more likely to support Labour due to the fact that they question established values and favour policies of a more radical nature. In accordance with this, it is argued that as people age they are likely to have acquired some element of wealth and an improving standard of living with the result that the desire to maintain the circumstances which are considered to have brought this about is strong. Therefore, it is believed that Conservative policies with their emphasis on wealth creation and the maintenance of the status quo hold more appeal for voters as they grow older.

However, it should also be noted that middle class voters, the great majority of whom vote Conservative, tend to live longer than working class Labour supporters and this will further accentuate the tendency for the more senior age categories to contain a high concentration of Conservative voters.

The 1992 General Election results fit well within this analysis as the Conservatives led Labour among all age groups except 18–24 year olds. However, it is a dramatic reflection of the change in Labour's fortunes that at the 1997 General Election the Conservatives only led Labour in the 65+ category. One of the most remarkable features of the 1997 General Election was increased support for Labour from middle aged voters. In 1992, the Conservatives enjoyed a clear lead of 9 per cent over Labour within the 35–54 age group. This contrasts with Labour's significant leads over the Conservatives in both the 30–44 and 45–64 age groups at the 1997 General Election.

The statistics for the 1992 and 1997 General Elections still show Conservative support advancing with age. However, there has been a transformation in support for Labour across the mid-range age groups which lends credibility to Labour's claim that it has broad-based appeal for all voters.

## Religion

The work of Anthony Heath and others suggests that a significant connection still exists between Church of England attendance and support for the Conservative Party. However, it is likely that this has little to do with religion and is a further manifestation of the influence of social class and the neighbourhood/locality effect.

Also, Roman Catholic voters tend to support Labour. This is believed to arise from the Irish, working class origins of a significant proportion of that vote.

## Ethnicity

Ethnic minorities account for approximately 5.5 per cent of Britain's population and there is clear evidence that much of this vote is cast in favour of the Labour Party. Political survey data suggests that, at the 1992 General Election, 79 per cent of ethnic minority voters voted Labour, 10 per cent voted Conservative and 9 per cent voted Liberal Democrat. With the 10.2 per cent national swing towards Labour, it is likely that this position of strength will have been further consolidated at the 1997 General Election.

Within ethnic minorities, members of the Afro-Caribbean community have recorded the strongest support for the Labour Party (86 per cent). Support among Asians exists at a lower level (67 per cent).

However, despite the formidable degree of Labour support which exists, evidence has accumulated that Asians engaged in non-manual work may be increasingly inclined to transfer their allegiance to other parties.

In attempting to explain the strong element of support that exists for the Labour Party within ethnic minorities, a number of reasons can be advanced.

- Black people identify strongly with the Labour Party as being pro-working class and therefore in a position to advance the material prosperity of ethnic minorities.

- Labour is considered by many members of ethnic minorities to have more liberal attitudes with regard to race relations and immigration than the Conservative Party.

- There is a tendency for black people to be concentrated in a comparatively small number of constituencies, many of which have become Labour strongholds. This has allowed a close relationship to develop between local Labour Party organisations and ethnic minority communities.

# Short-Term Influences

## Floating Voters and Electoral Volatility

With evidence accumulating of partisan dealignment and class dealignment resulting in reducing support for the two major parties, political commentators have become increasingly interested in the short-term factors which cause changes in voting behaviour.

At a time when social factors acting over a lengthy period of time are reducing in significance (although they remain important), a greater proportion of the electorate is becoming comprised of floating voters and therefore open to influence.

Estimates indicate that during the four weeks of the election campaign leading to the 1992 General Election, as many as 11.1 million voters changed their minds about how to vote. However, many of these changes cancelled each other out.

The 1997 General Election which produced a 179 seat majority for Labour, was very different. It has been estimated that as many as 3.2 million people who had voted Conservative in 1992 switched to another party.

Against that, the Conservatives could attract only 500,000 votes from other parties. This situation was reflected by an average swing to Labour of 10.2 per cent throughout the country.

Furthermore, approximately 2.8 million voters who voted at the 1992 General Election died prior to the 1997 General Election. This factor will also have made a significant contribution to the decline in the Conservative vote.

DIAGRAM 12

### 1992 and 1997 General Elections

**Changes in Support for the Major Parties
(approximate figures, millions of votes)**

|  |  | 1992 | 1997 | Net Change |
|---|---|---|---|---|
|  | Labour | 11.6m | 13.5m | +1.9m |
|  | Conservative | 14.0m | 9.6m | -4.4m |
|  | Liberal Democrats | 6.0m | 5.2m | -0.8m |

Floating voters are extremely important because, as a result of their willingness to switch parties, they generate the electoral swings which lead to changes of government. Political research has shown that although a substantial proportion of eventual voters for the two major parties determine how they will vote before the election campaign, a significant percentage make their minds up during the election campaign. In recent general elections, it has been observed that the Liberal Democrats have less of a 'hard vote' which they can count on with the result that the Party is very exposed to the vote-switching activities of floating voters.

The 1997 General Election revealed a high level of electoral volatility with the unusual feature emerging that Conservative voters were willing to switch directly to Labour. As has been noted, it is estimated that approximately 1.4 million voters transferred their allegiance directly from the Conservative Party to Labour.

DIAGRAM 13

## Responses to the Question:

**When did you decide which party to vote for at the 1997 General Election?**

|  | 1992 % | 1997 % |
|---|---|---|
| Today | 11 | 11 |
| During last week | 12 | 14 |
| Since election called | 19 | 18 |
| Before election called | 57 | 55 |
| Not sure | 3 | 3 |

*Source: NOP/BBC Exit Poll*

# The Rational Choice or Consumer Voting Model

Increasing recognition of electoral volatility and the importance of short term factors has led to a detailed examination of key influences on voters in the run up to elections.

Many of the explanations of short term influences on voters take the view that they operate in a rational way and select the party with the policies that they consider will best protect and advance their interests. This is known as the rational choice or consumer voting model and it stresses the importance of instrumental voting which involves voters acting like shoppers in a political market place looking for the best deal and voting accordingly.

# Issue Voting

This suggests that voters choose parties by considering their respective positions on the main issues. Supporters of this view consider that Labour's failure at recent general elections was due, to a significant extent, to the unpopularity of its position on key policy areas such as trade union reform, taxation, nationalisation and defence. In contrast, proponents of the issue voting explanation argue, the Conservative Party was identified with a range of policies which voters considered had the potential to increase material prosperity. These policies included privatisation, advancing share ownership, reducing levels of taxation and the sale of council houses.

One of the difficulties experienced by supporters of issue voting as an explanation of short term voting behaviour is that, during the 1987 General Election campaign, the Labour Party was ahead on a number of the main issues which were considered important by voters including employment, health and education but it still lost the election. Again, in the 1992 General Election, Labour led on these issues but, despite increasing its share of the vote, the Labour Party again lost the election.

However, it is worth noting that, at the time of the general elections referred to, those political surveys which were conducted indicated that the majority of voters considered the Conservative Party more able to generate increased prosperity than Labour.

In preparing for the 1997 General Election, Labour set out to rid itself of a tax and spend image which had proved costly in terms of electoral support. The Labour strategy was to reassure voters that no large scale spending commitments requiring increases in personal taxation would be made. Nevertheless, in order to reinforce Labour's traditional advantage over the Conservatives on issues such as employment, health and education, it was important that Labour should be able to demonstrate its capacity to implement policies in those areas which would lead to social improvement. Consequently, the concept of a windfall tax on private utilities was developed as a means of financing strategic policy objectives which was less likely to alienate voters.

## Competence

According to this view, voters are driven by self-interest and will support the political party which they consider most likely to improve their standard of living and that of the communities to which they belong. It is argued that Labour's defeats in 1987 and 1992 were partly due to the fact that voters thought they were more likely to prosper under a Conservative administration.

In analysing the 1992 General Election, commentators have judged the fact that Labour found it difficult to alter its negative image as a party of high taxation to be of considerable significance.

It is noteworthy that opinion polls taken immediately prior to the 1992 General Election found that only 47 per cent of voters considered that the Conservatives were competent to manage the economy but that this figure was 7 per cent higher than that for Labour.

However, it is clear that voters' assessment of a political party's capacity to deliver an improving economy is in part based on past experience of its actions while in office.

In this regard, Labour found it difficult to erase memories of its period in office (1974-79) when high rates of inflation and increasing industrial action leading to the infamous 'Winter of Discontent' were directly associated with Labour's economic management.

Part of the Labour Party's strategy in responding to such a negative image has been to reinvent itself as 'New Labour' a party which has reformed and modernised to the extent that, in the view of its leadership, the record of past administrations cannot be considered relevant. Evidence available from opinion polls conducted during the run-up to the 1997 General Election suggest that Labour was successful in bridging the gap which existed between themselves and the Conservatives over the issue of economic competence.

At the 1987 and 1992 General Elections, the Conservative Party benefited from the so-called 'feel good' factor whereby many voters discerned that their standard of living was improving. In the run-up to the 1992 General Election, there was a strong correlation between the MORI Economic Optimism Index and the Conservative lead over Labour. However, it is significant that, despite the relative strength of the economy prior to the 1997 General Election, a nil correlation between economic optimism and Conservative support was discerned during the six month period prior to the election. This suggests that the 'feel good' factor had ceased to operate in the Conservatives' favour. It is possible that this was due to the fact that voters had been reassured that Labour could run the economy effectively and to the prominence of other issues in the minds of voters.

## Leadership Style

It is recognised that perception of leadership style is one of the short term factors influencing voting behaviour. In recent general elections, there has been more media attention paid to the personalities of party leaders. Therefore, it is likely that opinions formed by voters concerning party leaders will result in an increasing number of votes being won or lost.

Most commentators agree that during the run-up to the 1992 General Election, the Conservative Party benefited from the fact that it elected a new leader, John Major, who was regarded by many voters as more 'trustworthy' and 'straight-forward' than Neil Kinnock, the Labour leader at that time. Since then, the relative popularity of Labour's new leader, Tony Blair, elected as leader in 1994, contrasted with voters' assessment of John Major and

boosted Labour's opinion poll ratings through to the general election.

However, it should be remembered that perception of leadership is only one factor influencing voters. As the table below shows, only 7 per cent of voters identified party leadership as being a determining factor at the 1992 and 1997 General Elections.

DIAGRAM 14

| Reasons for Voting: | | |
|---|---|---|
| | **1992**<br>% | **1997**<br>% |
| Party's policies | 41 | 45 |
| Usually vote for that party | 20 | 20 |
| Dislike another party | 18 | 15 |
| Party leader | 7 | 7 |
| Local candidate | 5 | 4 |
| None of these | 6 | 10 |

*Source: Adapted from 1992 NOP/BBC Exit Poll, 1997 Harris/Independent*

# Election Campaigns and Party Image

There is little doubt that the election campaign has a significant impact on the outcome of general elections. It has been estimated that 25 per cent of the electorate decided how they would vote during the final week of the 1997 General Election campaign and it is statistics such as those which justify the degree of effort that the parties expend on their respective campaigns.

During the course of an election campaign, each of the parties seeks to gain extensive media coverage and ensure that its policies and leaders are reported on favourably. However, all of the parties are aware that party image can prove more significant than reference to any particular set of policies. Promoting the party image involves making clear the general principles for which the party stands.

In this regard, each of the parties has sought to ensure that they are seen to be supportive of the family as an institution. It has been established that family concerns are often uppermost in the minds of voters when they decide how to cast their vote.

A number of observers attribute the failure of the Conservative Party at the 1997 General Election to the fact that its image became tarnished as a result of a number of significant developments. The 1997 General Election campaign will be remembered for the sleaze factor which forced the Conservative Party to adopt a defensive stance during the first two weeks of its campaign. Also, the election campaign exposed Conservative divisions over Europe and greatly contributed to the image of a divided party.

*Tony Blair on the campaign trail*

DIAGRAM 15

## Responses to the Question:

In your view, which of the political parties has run the most effective campaign so far?

|  | | 30 March 1997 % | 22 April 1997 % | Change |
|---|---|---|---|---|
|  | Conservative | 13 | 11 | -2 |
|  | Labour | 31 | 36 | +5 |
|  | Liberal Democrat | 28 | 13 | -15 |
|  | Other/None | 28 | 40 | +12 |

*Source: MORI*

## Summary

A detailed analysis of voting behaviour in Britain today suggests that partisan dealignment, whereby support for the two major parties is declining, is an important development. Part of this decline in support is due to the fact that traditional class loyalties are breaking down as a result of Britain's changing social structure.

As these long term social influences reduce, the impact of short term factors linked to the rational choice or consumer voting model becomes more important.

In this context, the 1997 General Election is of considerable significance. Labour's achievement in establishing a huge overall majority has provided further evidence of the declining importance of long-term social influences as large amounts of voters will cast their votes in a way that their class background did not predict. The fact that so many voters were willing to switch support directly from the Conservative Party to Labour indicates increasing electoral volatility and the further erosion of party loyalties and class-based voting.

STUDY TOPIC 2

# Electoral Systems – What Effects do they have upon the Distribution of Power?

## Britain and Representative Democracy

Britain has a democratic system of government. The term democracy is derived from the ancient Greek words demos meaning 'the people' and cratos meaning 'power'. In a representative democracy, citizens elect representatives to make decisions for them. This is in recognition of the fact that the complexities of governing a modern nation state like Britain are such that it would not be possible to allow all citizens a direct say in determining public policies. Therefore, electoral systems serve the purpose of legitimising governments by ensuring that established procedures exist to elect representatives who will run the country in the interests of the people. The development of democracy is viewed as crucial in maintaining stability within countries. As a result of the operation of democratic systems of government, countries can accommodate significant political and constitutional change in a gradual, peaceful way.

*Source: Collins Softback English Dictionary*

**democracy** (dɪˈmɒkrəsi) *n., pl.* **-cies 1.** government by the people for their elected representatives. **2.** a political or social unit governed ultimately by all its members. **3.** the practice or spirit of social equality. **4.** a social condition of classlessness and equality. **5.** the common people, esp. as a political force.

## Participation

It is generally recognised that representative democracy functions best when there is active participation on the part of the electorate. Obviously, there is a key role for voters to play in turning out at elections to ensure that representatives are genuinely accountable to those who elect them. Representatives who fail to meet the expectations of voters must be made aware that they are liable to be replaced if democracy is, in reality, to bring power to the people.

In Britain, accountability is reinforced by the fact that MPs and councillors represent people living within set geographical areas known as constituencies or wards. This is intended to ensure that voters can identify a specific person whose role it is to note and act on their concerns and ensure that their views are represented when decisions are made.

However, there is much more to democracy than voting at elections. There is a need for voters to be well-informed about issues and to have the right to express their views on all matters that they consider important at times other than the run-up to elections. In recognition of this, countries such as Britain are 'liberal democracies' which guarantee a range of citizens' rights including freedom of speech, freedom of assembly, freedom of conscience and freedom from arbitrary arrest and imprisonment.

# The British Electoral System

First Past the Post (FPTP) is the popular name given to the electoral system which has traditionally been used in Britain for all elections. It is also known as the simple majority or plurality system.

To secure victory and win a seat in the House of Commons, a candidate must simply obtain more votes than any of the rival candidates. The winning margin need only be one more vote. Under FPTP candidates are not required to gain a majority of the votes cast. Consequently, candidates can and often do win seats with less than 50 per cent of the total vote.

At the 1997 General Election, the constituency of Winchester produced the closest result. Only two votes separated the leading candidates and the final result was only confirmed after two recounts and a period of nineteen hours had elapsed.

Therefore, although 42.06 per cent of those who voted were in favour of having Mark Oaten (Liberal Democrat) represent them, it can be pointed out that the majority, 57.94 per cent, preferred other candidates. Essentially, the expressed preferences of a minority of voters determined the representation of the majority.

Similar arguments apply regarding the national election result. The FPTP system facilitates the domination of British politics by two major parties and it usually secures an overall majority of seats for the leading party. Of the fifteen general elections held since the end of the second World War, no party has ever won fifty per cent of the total number of votes cast. At the 1979, 1983, 1987 and 1992 General Elections, the Conservative Party secured large majorities with, at most, 43 per cent of the vote. The 1997 General Election provided further evidence of the extent to which the existing electoral system reinforces the position of the leading party. The Labour Party achieved an overall majority of 179 seats on the basis of having received only 44 per cent of the national vote.

Also, a further by-product of this situation is the degree of disadvantage faced by minority parties. Third parties are often adversely affected because their support is spread across the country. This was most spectacularly demonstrated during the 1983 General Election when the Labour Party with significant geographical concentrations of support, mainly in the North, was able to secure 209 seats with 27.6 per cent of the vote. In contrast, the Liberal / SDP Alliance won only 23 seats with 25.4 per cent of the national vote.

DIAGRAM 1

| 1997 Winchester Constituency Election Result | | |
|---|---|---|
| Mark Oaten (Liberal Democrats) | 26,100 | 42.06% |
| Gerry Malone (Conservative) | 26,098 | 42.06% |
| Patrick Davies (Labour) | 6,528 | 10.52% |
| Peter Strand (Referendum) | 1,598 | 2.58% |

*(Note: in September, 1997, Gerry Malone won a High Court case to re-run the Winchester election. He questioned 55 ballot papers which were rejected as void. Mr Malone claimed that, if they had been counted, he would have retained his seat. In the re-run election, the Liberal Democrat candidate won again. This time, Mark Oaten secured a much increased majority.)*

DIAGRAM 2

| 1997 General Election Result | | | |
|---|---|---|---|
| **Party** | **No. of Seats** | **% Vote** | **% Seats** |
| Labour | 419 | 44 | 63.5 |
| Conservative | 165 | 31 | 25.4 |
| Liberal Democrats | 46 | 17 | 7.0 |
| Others | 29 | 7 | 4.1 |

The 1997 General Election produced a good result for the Liberal Democrats with the Party making significant headway in terms of the number of seats gained. However, it is notable that even at this time of comparative success, 17 per cent of the national vote was only sufficient to secure approximately 7 per cent of seats.

In Scotland and Wales, the Conservative Party had to endure a disastrous result at the 1997 General Election due to the lack of geographical concentration of its support. The Conservative Party had no MPs returned in either Scotland or Wales, despite having secured the support of 17.5 per cent of Scots voters and 20 per cent of Welsh voters. This means that the huge amount of votes involved can be viewed as wasted in the sense that they have had no impact on representation.

The whole issue of wasted votes constitutes a major criticism of Britain's existing electoral system. It undermines the principle that all votes should be of equal value. Voters in a safe parliamentary seat where the sitting MP has a large majority are likely to consider themselves unable to influence the anticipated result when they cast their vote. This is in marked contrast to the position of voters in a marginal constituency where a small shift in support may prove sufficient to remove the sitting MP and change the political representation of the constituency. It is notable that floating voters within marginal constituencies can influence not only political representation within their particular constituencies but also the overall general election result.

In the run-up to the 1997 General Election, some commentators noted that the election result seemed to hinge on the voting decisions made by some 66,000 voters in the 57 closest marginals. Those voters, who constituted no more than 0.2 per cent of the total electorate, were considered to have votes of such high value that the major political parties had sought to ensure that their policies would be acceptable to them. Also, the election campaigns of the respective political parties during the 1997 General Election were designed to focus on the key marginals which could deliver the desired result.

Further demonstration of the fact that not all votes are of equal value is provided by statistics which show the average number of votes taken to elect a single MP for each of the three main political parties in Britain.

DIAGRAM 3

| General Elections of 1992 and 1997 (Approximate number of votes taken to elect a single MP) | 1992 | 1997 |
|---|---|---|
| Conservative | 41,942 | 58,182 |
| Labour | 42,646 | 32,219 |
| Liberal Democrat | 299,922 | 113,043 |

# Proportionality

The main criticisms which can be made of the First Past the Post electoral system revolve around the fact that it does not produce a proportional result. As has been noted, the existing electoral system acts to reinforce the position of the winning party and to support the domination of the British political system by two major parties. It ensures that votes will only influence representation if they exist in sufficient concentrations within constituencies to secure the election of an MP. This creates a democratic deficit in the sense that not all votes are of equal value and indeed some can come to be viewed as wasted.

It is often argued that an important test of the effectiveness of an electoral system within Britain's representative democracy is that it should ensure that the political composition of the House of Commons reflects the proportion of votes cast in favour of political parties at the general election.

The First Past the Post system clearly fails to meet this criterion in three important respects:

■ MPs are frequently elected on less than 50 per cent of the total constituency vote.

■ Since the Second World War, all British governments have been elected, sometimes with spectacular overall majorities, on a minority vote.

■ Third parties and minority parties are under-represented due to the geographical spread of their support. The FPTP system only rewards winners. Therefore, it is possible for a political party to amass a considerable amount of votes but few seats simply because it does not have the concentration of support in many constituencies which is required to win.

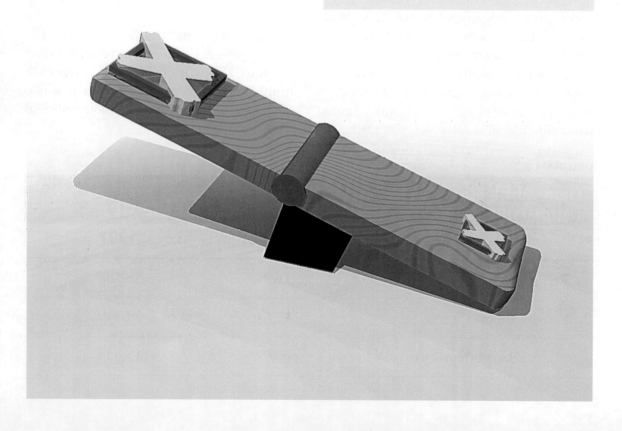

# Further Criticisms of the First Past the Post Electoral System

## Regional Imbalance

The First Past the Post (FPTP) system is claimed to have aggravated the situation in recent elections whereby Britain can be viewed, in electoral terms, as two nations: a predominantly Conservative South and a Labour North.

This has partly resulted from a concentration of Labour votes in the North which leads to large Labour majorities in safe seats so that many Labour votes are wasted. Conservative support in the South is more geographically spread while existing in sufficient concentrations to win a significant number of seats. As has been noted, Liberal Democrat votes are dispersed to such a degree that a significant proportion of that vote can be thought of as wasted due to the fact that it fails to influence representation.

Although the 1997 General Election radically altered the pattern of political representation in Britain, the arguments outlined above still hold. Despite the progress made by the Liberal Democrats, their share of the total vote would have entitled them to approximately 112 seats had a proportional result been generated. Also, the dominance of the Labour Party in Scotland and Wales was exaggerated by the fact that the First Past the Post system failed to take into account the significant support, albeit dispersed, that existed for the Conservative Party in those countries.

## Adversarial Politics

It is claimed that FPTP by removing the need for compromise, promotes a 'winner takes all' situation whereby governments press ahead with their respective programmes with little consideration for the views of other parties.

This is considered problematic in democratic terms due to the large number of votes invested in opposition programmes. If the policies and opinions of opposition parties can be safely ignored, it is possible that the majority of the electorate may not consider that it is being represented effectively.

In this regard, it is often pointed out that the Conservative Governments led by Mrs Thatcher as Prime Minister during the period 1979-1990 were able to introduce a series of radical measures despite the fact that the Conservative Party was only supported by a minority of British voters. The same argument can be applied to Mr Blair's Labour administration elected in 1997. With a majority of 179 seats, Mr Blair can reasonably anticipate being able to introduce new legislation without difficulty. However, Labour's current position of ascendancy is based on minority support (44 per cent of the electorate).

Recognition of those developments has caused some observers to contend that the FPTP system has the potential to undermine our representative democracy.

According to this view, voters may come to question the extent to which representative democracy is functioning effectively as their capacity to make politicians accountable to them is clearly diminished. Also, it should be noted that this situation has the potential to bring about radical shifts in the way the country is governed as one administration's programme is required to give way in entirety to another.

# Advantages of the First Past the Post System

The fact that the FPTP system has endured in Britain for so long indicates that it must have a number of strengths which are highly rated by British politicians and voters. In assessing Britain's existing electoral system, most commentators note that it scores highly in relation to each of the following aspects:

- Majoritarianism (producing a government majority)

- Representation and Accountability

- Simplicity

## Majoritarianism

It is often claimed that an effective electoral system is one which has the capacity to deliver a clear result in favour of a single party contesting a general election and allow a government to be formed. As has been noted, the FPTP system facilitates the domination of British politics by two major parties and it usually secures an overall majority for the leading party despite the fact that it has minority support within the country.

In this sense, the greatest weakness of FPTP, namely its inability to deliver a proportional result, becomes its greatest strength according to the standard of majoritarianism (producing a government majority).

Therefore, assessments of the effectiveness of FPTP as an electoral system are to a significant extent based on value judgement. Those who favour strong government based on the policies of a single party will tend to favour FPTP whereas those who consider the principle of votes of equal value to be paramount will reject the existing electoral system.

## Representation and Accountability

In Britain, there has traditionally been a strong emphasis on maintaining an effective link between voters and their elected representatives. The principle that Members of Parliament (MPs) represent all voters in a given constituency can be viewed as highly supportive of representative democracy as it ensures that voters can identify an individual who is required to take their interests into account when influencing decisions and is directly accountable to them at election time.

## Simplicity

The First Past the Post system is easy for all voters to understand and it produces a fast result. The process of voting is straightforward as the ballot paper simply requires that voters place a cross against their chosen candidate. For this reason, vote counting and analysis can be completed relatively quickly.

## Summary

The First Past the Post system can be viewed as effective in terms of the criterion of majoritarianism. It has the capacity to provide governments with a significant overall majority which makes them strong in the sense that they need not seek to establish compromises with any other political party.

However, there are concerns regarding the operation of FPTP and these are based on its failure to produce a proportional result. This deficiency, it is argued, detracts from Britain's representative democracy.

# Electoral Reform

Due to the fact that the FPTP system does not generate a proportional result and the implications of this for representative democracy, increasing attention in recent times has been paid to the issue of electoral reform.

Conservative Party domination throughout the 1980s and much of the 1990s has combined with the increasing importance of the Liberal Democrats as a third party to produce a number of developments relating to electoral reform.

## The Plant Committee

The Labour Party established the Plant Committee in 1990 to consider the issue of electoral reform. At that time, Labour was concerned that it might be unable to form a majority government in the near future and considered the options well worthy of examination.

The final report of the Plant Committee was published in April 1993 and it recommended reform of the electoral system in the sense of a move towards proportional representation for European elections, Scottish, Welsh or any regional assemblies, and an elected second chamber.

The 1994 elections to the European Parliament provided further evidence, if this was required, of the extent to which the First Past the Post system failed to deliver proportionality. In 1994, Labour won 62 seats within the European Parliament (72 per cent of Britain's available total) despite having received the support of only 44.2 per cent of voters. In contrast, the support of 16.5 per cent of all voters was only sufficient to win the Liberal Democrats 2 seats.

Accordingly, the Labour Party made two significant commitments to electoral reform within its manifesto for the 1997 General Election. The first commitment was that election to the European Parliament and the Scottish and Welsh assemblies would be based on proportional representation. The second commitment was to hold a referendum on the form of electoral system to be employed at general elections. Essentially, voters would be required to choose between the existing FPTP system and another system which would offer a more proportional result (possibly the Alternative Vote System).

Further to Labour's outstanding success at the 1997 General Election, there was some concern expressed that its interest in electoral reform might begin to wane.

In particular, the view was taken by some observers that the Labour Government might prove unable to introduce legislation during Autumn 1997 which would allow proportional representation to be used to elect MEPs (Members of the European Parliament) to the Strasbourg Parliament in 1999. However, in July 1997, the Government announced that a regional list system would be employed during the 1999 European elections.

According to some commentators, as voters come to accept the use of a proportional electoral system for the 1999 European elections, this will influence their decision in the referendum to be held on the electoral system for general elections.

The Government established an advisory commission during the Autumn of 1997 to choose a possible system to be used at future general elections which would produce a more proportional result. At the referendum to be held thereafter, voters would then be required to choose between the existing electoral system and the system recommended by the advisory commission.

However, other observers of the political scene take the view that Labour's agreement to adopt a form of proportional representation for the European elections represents a small concession which will allow pressure for electoral reform in terms of election to Westminster to be resisted. In this regard, they note that the arguments against proportional representation are much stronger when a government is being elected.

# Alternative Electoral Systems

In suggesting systems to replace FPTP, the recommendations which are made can be categorised as majority systems and proportional systems.

Majority systems would ensure that each winning candidate would require to be supported by at least 50 per cent of voters in a constituency. Proportional systems ensure that party representation in terms of seats in the House of Commons is closely linked to the level of support (percentage of the vote) for each party across the country.

## Majority Systems

### Alternative Vote System

It would be a comparatively simple matter to introduce the Alternative Vote System as a replacement for the existing British electoral system. This is because, as with the FPTP system, candidates stand for election in single member constituencies with one candidate being elected to represent each constituency.

With the Alternative Vote System, candidates are only elected if they receive more than 50 per cent of all votes cast. Should a candidate achieve this on the basis of voters' first preferences then that candidate is elected. However, as voters are required to rank candidates in order of preference on their ballot paper, second preferences can be taken into account if no candidate manages to reach the 50 per cent figure.

The process of taking into account second preferences involves the candidate who received the lowest number of first preferences being eliminated and votes being reallocated to second preference candidates. This procedure involving elimination and redistribution continues until one candidate reaches 50 per cent of the votes cast.

While this system ensures that winning candidates must secure at least 50 per cent of the vote and therefore be truly representative of their constituents in the sense that they are the most popular (or least unpopular) candidates, critics point to the fact that the Alternative Vote System fails to produce a proportional result. Nevertheless, the position of third parties, such as the Liberal Democrats, who regularly take second place in constituency elections is likely to be advanced to a significant extent as they will be many voters' second preferences.

At present, the Alternative Vote System is used to elect the Australian House of Representatives.

It should be noted that majority systems also exist in the form of the Second Ballot System and the Supplementary Vote System.

## Second Ballot System

This system also requires that candidates receive an absolute majority of votes cast before being elected. In the absence of this, the first ballot leads to a number of candidates being eliminated due to the fact that they have a low share of the vote.

One or two weeks later, a second ballot is held and candidates are elected on a First Past the Post basis. In some versions of this system, only two candidates are allowed to remain to ensure that the victorious candidate will have more than 50 per cent of the vote.

The Second Ballot System does not provide a proportional result but, in common with the other majority systems, it ensures that no vote is wasted as voters are aware that, should their first choice candidate be eliminated, they will still be in a position to influence the second ballot which will involve only leading candidates. Indeed, those candidates defeated in the first ballot may choose to endorse one of the remaining candidates in an attempt to secure their election.

A form of the Second Ballot System is used for elections to the French National Assembly and for French Presidential elections. In the 1993 French National Assembly elections, 90 of the 577 seats were elected in the first ballot and the second ballot normally involved only two remaining candidates.

## Supplementary Vote System

This is similar to the Alternative Vote System. However, instead of ranking all candidates in order of preference, voters are required to record only first and second preferences. Once again, candidates who receive more than 50 per cent of first preference votes are elected. Should no candidate achieve this then only the two leading candidates are allowed to remain in the contest, all other candidates are eliminated. The second preference votes from the eliminated candidates are then distributed to the remaining candidates and added to their first preference totals. The candidate who then has the greater number of votes is elected.

The Supplementary Vote System has the advantages that there is no time-lag between ballots and the process of voting remains straightforward with voters only being required to record first and second preferences. This system was devised by the Labour Party's Plant Committee and it is likely to command significant support from Labour members of the advisory commission established in Autumn 1997 to recommend a possible alternative to the existing electoral system.

## Summary

A significant advantage of majority systems when considered as a possible alternative to the existing electoral system is that they could be introduced in such a way that much of the existing electoral structure and its associated strengths would be retained.

Majority systems maintain close constituency links, produce results quickly and effectively and can be readily understood by most voters. Also, they have the effect of enhancing representative democracy by ensuring that all elected representatives are required to obtain more than 50 per cent of the total number of votes cast.

Furthermore, despite the fact that majority systems do not produce a proportional result, they do tend to favour third parties so that the relationship between the percentage of votes cast in favour of such parties and the percentage of seats they obtain becomes closer.

The above features explain why majority systems enjoy some degree of support from those who advocate reform of the existing electoral system.

# Proportional Systems

As their name suggests, proportional systems have the significant advantage that they ensure that the extent to which each political party is represented in the House of Commons directly reflects its degree of support in the country at election time. Therefore, it is argued that proportional systems are best placed to uphold representative democracy by ensuring that representatives are truly accountable and that no votes are wasted. However, opponents of proportional representation object to it on the following basis.

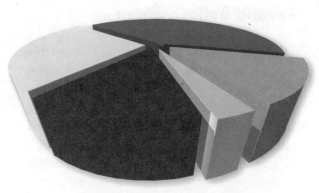

Firstly, they claim that it can reduce the quality of ongoing voter representation due to the fact that, at best, multi-member constituencies exist and this breaks the direct link between MPs and their constituents which is a feature of the present electoral system.

Secondly, and most damagingly, it is pointed out that proportional systems often fail to generate a clear-cut result in the form of single party government. Instead, coalition governments have to be formed which involve power being shared between two or more parties. In this regard, it is claimed that coalition governments give undue influence to small parties which may only represent the views of a limited amount of voters. Also, coalitions can often prove unstable should the junior partner choose to switch allegiance to another large party. Such activity is sufficient to bring down a government and can produce a great deal of political instability.

This raises the issue that in the event of such instability and the constant need for compromise, voters may find that the party policies they supported at election time are not those which are subsequently implemented due to the need to find common ground with a junior party in a coalition. Also, it becomes more difficult for a government to be held accountable for its policies when they are the product of two or more parties.

A final area of criticism expressed by opponents of proportional representation is that it may lead to a sharp increase in the number of political parties. It is claimed that such a climate can provide encouragement for extremist parties which may have the ultimate aim of subverting democracy.

In making a response to these points, supporters of proportional representation argue that its multi-member constituency basis further enhances representation by providing voters with choice not only between parties but between individual candidates representing the same party. Also, they take the view that the possible requirement to form a coalition government and the resulting compromises that larger parties may have to make will enhance political stability by reducing the major policy shifts which can arise within the present electoral system when a change of government takes place.

## The Party List System

List systems involve each political party preparing a list of candidates who will contest the election. Voters do not choose individual candidates but instead vote for a party with seats being allocated according to party lists. This means that a party which obtained 50 per cent of the total vote would be in the fortunate position of having exactly half of its candidates elected (the top half). Therefore, list systems are truly proportional as the percentage vote obtained by each party is calculated and seats allocated on a pro rata basis.

Party List Systems of varying complexity are used by many countries including Belgium, Italy, Luxembourg, Spain, the Netherlands and Israel.

The main criticism made of the Party List System is that it significantly strengthens the role of political party leadership but fails to support an effective link between voters and representatives.

The lists will be compiled by party headquarters with the result that the party leadership will have a significant degree of control over candidates. Whether or not they appear on the list and their position on it will be determined by the leadership.

In addition, voters will find it difficult to identify a particular person who represents them and may have to raise their concerns with party organisations rather than an individual representative.

In recognition of this, most of the countries which use list systems including Italy and Spain, prepare regional lists in an attempt to introduce some element of a direct link between voters and representatives.

However, a small group of countries including Israel, Luxembourg and the Netherlands treat the whole country as one constituency when vote counting and allocation of seats takes place.

## Single Transferable Vote (STV)

This is the most complex of the proportional representation (PR) systems but it also commands significant support. It is favoured by both the Electoral Reform Society and the Liberal Democrats. Under STV, the country is divided into multi-member constituencies each of which may elect three, four or five Members of Parliament. Political parties may put forward as many candidates in each constituency as there are seats to be contested.

Voters record on the ballot paper their support for candidates in order of preference. If they wish, voters can rank order all candidates but some may choose to support only one or two candidates and cast votes in their favour.

The formula for working out the quota of votes that a candidate would need to secure election is shown below:

$$\frac{\text{Number of Votes Cast}}{\text{Number of Seats} + 1} + 1$$

Accordingly, in a five member constituency within which 300,000 votes were cast, the number of votes required to meet the quota would be as follows:

$$\frac{300,000}{5 + 1} + 1 = 50,001 \text{ votes}$$

Should a candidate reach the stated quota on voters' first preferences then that candidate is elected. Those candidates who receive more votes than the quota requirement have their second preference votes distributed to the remaining candidates with the result that some of those candidates may achieve the quota figure and so the process continues.

However, should the allocation of second preference votes in this way prove insufficient to bring more candidates above the quota figure, then those candidates who have the least first preference votes will be eliminated and their supporters' second preferences taken into account.

This process of reallocating votes continues until successful candidates have been identified for all of the available seats. In this way, the STV system ensures that votes are not wasted.

The main criticism made of STV is that the process of generating a result may prove to be complex and involve a number of stages at which votes are reallocated and new calculations made. Consequently, it is argued that the democratic process may be undermined if voters fail to understand the basis on which results are determined.

Furthermore, the fact that STV is based on multi-member constituencies is criticised as it is claimed that this weakens the link between voters and their representatives.

However, in response, supporters of STV claim that voting is quite straightforward and note that political parties are more likely to select a range of candidates to contest multi-member constituencies and that this should act to enhance the representation of both women and ethnic minorities. Also, it is contended that voters in multi-member constituencies will be able to choose the representative to approach with any concerns that they have. In contrast, within single member constituencies, some voters will be obliged to obtain support from a representative who holds opposing political views.

Although the STV system does not produce an exactly proportional result, it establishes a very close link between political support in the form of votes cast for a party and representation (the number of seats it obtains).

The STV system is currently used in Malta, the Irish Republic and Australia (for elections to the Senate).

## Additional Member System

The Additional Member System (AMS) attempts to bring about an ideal situation whereby the benefits of proportional representation are obtained without a substantial amount of sacrifice in terms of representation of constituents.

The Additional Member System currently operates in Germany and it involves half of the seats in the legislature being subject to direct election on a First Past the Post basis and the remaining half on a regional Party List basis. This has the effect of producing a proportional result overall.

The individual elector has two votes, one for the candidate and one for the political party. As candidates are elected by means of the First Past the Post system, they are topped up by members from the respective party lists in proportion to the overall percentage vote that the party has obtained.

In Germany, to prevent the rise of extremist parties, political parties are required to obtain at least three constituency seats or a 5 per cent regional vote before they qualify for 'additional members' elected from party lists.

The percentage of seats won by each party in the constituency elections is compared with the percentage vote for the party across the country. In the event that a discrepancy exists, this is corrected by a further allocation of seats to the party from regional party lists.

The Additional Member System has the advantage that it not only produces a proportional result but it retains a clear link between voters and their represent-atives. It is this feature which caused the Plant Committee, set up by the Labour Party to examine electoral reform, to recommend AMS as its preferred form of proportional representation. This was taken a step further in October 1995 when the Scottish Constitutional Convention determined that election to a future Scottish Assembly would be by AMS.

According to the model developed, there will be 129 Members of a Scottish Parliament (MSPs) elected by an Additional Member System. Seventy three MSPs will be elected by First Past the Post from the existing Westminster constituencies and the number will then be topped up proportionately with the remaining 56 MSPs chosen from regional party lists based on Scotland's eight Euroconstituencies.

Critics of the Additional Member System point to the large size of constituencies in Germany and the difficulty of ensuring that all constituents are represented effectively. Also, it is clear that the adoption of regional party lists places more power in the hands of political party headquarters.

## Summary

To a significant extent, the electoral system which a country has reflects its historical path of political development. No electoral system is perfect as each has an element of advantage and disadvantage when compared with possible alternatives.

The programme of constitutional reform proposed by the new Labour Government which involves the use of proportional representation for European elections and the election of the Scottish Assembly and includes the promised referendum on the nature of the electoral system to be used for Westminster elections makes this one of the most significant periods in the history of electoral reform.

It can be argued that the advantages of proportional representation in the context of the European elections and elections to the Scottish Assembly outweigh the disadvantages as no national government is being elected. However, it remains to be seen whether the electorate will be convinced that a new system should be put in place to replace First Past the Post and elect a future government. To date, the prevailing view has been that arguments relating to strong government are of greater importance than those made regarding the possible undermining of representative democracy.

At this point in time, it seems likely that the advisory commission, established by Labour in Autumn 1997 to recommend a possible system to be used at future general elections, will opt for a majority system such as the Supplementary Vote. This is the system which is likely to command the support of Labour members of the advisory commission and there are early indications that the Liberal Democrats are prepared to end their traditional support for the STV system in order to secure some limited element of electoral reform.

A majority system, such as the Supplementary Vote, would produce a more proportional result and significantly improve the position of the third party in British politics. However, it should be noted that any system recommended by the advisory commission would have to be supported by the electorate in the promised referendum on electoral reform.

STUDY TOPIC 3

# How Does the Media Shape Political Attitudes?

## Introduction

The phenomenal growth of the media, in Britain and throughout the Western World, during the last thirty years has meant that its influence on the political process has become the subject of concentrated study. A number of surveys conducted in Britain have shown that more than sixty per cent of the adult population consider television to be their main source of political information. A further twenty five per cent of adults identify the press as the source which they draw upon to the most significant extent for such information.

Most initial theories relating to media influence on the political process within democratic societies led to the conclusion that it was, on the whole, both positive and favourable. The view was taken that by encouraging a greater awareness of political issues among the general public, the media acted to facilitate the democratic process. Furthermore, it was argued that the capacity of the media to influence public opinion is very limited due to the public's capacity to be selective.

According to this interpretation, members of the public were most receptive to information and comment which confirmed existing views and would act to reinforce established loyalties. At a later stage, this rather narrow view of the role of the media was broadened to take more account of the entertainment function that the press, radio and television could provide.

In recent times, theories about the role of the media which suggest that they are no more than neutral channels of communication have become subject to increasing challenge. Firstly, it has been noted that firm party loyalties based on social class and other influences are being eroded. Consequently, as the number of floating voters increases, it is contended that the capacity of the media to influence public opinion on political issues and ultimately electoral choice is enhanced. Also, the actions of both leading politicians and prominent individuals within the media are such that they clearly consider the role of the media to be of great importance not only in communicating information but also in persuading and thereby forming and changing public perceptions.

In this context, a number of observers have concluded that the high quality of Labour's 1997 General Election campaign, conducted by their campaign manager, Peter Mandelson, played a significant part in securing Labour's sizeable overall majority. It has been noted that Labour had more than one hundred staff working within its Millbank base immediately prior to and during the election campaign.

Indeed, both leading parties made such attempts to manage the media and thereby ensure that their policies and views received prominent coverage during the 1997 General Election campaign that their campaign bases are said to have resembled sophisticated news services designed to quickly assimilate and generate information.

## Interpreting the News

In recognition of such developments, most modern accounts of media influence note that the media does not simply report the news but that it is powerfully placed to provide interpretations of it. Furthermore, the media has the capacity to influence the political agenda by choosing certain issues to be highlighted and by projecting persuasive images such as the 'loony left' or an 'indecisive' John Major.

With regard to the opinion forming capacity of the media, it is often commented that members of the public are highly susceptible to such influence. It is noted that the vast majority of the population derive their information about politics from the mass media and that they often have no alternative but to trust news reporting as their lack of experience of politics makes it impossible for them to assess the extent to which it is comprehensive, accurate and impartial.

However, it is important to recognise that the passivity of readers, viewers and listeners can be, and often is, overstated by those who attempt to assess media influence. It should be remembered that a range of factors such as social class, education and geographical location as well as the related influences of family, friends and colleagues act to help determine the political predispositions of individuals. Therefore, the media will have different effects on different people.

Also, uniformity is not normally a feature of media news coverage and interpretation within democratic societies. Consequently, it is reasonable to take the position that since most people have access to more than one media outlet this should be sufficient to ensure that no single media product can exert undue influence on public opinion.

Nevertheless, there is widespread acceptance that the role of the media as an opinion former is already significant and that developments within the media industry are likely to further advance this position of influence.

## Ownership and Control

Technological developments within the press and broadcasting are such that they have acted to concentrate ownership of the media in the hands of a few multinational companies with global reach and enormous investment power. Only six multi-national companies own all mass circulation newspapers in the United Kingdom and the ascendant position of Rupert Murdoch and his News International empire is such that it owns 35 per cent of Britain's national press.

Furthermore, these large corporations have heavily invested in the revolution that satellite and cable technologies have created within the broadcasting industry. In particular, digital terrestrial television has the potential to make the information superhighway a reality with television becoming the vehicle by means of which shopping, banking, internet access and videophoning are conducted within the home.

Therefore, it seems likely that the media's sphere of influence will expand but that ownership of the media will become further concentrated in the hands of a small number of multinational companies. For this reason, it is important to reflect on how the major players in the media industry use the power currently at their disposal.

According to some radical interpretations, power is used by the media to support the interests and values of dominant groups within society with the result that those who are to the left of the political spectrum such as socialist parties and trade unions become marginalised in the sense that they find it difficult to obtain favourable news coverage of their activities.

One of the most active groups of social researchers in recent years who have taken this position is the Glasgow University Media Group. This group has argued consistently that it is able to detect such bias within the British media.

However, a number of commentators take a broader view which attaches greater significance to the commercial imperatives which drive media corporations. This involves them being thought of simply as large business organisations seeking to promote social and political conditions which will advance their commercial interests. This interpretation would cast media corporations as essentially profit orientated bodies which will support whichever party or viewpoint is perceived to be of commercial advantage to them. Within this analysis, media corporations

DIAGRAM 2

## Illustration of the potential of digital television.

*The current television broadcast sends a picture broken down into 625 lines with an aspect ration of 3 x 4, whilst High Definition Television (HDTV) sends the picture using 1125 lines with an aspect ration of 9 x 16. One benefit of HDTV is the pitcure is over four times the size of conventional broadcast television.*

consider the propaganda support that they can provide for particular parties or viewpoints as an asset which can be used as a bargaining counter when meeting with politicians and other influential groups.

### The Media and Democracy

In general terms, it is often stated that the relationship between politicians and the media is one of mutual dependency. Politicians need the media to communicate their messages and the media actively require a stream of interesting news items to inform, interest and entertain their readers, listeners and viewers.

At best, the activities of the media act to uphold democratic traditions and institutions by ensuring that the public is made aware of the views and activities of their political representatives. The media also encourage participation in the political process by ensuring that important issues are understood.

However, it can also be argued that media activities can prove damaging to democracy due to the potential for manipulation of news by powerful commercial interests. A further development of this view that media activities can undermine the democratic process is based on the efforts made by media sources to ensure that political coverage is entertaining. It is considered that this emphasis has led to an undue concentration on items with a human interest slant, e.g. the personalities and personal lives of politicians, which has acted to trivialise politics and disillusion the public.

That the media is a powerful influence within the political system cannot be challenged; the extent to which it is an influence for good or ill will ultimately depend on the demands that the public makes of media provision.

# The Press

## The British Press: Structure and Developments
### Popular and Quality Press

At present, Britain has ten national daily newspapers and nine national Sunday newspapers. In general terms, the British press can be divided into two distinct categories; the quality (broadsheet) press and the popular (tabloid) press. The quality press is intended to cater for a mainly middle class readership and it includes such titles as The Daily Telegraph, The Guardian, The Financial Times, The Independent and The Times.

The great majority of tabloid readers are working class. However, it is notable that the Daily Mail and the Daily Express have a higher proportion of lower middle class readers than papers such as The Mirror, The Sun and the Daily Star whose readership is mainly working class.

Britain has a small but growing readership of quality newspapers. There are five quality national daily newspapers in Britain and this represents an impressive total in relation to the size of the population.

In general terms, the press is well supported in Britain. A recent survey conducted by French researchers established that British people bought more newspapers per head of population than many of their European counterparts. However, it was noted that Britons are highly distrustful of the accuracy and reliability of newspaper content.

This survey can be linked to the view expressed by some commentators that there are two main types of newspaper reader in Britain. According to this interpretation, tabloid readers (who constitute the great majority of newspaper readers) have limited understanding and experience of politics with the result that they are often dependent on television for much of their political information. In contrast, readers of the quality press are considered to have, in the main, a high level of political interest and participation.

DIAGRAM 3

## Tabloid Readership: Social Class Analysis (Percentages)

| | AB | C1 | C2 | DE |
|---|---|---|---|---|
| Daily Express | 20 | 34 | 26 | 20 |
| Daily Mail | 24 | 32 | 25 | 19 |
| The Mirror | 6 | 18 | 36 | 40 |
| Daily Star | 4 | 14 | 38 | 44 |
| The Sun | 5 | 17 | 35 | 43 |

*Source: Watts, 1997*

DIAGRAM 4

## The Popular (Tabloid) Press: Circulation Statistics (July 1997)

| Daily Newspaper | Circulation |
|---|---|
| Daily Express | 1,226,466 |
| Daily Mail | 2,217,123 |
| The Mirror | 2,330,450 |
| Daily Star | 738,412 |
| The Sun | 3,811,529 |

*Source: ABC*

DIAGRAM 5

## The Quality (Broadsheet) Press: Circulation Statistics (July 1997)

| Daily Newspaper | Circulation |
|---|---|
| Daily Telegraph | 1,093,582 |
| Financial Times | 326,084 |
| The Guardian | 406,478 |
| The Independent | 258,386 |
| The Times | 758,682 |

*Source: ABC*

# Ownership

The national British press is owned by a few large business concerns. Approximately 80 per cent of newspaper circulation is controlled by three large conglomerates. The largest of these is Rupert Murdoch's News International which accounts for fully 35 per cent of the newspaper market. The other major players in the British newspaper industry are the Mirror Newspaper Group and United Newspapers.

Despite the fact that new printing technology has supported an increasing number of publishing ventures and publications, ownership of the British newspaper industry remains highly concentrated. Indeed, The Independent, which was established in 1986, was the first quality newspaper to be launched in Britain in 113 years. Also, the Today newspaper (which closed in November 1995) represented an attempt by its founder Eddie Shah to use the cost advantages generated by new printing technology to gain a foothold in the tabloid daily newspaper market. Prior to closure, the Today title became part of the News International group.

Concern regarding the high concentration of ownership which exists within the newspaper industry centres on the fact that the press is independent of government control and is in a powerful position to influence public opinion.

Ownership of the press is characterised by powerful proprietors who have traditionally attempted to influence the voting intentions of their readerships by favouring a particular political viewpoint. In this regard, it is often argued that the Conservative Party has a significant advantage over its political rivals as its pro-business policies have been viewed by the major newspaper producers as supportive of their commercial interests.

Newspapers are well placed to influence their readers. They can decide on the news stories to be covered, the amount of space that each item will be given, its position within the publication and the editorial line which will influence the way in which the story is presented and how it is likely to be interpreted by readers.

DIAGRAM 6

## Ownership of British Daily Newspapers

| Daily Newspaper | Owner |
| --- | --- |
| Daily Express | United Newspapers |
| Daily Mail | Associated Newspapers |
| Daily Star | United Newspapers |
| Daily Telegraph | Hollinger |
| Financial Times | Pearson |
| The Guardian | Guardian Media Group PLC (Scott Trust) |
| The Independent | Newspaper Publishing PLC |
| The Mirror | Mirror Group Newspapers |
| The Sun | News International |
| The Times | News International |

# The Press and Influence

The capacity of the tabloid press to influence public opinion has been a particular area of concern. The development of tabloid journalism has to some extent been influenced by television. Television attracts large audiences, is capable of providing news which is the latest available and is required to be impartial.

In response to this, the newspaper industry has had to develop its own distinct identity. With regard to the quality press, its capacity to provide in-depth political coverage and analysis makes it attractive to readers who have a strong interest in political affairs. The response of the popular press has been to focus on the entertainment that newspapers can provide in the form of human interest items. Consequently, to the extent that politics is dealt with, there is a tendency to concentrate on personalities and party political content.

The commercial drive to retain the loyalty of readers and advertisers has meant that newspapers have become involved in fierce price wars and journalists have come under increasing pressure to obtain exclusive stories. Also, every attempt is made to present stories in the most eye-catching way possible. The result has been the growth of chequebook journalism and an increasing emphasis on the sensational, the trivial and stories of a spurious nature.

# Newspapers and Elections

An increasing number of observers have claimed that the national press constitutes a significant influence on voting behaviour and election results. Subsequent to the 1992 General Election, such arguments were lent additional weight when the Sun newspaper ran its front page headline, "It's The Sun Wot Won It".

On the day of the 1992 General Election, The Sun had attempted to discourage readers from voting Labour by running a nine page special which incorporated the front page headline, "If Kinnock wins today, will the last person to leave Britain please turn out the lights".

The Sun's attempt to influence the outcome of the Election appeared to prove very successful. In 1992, Sun readers constituted more than one fifth of the electorate and more than one third of the 'don't knows'. Despite the fact that the majority of Sun readers were considered to be Labour supporters, only 36 per cent voted Labour.

The Sun headlines prior to the 1992 General Election represented the culmination of a series of attacks on Labour primarily by the tabloid press. Labour policies on taxation, Europe, proportional representation and immigration were attacked relentlessly during the course of the election campaign with the result that Neil Kinnock, leader of the Labour Party at that time, attributed the loss of the election to hostile press coverage. He was not alone in this assessment. Alistair McAlpine, a leading member and former treasurer of the Conservative Party, referred to the editors of The Sun, Daily Mail and Daily Express as the 'real heroes' of the campaign.

During the 1992 General Election campaign, Labour faced an uphill struggle as a result of what Guardian correspondent, Martin Linton, has referred to as the 'press deficit'. Linton noted that 70 per cent of all national newspapers had supported the Conservatives during the 1992 General Election campaign as opposed to 27 per cent favouring Labour. The resulting press deficit of 43 per cent ensured that the great majority of voters were being presented with an adverse view of Labour immediately prior to the 1992 General Election thereby increasing the prospect of defeat.

Linton commented that, during the period from 1945 through to October 1974, Labour had faced press deficits that varied between 10 and 18 per cent. During that time, he noted Labour had been successful on five occasions but that the Labour Party had never won a general election with a press deficit in excess of 18 per cent. In analysing the contribution of The Sun newspaper to Labour's defeat, Linton noted that its efforts had produced a crucial 8 per cent swing to the Conservatives among Sun readers.

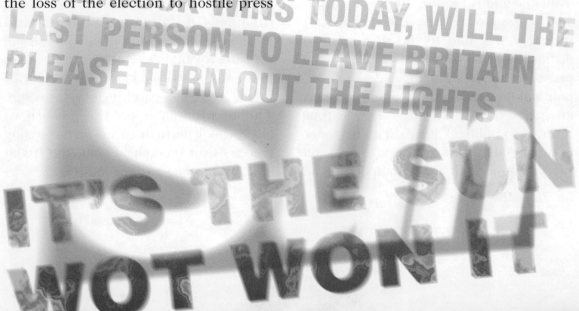

## 1997 General Election

A remarkable series of events led to Labour being able to reverse the adverse trend of press coverage at the 1997 General Election. At this election, 60 per cent of Britain's national daily newspapers advised their readers to vote Labour. It was the first time in well over a generation that most newspapers opted to support Labour.

Mr Major witnessed a general erosion of press support for the Conservative Party and its policies and, in particular, his leadership of the Party after the 1992 General Election.

It is generally agreed that the humiliating circumstances of Britain's withdrawal from the European Exchange Rate Mechanism (ERM) in September 1992 was the start of this process. Thereafter, some of the Conservative Party's leading press supporters, including the Daily Mail and the Daily Telegraph, became openly critical of the Government's handling of the economy and this placed added pressure on Mr Major.

Furthermore, the Conservative Party was burdened by sleaze allegations which led to several resignations from government during Major's premiership and culminated in the 'cash for questions' scandal which led to a series of setbacks for the Conservative Party during the early stages of the 1997 General Election campaign.

In June 1995, in response to internal party conflict and in an attempt to unify the Conservative Party in the face of increasing Eurosceptic dissent, John Major resigned the leadership and sought re-election. During the ensuing leadership campaign, almost all of the Conservatives' traditional allies within the press supported John Redwood, a leading Eurosceptic, but they failed to secure their objective when Conservative MPs re-elected John Major.

Press hostility towards Mr Major's Conservative Government combined with the election, in 1994, of Tony Blair as leader of the Labour Party and the on-going development of New Labour policies to make the Labour Party a more attractive prospect as viewed by the leading press conglomerates. Labour enjoyed a commanding lead over the Conservatives in opinion polls and a number of observers noted that the Labour Party's position on ownership regulations seemed more favourable to the leading players in the newspaper industry than those of the Conservative Party.

In July 1995, Tony Blair met with Mr Murdoch and senior executives within the News International organisation to discuss a range of matters relating to the media industry. By March 1997, relations between between News International and the Labour Party which had been soured by the Wapping industrial dispute, had improved to the extent that The Sun newspaper, in response to Rupert Murdoch's directive, declared its support for Labour. Further support for Labour came from the News of the World, News International's leading Sunday newspaper.

**The Independent**

**MAJOR'S BIG GAMBLE PAYS OFF**

**The Sun**

**It's Worse Than That, He's Won**

Consequently, the position of the Labour Party, in terms of press support, had been transformed from that which existed in the lead up to the 1992 General Election.

The research organisation MORI established, during the run-up to the 1997 General Election, that 56 per cent of Sun readers intended to vote Labour. This contrasted with the 36 per cent who ignored the newspaper's advice in 1992 and decided to vote Labour.

The fact that newspapers are perceived by politicians to have significant influence on voting intentions can be gauged from the fact that Mr Murdoch, owner of News International, during a visit to Britain which took place in February 1997, was invited to meetings with Britain's leading politicians. This involved meeting Mr Major, then Prime Minister, at Chequers where it is reported Rupert Murdoch was

urged to maintain News International's support for the Conservative Party. He also met with Mr Blair and Mr Gordon Brown. The subjects discussed included Labour's economic policies and approaches to welfare reform.

With reference to press influence, there is a tendency for commentators to concentrate on the popular (tabloid) press. However, it is important to recognise that quality national newspapers with their in-depth political coverage are highly influential as the opinions expressed within them are noted carefully by leading politicians and civil servants involved in the policy process. Consequently, politicians frequently contribute to the pages of quality newspapers to make their views known and to respond to points made within articles, editorial comment and letters written by readers.

**DIAGRAM 8**

## British Daily Newspapers and Political Party Support

| Daily Newspaper | 1992 | 1997 |
|---|---|---|
| Daily Express | Conservative | Conservative |
| Daily Mail | Conservative | Conservative |
| Daily Star | None | Labour |
| Daily Telegraph | Conservative | Conservative |
| Financial Times | Labour | Labour |
| The Guardian | Labour | Labour |
| The Independent | None | Labour |
| The Mirror | Labour | Labour |
| The Sun<br>The Sun (Scotland) | Conservative<br>SNP | Labour<br>Labour |
| The Times | Conservative | Conservative |

# The Lobby System

Politicians have the capacity to influence the press. The major political parties have found an increasing role for media specialists, often referred to as 'spin doctors' who are employed to obtain favourable media coverage whenever possible and limit the capacity of potentially damaging news items to undermine their particular party. With this in mind, it can be argued that the lobby system provides an important way in which government politicians can influence the press directly.

Approximately 150 journalists at Westminster are known as lobby journalists. This means that they have access to the Members' lobby and other parts of the Palace of Westminster which are normally off-limits to members of the public and they benefit from confidential briefings given by Ministers and information officers. This information is provided on an unofficial basis with the result that the comments made must not be attributed to any specific individual.

The benefits of this arrangement seem clear. The journalists involved benefit from a continuous flow of political information with the general public being made aware of matters which might not be reported under normal circumstances. In this way, it is possible to interpret the lobby system as being a feature of open government and, therefore, good for democracy.

However, a number of commentators take the view that the adverse effects of the lobby system outweigh the benefits. They claim that it places the government of the day in a powerful position to manage the news and reinforces the position of 'spin doctors' whose role it is to ensure that government activities are reported in a favourable way.

In this regard the capacity of Bernard Ingham, when serving as Mrs Thatcher's Press Secretary, to influence the lead items in the tabloid press is often referred to. During the period 1986-90, The Guardian, The Independent and The Scotsman refused to participate in the lobby system in protest at what they regarded as news management activities.

Furthermore, critics of the lobby system take the view that it undermines the investigative role of journalists and reduces their position to that of purveyors of government information.

# The Press and Privacy

An analysis of media coverage during the 1997 General Election campaign revealed that the economy had received 5 per cent and taxation 10 per cent whereas sleaze was far ahead of both major concerns with coverage amounting to fully 18 per cent.

News stories which are based on allegations against politicians or revelations about their private lives are often seized upon by the tabloid press, in particular, because of their human interest element which attracts readers.

However, as such adverse coverage of the political scene in Britain has grown in both frequency and intensity, it is notable that public respect for and confidence in politicians has declined. All recent indications suggest that politicians who become the subject of such press coverage are liable to lose the support of significant amounts of voters.

The determination of the tabloid press to obtain stories about leading public figures and to be first to publish them has led to increasing concerns about the intrusive activities of the press. Chequebook journalism, the use of telephoto lenses, door stepping, bugging and other such questionable activities have become part of the stock-in-trade of tabloid journalists under increasing pressure to break exclusive stories.

In response, increasing consideration

has been given to the use of statutory controls on the press. In 1993, the Second Calcutt Report, produced by the committee chaired by Sir David Calcutt, recommended that legislation be introduced in an attempt to outlaw some of the more extreme activities of the press and thereby protect privacy. It also recommended that victims of intrusive press behaviour be compensated. However, the Government opted to continue to encourage the press to self regulate its activities.

With the election of the Labour Government in 1997, the issue of privacy and press controls is being reviewed and it seems likely that journalistic activities which are considered to constitute an invasion of privacy, such as door stepping, will be outlawed.

The whole issue of media control is highly controversial. Although the protection of individual privacy is a worthwhile objective, the Government must ensure that any law passed to achieve this does not lead to an erosion of democracy by restricting the investigative activities of journalists and promoting secrecy. This helps to explain why successive governments have been slow to act on this issue.

## Restrictions on the Press

The Official Secrets Act has the effect of deterring journalists from writing articles based on official information which has not been released by Ministers for official disclosure. In its modern form, this Act only protects certain categories of information which include that relating to defence, security and intelligence and law and order.

A further restriction on journalistic activities is the D Notice system which is designed to prevent publication or broadcasting of defence information thought to be sensitive.

The D Notice system is operated by a committee consisting of officials and journalists who issue private written warnings to newspapers whose activities are considered to warrant such intervention.

Some commentators have concluded that the combined effect of the Official Secrets and the D Notice system is to make Britain one of the most restrictive countries in terms of press freedom in the Western World. They point out that the Official Secrets Act provides the means by which Ministers can maintain secrecy through the simple expedient of classifying as secret certain information which they do not wish to enter the public domain.

Furthermore, the press is restricted by legislation relating to copyright and libel. It is argued that this protects the interests of wealthy organisations and individuals who can operate a degree of censorship by threatening recourse to the legal system and the pursuit of appropriate damages. In contrast, the majority of the population who cannot afford this course of action are unable to take advantage of the protection that the law affords.

# Television

## Public Perception and Regulation

A significant majority of the adult population in Britain depend on television as their main source of information. A number of studies have shown that, in general terms, television coverage of political issues is thought to be accurate, reliable and trustworthy. The much lower approval rating for newspapers is in sharp contrast to this finding.

Public confidence in the quality of television output is based, at least in part, on the strict controls exerted over television broadcasters. The British Broadcasting Corporation (BBC) and the Independent Television Commission (ITC), which regulates the output of commercial television companies, are required to ensure that their coverage of political issues is characterised by a respect for accuracy and an impartial approach.

The BBC's Royal Charter, which was first granted in 1926, provides for a structure whereby the organisation is controlled by a government-appointed Director-General and Board of Governors. BBC funding is largely derived from the annual television licence fee which is set by the government. The BBC's founding Charter prohibits political advertising and requires the organisation to observe political impartiality.

Commercial broadcasting is regulated by the Independent Television Commission (ITC) whose administrators are also subject to government appointment. Under the terms of the 1990 Broadcasting Act, the ITC is required to ensure that all commercial television companies licensed by it meet legal requirements relating to balanced and impartial coverage.

## Political Coverage

The potential for television broadcasting to influence political attitudes is enormous. According to the recent report entitled, 'Cultural Trends in the 90s', published by the Policy Studies Institute, the average person in Britain watches television for 25.2 hours each week. Furthermore, research conducted by the Broadcasters' Audience Research Board

(BARB) established that, in 1995, fully ninety six per cent of the population watched television at least once per week.

Of the total amount of television output, approximately twenty per cent is devoted to news and current affairs programmes which often deal with sensitive and controversial political issues. In the run-up to a general election, televised coverage of political issues intensifies and it is estimated by BBC News that fully two thirds of the population (36 million) tuned in to its daily coverage of the 1997 General Election campaign.

Nevertheless, evidence exists that the general public often consider the concentrated emphasis on politics that exists when a general election is imminent to be somewhat unattractive. During the 1997 General Election campaign, ITN's News at Ten lost approximately ten per cent of its normal audience and the BBC reported that its flagship news programme, Nine O'Clock News, had lost fully 1.5 million viewers (25 per cent of its normal audience).

In attempting to explain seeming public disinterest in general election campaign coverage, the requirement that broadcasts dealing with political matters should be demonstrably objective is often blamed for causing televised reports to be rather bland and mundane.

The strategy adopted by the BBC and commercial television companies tends to be that of ensuring that the three major political parties, Conservative, Labour and the Liberal Democrats receive broadly equal coverage in terms of the extent to which their parties feature in news broadcasts. This is related to the particular sensitivities of party leaderships at election times who wish to ensure that the electorate is made fully aware of the messages that the party wishes to communicate and of its particular activities during each day of the campaign.

Television broadcasters have to be seen to be doing everything in their power to produce output which will be generally perceived as accurate and impartial as they will almost inevitably face allegations of bias at some stage during the campaign. For example, prior to the 1997 General Election campaign, Brian Mawhinney, then Conservative Party Chairman, demanded a meeting with the BBC to discuss his fears that their journalists were waiting with "eager anticipation" for a Labour victory. This subsequently provoked an angry response from Labour, fearful that such comments might generate an element of Conservative advantage, as reflected in the statement made by party leader Tony Blair that television news programmes create a "conspiracy against understanding".

There seems to be some degree of agreement on the part of broadcasters that televised reports of the 1997 General Election campaign were unsatisfactory. In attempting to analyse the reasons for this, Richard Tait, editor-in-chief of Independent Television News (ITN), attributed viewer dissatisfaction with televised election coverage to the news management activities of the leading political parties and the "stop-watch approach" to television coverage of political issues which necessitated broadly equal broadcast time for each party regardless of the intrinsic newsworthiness of the issues being dealt with.

The emphasis on balance between the major parties is further reinforced by the fact that the time made available for party election broadcasts is strictly regulated to ensure that no element of unfair advantage exists.

However, the explanation for the seeming disinterest of a large section of voters in televised election coverage may well be more complex than disenchantment with the quality of news and current affairs programmes. A number of political surveys conducted during the run-up to the 1997 General Election established that as many as seventy per cent of voters had decided which party they would wish to see form the new government prior to the start of the election campaign.

Therefore, despite the potential that television has to exert political influence, it seems likely that many voters simply have their existing attitudes reinforced by focusing on those elements of coverage which relate directly to their established political opinions. The requirement that television broadcasters meet appropriate standards of accuracy, balance and impartiality serves to ensure that voters who remain undecided will be given every opportunity to make up their own minds free from any overt influence brought to bear by televised political coverage.

Nevertheless, politicians remain highly sensitive to the role that television can play in establishing a positive image of their party in the minds of voters. There is an awareness that traditional party loyalties based on social class and other such influences are waning with the result that voting behaviour has become more volatile. Furthermore, the impact of televised advertising on consumer preferences acts as a constant reminder to politicians of the potential power of television. A number of research studies have concluded that voters are much more likely to believe what they see on television as opposed to what they read in newspapers due to the exceptional impression made by televised images.

## Information Technology and Television

The development of new technology which will affect the broadcasting industry makes it difficult to assess the future political impact of television. Services provided by satellite television and cable television companies have already ensured that British viewers can access a range of programmes which extends far beyond those offered by the BBC and the commercial television companies operating within the independent television regions.

However, the situation will become even more complex from 1998 onwards with the digital television revolution which will transform traditional views about television.

Digital television provides a sharper picture, CD sound and access to hundreds of channels by means of pay-per-view programmes. Furthermore, television will become a means of accessing, by means of a telephone link, a large number of services including home banking, home learning, home shopping, video games entertainment, internet surfing and video-phoning.

*BBC Online Web Page*

During 1998, more than 200 digital terrestrial channels will be made available by British Digital Broadcasting (BDB) and, in addition, 200-plus satellite digital channels will be provided by Rupert Murdoch's BSkyB. BSkyB will also be responsible for manufacturing the set-top decoders which will be needed to enable existing television sets to receive digital transmissions.

It is proposed that the Independent Television Commission (ITC) and the Broadcasting Standards Council (BSC) will be responsible for regulating the output of the new channels. However, a number of commentators have expressed fears regarding the capacity of those regulatory bodies to control such diverse televised output effectively.

Furthermore, concerns exist that a few major players will dominate television broadcasting in the same way that concentration of ownership exists within the newspaper industry. The dominant position of Mr Murdoch's News International within the British newspaper industry and the increasing influence of BSkyB in satellite broadcasting are often cited as justification for such fears.

# Television and Political Parties

While it is reasonable to argue that impartiality requirements have done much to ensure that the power of television is not misused to manipulate voters, there can be little doubt that the medium of television has radically altered the ways in which political parties communicate with the electorate.

## The Importance of Image

There is clear evidence that election campaigns have become more presidential in style. The extent to which television focuses on political personalities necessitates that party leaders' appearance, speech, dress and manner should be such that voters' confidence can be won on the basis of a series of short, well-managed television appearances. Such is the emphasis now placed on the image of the party leader that some commentators consider an effective media presence to a be a prerequisite for appointment to the

position of leader. This element of television influence is generally considered to be unfortunate as it may rule out individuals with otherwise excellent leadership qualities.

## Media Events

Media concentration on leadership has also had the effect of marginalising local Parliamentary candidates and local political issues as there is a tendency for television reporters, in particular, to concentrate their energies, during election campaigns, on reporting media events arranged by party headquarters at which leading party figures will communicate policies on issues of national importance. At these staged rallies, politicians will often be joined by prominent entertainers and sports personalities to ensure that the event will command significant media attention.

## Soundbites

A further effect of television coverage is that lengthy speeches to party members have given way to concise statements written for the party leader, at least in part, by professional speech writers whose task is to incorporate short, memorable fifteen to thirty second 'soundbites' which it is hoped will be given extensive coverage in televised news broadcasts. As a result, the real audience for leading politicians when delivering a speech is often the electorate as a whole rather than those attending the event.

## Spin Doctors

During election campaigns professional media managers (or 'spin doctors'), such as Labour's Peter Mandelson, will seek to arrange each day so that positive media coverage of party activities is maximised. As a result, each day of the campaign will be scheduled in such a way that party

news conferences allow sufficient time for national television news reports to be prepared. Furthermore, a range of appropriate photo-opportunities will be put in place for leading party spokespersons.

It has become common practice for the major parties to plan election campaigns to allow each day to be devoted to a single issue with the instruction that all party spokespersons should remain 'on message' throughout the day. However, from time to time, a difficult issue will arise which requires the party leadership to make a response. At that point the role of party 'spin-doctors' becomes crucial as their task is that of interpreting events in a manner which is favourable to the party (or, at least, serves to limit damage to the party's image) and securing prominent media coverage for this version of events.

## Narrowing the Focus

Some observers take the view that, by concentrating on personalities and sensational issues, television can act to devalue the political process. In this regard, the prominence of sleaze allegations during the 1997 General Election campaign is often referred to. Also, it is noted that the number of politicians gaining national media coverage is declining. During the early stages of the 1997 General Election campaign, just ten frontbench politicians from the three major parties accounted for fully 87 per cent of media attention.

The influence of television is not restricted to general election campaigns. It is significant that some politicians seem to relish the opportunity to debate important issues on televised current affairs programmes rather than explore them in depth within the House of Commons. To some extent, the decision to televise the House of Commons in November 1989 (made permanent as a result of a free vote in July 1990) provided an opportunity to extend the educative and information giving roles of the House of Commons. In this regard, television coverage of select committees is generally considered to have been successful. However, the adversarial exchanges between the Prime Minister and the Leader of the Opposition at Prime Minister's Question Time with their inevitable emphasis on the personalities involved gain most consistent television coverage in national news programmes.

## Summary

Television is such a powerful medium that it has profoundly changed the ways in which political parties seek to communicate their views. All major political parties recognise that the extensive access to the electorate provided by television necessitates that strategies be put in place to ensure that communication of party policies is effective.

However, the nature of television with its concentration on short, easily understood, messages with visual impact has led some political commentators to conclude that it has generated an emphasis on party leaders, party image, 'soundbites' and media management which does little to support the democratic process.

Those who oppose this view would argue that television contributes greatly to democracy by ensuring that all viewers have access to high quality, interesting, balanced and objective reports. This, it is claimed, places voters in a strong position to make an informed choice.

One thing is certain, digital television technology will result in the already central role of television in the lives of many British people being further extended. It seems certain that viewers will enjoy more choice than ever before and their expression of preferences, in terms of the programmes that they are prepared to pay for, will ultimately determine the quality of television output.

# Political Parties and their Policies

STUDY TOPIC 1

## What function do political parties play in a democracy?

### Political Parties

It is almost impossible to imagine that a modern democracy like Britain could operate effectively without political parties playing a central role in the political system. For centuries, parties or groups of MPs in Parliament have worked to represent similar interests and discuss shared principles. However, it is only in relatively modern times that the idea of a political party based on national organisation, with its members participating in a range of activities from policy-making to contesting elections, has become established.

Towards the last quarter of the 19th Century, the then two major parties, the Conservatives and the Liberals, began developing associations in each constituency in order to gain support for their candidates at elections from the growing mass electorate. Nowadays, those parties and the Labour Party have organisations which take account of both the parliamentary nature of their activities and the need to organise throughout the country to develop appropriate policies and communicate these to voters. Other parties which have been successful in gaining seats in Parliament, such as the Scottish National Party, organise themselves in a similar way.

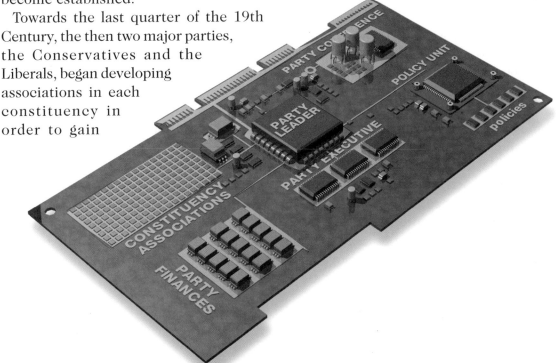

## Pressure Group or Political Party?

People join political parties because they consider themselves to have something in common with other members, i.e. similar views or the same interests. However, it is simplistic to define a political party as a group of like-minded people. Pressure groups also meet this criterion and although both pressure groups and political parties operate within the political system, a party is not a pressure group.

- A pressure group may have a policy or policies which it wishes to see implemented but which may relate to an area of special interest, e.g. protecting the environment. In addition, its activities are usually restricted to educating the public about its policies and influencing the government to adopt its policies or change existing ones.

- A political party addresses the whole range of government policies and does not restrict its interest to one single issue or area of policy. A party does not seek simply to influence the government but to develop its own policies in order to win power and put these policies into practice, i.e. to become the government.

Some parties may, at times, appear to act in a similar manner to pressure groups. For example, in the past, the Scottish National Party (SNP) stood simply for independence for Scotland. As it became more popular with voters and had to address the concerns of its supporters on a number of issues, the SNP developed a range of policies, not only to be implemented after independence but also to take account of the situation prior to independence, e.g. in local government. However, even if the Party had remained a single issue organisation, the very fact that its objective is to win political power and establish a new political state is sufficient evidence to confirm the SNP's status as a political party.

In the 1997 General Election, the Referendum Party, which had one overarching policy (to allow the British people the right to decide in a referendum whether or not to remain in the European Union) and the Natural Law Party, which drew its inspiration and philosophy from Eastern mysticism, both put up candidates in hundreds of constituencies. By focusing on a narrow range of issues, those two parties could also be regarded as behaving like pressure groups.

Nevertheless, distinguishing features exist. The aim of the Referendum Party was to gain power to implement its single policy and the Natural Law Party had developed policies which covered the whole range of government activity. Consequently, both organisations can safely be regarded as political parties.

Another development in the 1997 General Election was the decision by anti-abortion candidates to stand under the banner of the Pro-Life Alliance. This organisation aimed to win votes from sitting MPs or candidates who supported abortion. As this tactic was designed to promote a single issue rather than win seats, the Alliance is clearly a pressure group despite the fact that it is involved in the electoral process.

To summarise, a political party is made up of a group (sometimes a very large group) of people who support policies which cover the whole range of government activity. It seeks not to influence the government but to take office and enact its own policies.

## The Function and Role of Political Parties

Parties give ordinary citizens the opportunity to participate in the political process. Party members take part in the selection of candidates, who are nominated from within the party, to stand for election to Parliament and to local councils. Their election campaign expenses are met from party funding and the party provides workers to campaign on their behalf. In the 1997 General Election, out of 659 MPs elected, only Martin Bell did not belong to a party. It should be noted that he was helped indirectly by Labour and the Liberal Democrats who decided not to put up candidates against him so that he could maximise the vote against the sitting Conservative MP for Tatton, Neil Hamilton.

By giving ordinary citizens with no or limited financial means the opportunity to stand as candidates, parties are a vehicle for the recruitment of potential political leaders. Tony Blair, William Hague, Paddy Ashdown and Alex Salmond were at one time ordinary individual members of their party. Political parties have provided the country with its leaders and alternative leaders.

As campaigning organisations, both at and between elections, parties help to educate the electorate in the important issues of the day and provide alternative views on these issues. At elections, they also help to mobilise the electorate to make the effort to vote, thereby maximising participation in the electoral process.

As mentioned above, parties are groups of like-minded people but, within each party, there can be many different points of view. The party gives the proponents of these varied viewpoints the discipline to reach agreement and present a common policy to the electorate. In this way, differing points of view are reconciled and the resulting policy entered into the political process. In the absence of this development, diverse elements within each party could become splintered and marginalised rather than playing a meaningful role in political activity.

The different policies which each party presents to the electorate gives voters a clear choice of alternative programmes for government. If a government does not fulfil its policy commitments then it can be held accountable by the electorate who have various alternative parties from which to choose. Without a party system, such accountability and choice of alternatives would not be available.

Party organisation in Parliament adds to this idea of accountability and choice. The Whip system ensures discipline among MPs of the same party. Consequently, the governing party should be able to govern effectively and implement its policies while the other parties maintain effective opposition. Furthermore, the two party system not only presents the electorate with a range of choices but the choice between the current government and the alternative government, the Official Opposition.

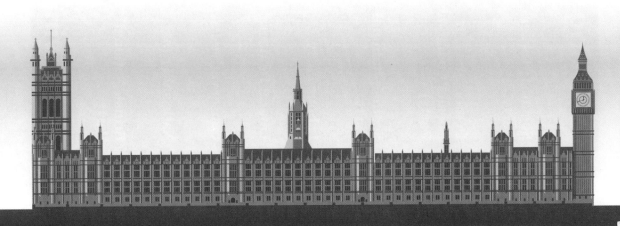

# The Political Spectrum – from Right to Left

All parties have a set of basic beliefs about the nature of politics. It is from these beliefs or ideology that a party's policies are derived. Policy development allows political parties to react to situations and tackle problems as they arise in real life. It is traditional, when trying to explain a party's ideology, to speak of it as being left wing, right wing, on the left or right of the political spectrum, or in the centre. This tradition is based on the seating arrangements within the French Estates General in 1789. Those who favoured the status quo, which involved keeping social and political conditions as they were, sat to the right of the King. Those who favoured radical change were seated to his left. In between, sat those who wanted some change but at a more moderate pace than those on the left.

If this model is applied to modern Britain, a basic representation of the political spectrum emerges. The far left is occupied by Trotskyist revolutionary groups. Moving towards the centre are the parties of the Democratic Left (former Communist Party). To the left of centre are the Labour Party and the Scottish National Party with the Liberal Democrats being placed at the centre of the political spectrum. The Conservative Party occupies the right of centre and the National Front and British National Party (who favour racist and fascist policies) are found on the far right.

## Political Parties – Right or Left?

However, this representation of the political spectrum is somewhat simplistic. The two main parties, Conservative and Labour, have always been broad coalitions of individuals with differing views. For example, in the early 1980s, the Labour Party accommodated individuals and groups whose views ranged from the far left Trotskyist Militant Tendency to the centrist Social Democratic Alliance. The latter's members could have fitted quite happily into the Liberal Party and, indeed, by 1988, most of this group had become members of the Liberal Democratic Party.

The Conservative Party, too, has been the political home of individuals whose views could span the section of the political spectrum ranging from the centre to the far right. The Monday Club was established in 1961 to promote an anti-black immigration policy and a nationalistic defence policy – very similar to those of the far right groups. The Bow Group and the Tory Reform Group, on the other hand, have members who could feel at home in the Liberal Democrats or with certain elements of New Labour.

## The Political Spectrum

left wing — Socialist Workers' Party — Democratic Left (former Communist Party) — Scottish National Party — Labour Party — Liberal Democrats — Conservative Party — National Front — British National Party — right wing

## Economic Policy –
## Blurring the Differences?

Complicating matters further is what appears to be the disappearance of major economic policy differences between the Labour Party and the Conservative Party. The former used to be clearly identified with, the promotion of equality by using taxation to redistribute wealth, increased welfare benefits and support for trade unions and nationalisation. The Labour Party has now moved significantly away from these and has accepted most of the changes made by the Conservatives during their eighteen years in power. Indeed, some commentators have suggested that the Liberal Democratic Party, the traditional centre party, is more left wing in its economic and social policies than Labour and should act as its conscience on these matters.

More confusing still, if the traditional view of the political spectrum is accepted, is the role of the Conservative Party in recent times. As a right wing party, it would normally be expected to support the status quo. However, under Mrs Thatcher's leadership it developed and implemented a range of radical social and economic policies which generated significant change. In reaction to this, the Labour Party and anti-Thatcherite Conservatives (the so called 'wets') were left to defend established social and economic policies.

## Europhiles and Eurosceptics

In order to understand British political parties it should be realised that the political spectrum of left, right and centre is to some extent reflected by each individual party.

After the 1997 General Election, this political situation became even more confusing. The main divide in the Conservative Party is between Europhiles, who favour further economic and political integration with the European Union, and Eurosceptics, who oppose any further integration and are even hostile to membership of the EU itself.

In the Labour Party, the mainstream of the party (popularly known as New Labour) support Tony Blair's reforms. This group consists of

people drawn from both the right and left wings of the party. However, New Labour supporters coexist with the section of the party which calls itself Old Labour. This group is characterised by such prominent Labour figures as Tony Benn who still emphasise the importance of socialist policies.

Despite this complexity, the advantage of using terms like left, right and centre to describe the political spectrum is that most people are familiar with them. Labour is still regarded as left wing, the Conservatives as right wing and the Liberal Democrats as being at the centre. Even the new groupings and alignments within the two main parties are being referred to in the familiar right, left and centre terms by the media, the public and the parties themselves. Such familiar terms are more meaningful to people than the small print of policy differences that separate parties and groups within parties. They are a shorthand way to describe political divergence and that is why they will continue to be used by politicians, media commentators and the general public.

# Conservative Party Organisation

The history of the two main parties provides some explanation of the difference in their structures and the distribution of power within them. Strictly speaking, the Conservative Party is made up of Conservative members of the Commons and Lords. It originated inside Parliament in the 19th Century and formed an organisation outside Parliament to support it in the country as a whole. After its defeat in the 1997 General Election, the Party established a commission to examine its structure and recommend any changes.

## The Constituency Association

At constituency level in the Conservative Party, the constituency association is responsible for recruiting members. In fact, there is no national membership system as there is in the Labour Party - members belong to their local association. This makes it difficult to determine national membership (estimates vary from 750,000 to as low as 250,000). Even if the higher estimate is accepted, this still constitutes a big fall from the 1950s, when estimates of 2,000,000 members were made.

Other parties have seen a similar decline in their memberships but the Conservative Party has become sufficiently alarmed to consider the development of a national membership system and embark on a recruitment drive.

The constituency association is responsible for selecting candidates, both to contest the constituency in parliamentary elections and to contest wards within the constituency in local council elections. The association is also responsible for fund-raising and campaigning between elections and sends representatives to area councils, e.g. the West of Scotland Area Council, and to the annual conference. Over half the associations have full-time agents who provide professional assistance.

In Scotland, which has a separate organisation, constituency associations are also represented at the Scottish Conservative and Unionist Council. There is also a Scottish party conference. The National Union of Conservative Associations coordinates constituency associations in England and Wales. It has a Central Council consisting of Conservative peers, Members of the European Parliament, prospective MPs and regional representatives. Probably the most important function of the National Union is to organise the annual party conference.

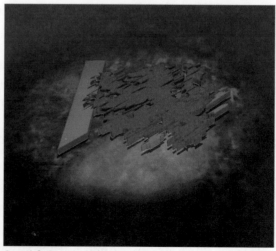

*Scottish Conservative Party Logo*

## The Party Conference

The conference consists of a series of debates followed by replies from government ministers or opposition spokespersons, depending whether or not the Conservative Party is in power. The subjects for debate are selected from resolutions received from constituency associations. These are vetted carefully by the organisers and no resolution which might be harmful to the party leadership is chosen. The highlight of the conference is the party leader's address. This is received enthusiastically by the representatives and a long, standing ovation is always given.

The conference does not make party policy as its purpose is to rally the representatives present and send them back to their constituencies to convey their enthusiasm to others. Probably most important in this age of television, it is an occasion for the party to demonstrate to the electorate its unity of purpose and its loyalty to the leader.

## Central Office

This is the professional, full-time wing of the party. Its headquarters are in Central Office in London. There is a Central Office in Edinburgh for the Scottish Party. It is run by the party chairman and other senior officials appointed by the leader. Central Office offers advice to constituency associations on matters like political education, campaigning and fund-raising. It provides training for constituency agents. However, its most important role is to act as a bridge between ordinary members and the Party's MPs. All of these functions are evident during the course of election campaigns which are run from Central Office. The campaign is coordinated and directed by the party chairman (in the 1997 General Election, it was Brian Mawhinney MP) who is always a member of the Cabinet or Shadow Cabinet.

## The Party Leader

At the apex of the party organisation is the party leader. The leader is in charge of all appointments to the front bench, either in or out of government, and also appointments to all full-time positions in the professional wing of the party. The leader is elected by Conservative MPs only, although constituency association chairpersons, Members of the European Parliament, Peers and National Union officials are consulted. Subsequent to the 1997 General Election defeat, when there were only 165 Conservative MPs and none in either Wales or Scotland, there were calls to allow a wider franchise. This is to be examined by the commission formed to report on party organisation.

*William Hague, Leader of the Conservative Party*

## The 1922 Committee

One part of the party over which the leader has no formal power is the 1922 Committee (the organisation of backbench Conservative MPs). It meets weekly and elects its own chairperson and executive. The leader may attend by invitation only. In normal circumstances, the 1922 Committee is loyal to the leader but if the party's popularity is low and MPs are worried, their concerns will be reported to the leader by the 1922 Committee Executive. It would be a foolish leader indeed who did not listen to and address these concerns because, in the end, retention of the position is dependent on the support of these MPs.

## Party Income

The Conservative Party receives its income from a levy on constituency associations and from donations made by companies and individuals. There are also donations from organisations such as the Aims of Industry and United British Industrialists (UBI), which are financed by some private companies. The Conservatives' opponents often refer to these organisations as fronts for the party. Such donations remain confidential if the donors so wish although this has caused some controversy. The party's opponents claim that it is a way for business to buy influence with the party, especially when in government. There have been claims that the party receives donations from both individuals and companies abroad.

Whatever the truth of these claims, after the 1997 Election, it was expected that the Labour Government would place restrictions on donations from abroad to political parties and require parties to reveal their sources of revenue.

It was also expected that the subject of funding for parties would be referred to the Committee on Standards in Public Life – a body established by the previous Conservative Government to investigate allegations of corruption and wrongdoing by MPs and others in public life. If action is taken to restrict or cut off sources of Conservative Party finance, it could be very serious. Although the Conservative Party managed to clear a deficit of £20 million before the 1997 Election, the election campaign was rumoured to have cost the party £28 million. However, new leader, William Hague, has already announced that the party will no longer accept donations from abroad and that all donations over £5000 will be made public.

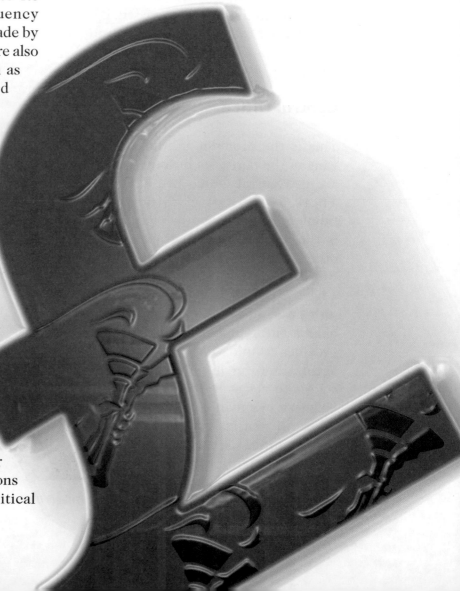

# Labour Party Organisation

The Labour Party was formed as a result of the activities of several organisations outside Parliament which came together to secure the election of MPs to represent the interests of working people inside Parliament. Labour MPs and Peers are the Parliamentary Labour Party.

## Labour Party Membership

Membership of the Labour Party is more complicated than in the Conservative Party. There are two types of membership (individual membership and affiliated membership).

Someone wishing to be an individual member applies to Party Headquarters, Millbank Tower, in London. The application is then sent to that person's local Constituency Labour Party (CLP) which decides whether to accept the application. Once the application is accepted, the new member is allocated to a local Labour Party branch in a particular area of the constituency (usually based on a local government ward). Individual membership of the Labour Party had fallen from an estimated 750,000 in the 1950s to just over 200,000 in the early 1990s. By 1997, this had increased to almost 400,000 a target the Party set itself.

## The Constituency Labour Party

The CLP is run by a General Committee, a body on which not all individual members of the CLP can sit. This is the source of the idea of affiliated membership.

The General Committee consists of delegates elected by Labour Party branches and other organisations which are permitted under national rules to affiliate to the party. These organisations are local branches of trade unions, the Cooperative Party (the sister party of the Labour Party, which won 26 seats at the 1997 Election), and socialist societies, like the Fabian Society. Essentially, the organisations which came together to form the party in 1900.

These organisations are permitted to elect a number of delegates to represent them on the General Committee, depending on how many members they have resident within the constituency. Such members are the affiliated members of the party.

If the CLP wishes, it can establish Women's Sections and branches of Young Labour for appropriate individual members. These bodies can also elect delegates to the General Committee.

The CLP has much the same functions as the Conservative Constituency Association. It elects candidates for parliamentary and local government elections. It raises funds and recruits members. It organises campaigns between elections and has political education

*Tony Blair, Leader of the Labour Party*

meetings for members. Very few CLPs employ full-time agents nowadays. Each CLP is entitled to elect delegates to represent it at the party's annual conference and at the annual conference of its regional council or, in Scotland, of the Scottish Labour Party.

## The Annual Conference

The annual conference is composed of delegates from the CLPs and from the organisations permitted to affiliate to the party. The conference consists of a week of debates which focus on general topics, such as foreign affairs, the economy and health. Resolutions from CLPs, Local Party Forums and affiliated organisations are debated within these general headings as are reports from the party's Policy Forum. A member of the National Executive Committee (NEC) and the Cabinet minister or opposition spokesperson responsible for each area of policy also have an opportunity to speak before conference votes on the resolutions and reports.

The voting is by show of hands but, if requested by delegates, a card vote is taken. Each delegate places a card into a ballot box, on which is written the number of votes each CLP or organisation is allowed. This figure is dependent on its number of affiliated members. A CLP has a minimum of 1000 votes, while some of the largest trade unions have over 1,000,000. This has led to charges, and not just by its opponents, that the trade unions have too great an influence on the party.

## Voting at Conference

There have been changes made to party rules which have diminished the weighting given to trade union votes at the conference. In 1997, this was 50 per cent of the total, even though, going strictly by numbers, they were entitled to 90 per cent. Tony Blair would like to move to a system of one-member, one-vote in future.

This description of open debates and voting gives the impression that the Labour Party conference is more democratic than that of the Conservatives. On paper, this is true. Resolutions are not vetted, debates are open and voting does take place and can influence party policy.

*Tony Blair at a press conference*

However, it is recognised that the conference nowadays is just as much stage managed as a show of unity and a televised event as its Conservative equivalent. Certainly, delegates may still be able to say something from the rostrum which is embarrassing to the leadership. However, the days are gone when someone like Denis Healey, the Chancellor of the Exchequer in the 1970s, was granted only three minutes to address conference on a major financial crisis, amid loud booing from delegates – a public relations disaster. A new discipline among delegates, born out of the frustration of 18 years opposition and the desire to present a united face on the nation's TV screens, would make such an occurrence highly unlikely nowadays.

Other ways in which the conference has developed as an opportunity to gain good publicity include rule changes which allow front bench spokespersons the right to address debates. These are complemented by unwritten (and unlikely to be admitted) practices like the chair calling only those speakers who conform to an unwritten dress code.

## The Parliamentary Report

As with the Conservative conference, the highlight is the leader's speech, officially known as the Parliamentary Report. This serves the same function as a rallying call to the delegates, an opportunity to show loyalty to the leader and to allow the leader to broadcast to the nation with the image of a totally united party. The length of the standing ovation for the leader now rivals that given by Conservative delegates.

## The National Executive Committee

The National Executive Committee (NEC) has no equivalent in the Conservative Party. There are sections for representatives of CLPs, elected by a postal ballot of all individual members, for women and for Young Labour representatives, elected by their own conferences, and for trade unions and Socialist Societies, elected by these organisations. The leader and deputy leader of the party are also members.

At its monthly meetings, the NEC is responsible for looking after party affairs between conferences and carrying out conference decisions. It has various sub-committees dealing with different aspects of party business including organisation, finance, home policy and international affairs. Throughout the year, in consultation with the leader, it initiates various campaigns on issues of importance at the time.

Also elected by the conference is the National Constitutional Committee, whose responsibility it is to deal with matters of discipline and to enforce party rules. It was established in the 1980s to investigate suspected members of the Militant Tendency who, it was claimed, were infiltrating the party.

## Full-time Professional Staff

To help carry out the work of the NEC and to deal with internal party matters, e.g. compiling the national membership list, full-time professional staff are employed at its headquarters, Millbank Tower. (The Scottish Party has its own HQ in Keir Hardie House, Glasgow.) Millbank Tower has many similar functions to those of Conservative Central Office.

- It is the bridge between CLPs and the leadership.

- It provides information about campaigns between elections.

- It gives advice on political education.

- It regularly sends out literature to CLPs and branches, keeping them up-to-date on party business and political matters in general.

## The Party Leader

The party leader is elected by postal ballot of all individual members, as is the deputy. In government, the leader is Prime Minister and is free to appoint the Cabinet and other government positions. In Opposition, the Shadow Cabinet must be selected from members of the Parliamentary Committee. This restricts the choice of Labour Opposition leaders in a way that the Conservative leader does not have to be concerned about.

All Labour MPs, not just backbenchers, are members of the Parliamentary Labour Party. This elects the Parliamentary Committee. Consequently, the Parliamentary Labour Party has more influence in opposition when front bench spokespersons are being appointed. It meets weekly and the leader attends by right of being a member. In government it can be an irritant to Labour prime ministers, especially when the government is unpopular and some direct criticism is made. However, this can be a good thing in that it allows criticism to be aired in private without the embarrassment of a public row.

Since there are so many alternative sources of influence in the party and, consequently, of possible dissent, it is frequently argued that it is more difficult for Labour leaders to exert control over their party than it is for Conservative leaders. However, successive leaders like Neil Kinnock, John Smith and especially Tony Blair have moved to eliminate these sources of discontent. This has been done by ensuring that people loyal to the leadership are elected to positions of influence and also control organs of the party, like the NEC. Up to and after the 1997 Election, Tony Blair probably dominated the Labour Party as much as any Conservative counterpart has been able to do and certainly more than any Labour leader before.

## Labour Party Finance

The Labour Party receives its finance from individual members' subscriptions (a proportion of which goes to each member's CLP), from donations (of which any above £5000 are published) and from fees from affiliated organisations, most notably trade unions. In 1996, trade unions provided 45 per cent of Labour's income. This represented a fall of 32 per cent over the previous eleven years. Trade union branches also contribute significantly to CLPs, through affiliation fees and some trade unions have an agreement with certain CLPs to help pay their administrative expenses and assist with the election expenses of candidates in Parliamentary elections.

Although the proportion of income from unions has fallen, it still represents a considerable amount and leaves the party again open to the charge of being controlled by the unions. Tony Blair would wish to see alternative sources of revenue being developed to reduce dependency on trade union finance. However, given the extent of the contribution that trade unions make to Labour Party funding, this is likely to remain an important source of income for the foreseeable future.

STUDY TOPIC 2

# In what ways do the ideologies of the main political parties differ?

Before examining the particular ideology of each of the four main parties in Scottish politics, it is worth identifying ideas and beliefs which they have in common.

- Firstly, the parties are all parliamentarian, i.e. they wish to achieve their aims through the ballot box. If they disagree with a law, they will accept this in most cases and work to change it by gaining power to legislate in future.

- Secondly, the parties are tolerant of their opponents. It may be hard to accept this once the weekly confrontation between the party leaders at Prime Minister's Question Time or during the heat of an election campaign have been witnessed. However, no major political party would wish when in power to remove the freedom of other political parties to criticise or promote alternative points of view.

- Thirdly, the parties believe in the freedoms of ordinary citizens – freedom of speech (including freedom of the media), of religion, of ownership of property and of association. Furthermore, all of the parties oppose discrimination on the grounds of race or colour.

- Fourthly, the parties all agree that foreign and defence policy should be conducted in the best interests of Britain – in the SNP's case, of Scotland – although there is often disagreement as to how this might be achieved.

## The Conservative Party

 The Conservative Party does not admit to having an ideology. It believes such a concept is alien to its being although such a stance could be argued in itself to constitute some form of ideology. Gaining power seems to have been the main principle in the history of the Conservative Party and, if this has been its aim, it has been very successful in achieving it (it has held or shared power for two-thirds of this century). The acceptance by the Conservative Party of the need to change its position on certain matters to gain power is all part of the Conservative belief in pragmatism rather than ideology.

There are two strands of thought which could be regarded as ideological and which have caused some disagreement in recent years – Thatcherism and One Nation Conservatism.

## Thatcherism

This strand of thought, as the name suggests, was dominant when Margaret Thatcher was leader and Prime Minister and had adherents in Mr Major's Government in the form of Michael Forsyth, John Redwood, Michael Portillo and Peter Lilley. It advocates the primacy of the free market economy and a radical reduction in the role of the state. This led to the privatisation of former nationalised industries, removal of government controls on prices, incomes and dividends, reductions in subsidies to industry and, at a local level, the sale of council houses. In accordance with this was a belief that people should be self-reliant, accept more responsibility for their own lives and enjoy increasing freedom of choice. Linked to the above was the intention to reduce social security although spending on this area actually rose in real terms during Mrs Thatcher's period in office. More successful was the reduction in all rates of income tax.

In addition, grant-maintained schools were successfully established, at least in England and Wales, to provide an alternative to local authority schools, and the Assisted Places Scheme was set up to allow children from lower income homes to attend private schools. With regard to foreign affairs, a vigorous defence of British interests was advocated particularly in dealings with the European Union and the former USSR.

## One Nation Conservatism

This is a belief that the Conservatives have to represent the whole nation, not just some sections to the exclusion of others, or the Party will not survive. It believes that some government intervention in the economy is a good thing, perhaps to help a new industry become established or to protect another whose closure might be harmful to the economy as a whole. There is also a belief among Conservatives who hold this view that the strong must look after the weak and that governments must tackle poverty if society is not to suffer from ill-health, crime and unrest. In addition, a distinctive approach to foreign affairs is taken, particularly with regard to dealings with the European Union (EU) and it

is in this particular area of policy that the biggest gulf between the two main strands of Conservative thought has developed in the 1990s. Adherents of One Nation Conservatism in the 1980s were named pejoratively 'wets' by Mrs Thatcher and her supporters. In John Major's Government, Kenneth Clarke, Michael Heseltine and Stephen Dorrell were included in this group.

## Eurosceptic versus Europhile

The Thatcherites might now be more aptly named Eurosceptics, i.e. they are against any further delegation of power from Westminster to the institutions of the EU. They also oppose a single European currency and any attempt by the EU to assume control of foreign policy for its members.

The 'wets' might now be more aptly named Europhiles. They favour a more conciliatory approach to the EU and support a single European currency at some time in the future. In addition, they would be prepared to allow some of the decision making currently exercised at Westminster to be undertaken by the EU if this was judged to be in Britain's interest. It was the failure of these two wings of the Party to resolve their differences which caused John Major's Government to become divided and contributed to the decisive 1997 General Election defeat.

## Unifying the Party

Nevertheless, there are some views shared by nearly all Conservatives which act to unite the Party. These include, support for law and order and a strong defence policy. There has never been any disagreement among Conservatives about the need to maintain nuclear weapons and retain NATO membership. Also, all Conservatives see themselves as being patriotic, both in dealings with other countries and in attitudes at home, e.g. a commitment to the monarchy and to the Union of Scotland, England, Wales and Northern Ireland. William Hague, who became leader after the 1997 Election defeat, promised to unite and rebuild the Conservative Party. The division between Eurosceptics and Europhiles may be his biggest obstacle to achieving this.

# Commitment to the Union

# The Labour Party

The Labour Party has always been regarded as being more ideological than the Conservative Party. Its 1918 constitution contained several clauses which outlined its purpose and its aims. Most famous of these was Clause 4, Part 4 which advocated the common ownership of the means of production, distribution and exchange. This came to be regarded by most members as an ideal, almost an issue of faith for some. It was, until 1995, (when a new Clause 4 was approved by a special conference, after a postal ballot of individual members) the one part of the constitution to appear on the party membership card. If put into practice, it would have meant the nationalisation of at least the biggest companies as well as of land and banks. This aim is what distinguished the Labour Party from others and identified it as a party which could be described as socialist.

However, Part 5 of the old Clause 4 also defined one of the party's aims as to form an administration in Parliament, i.e. to win elections and be the government. Many party members have regarded a commitment to the large-scale nationalisation implied in Part 4 and the objective of winning elections in Part 5 as contradictory. They believed that the implications of Part 4, if offered in a manifesto to the electorate, would prove unpopular and result in electoral defeat.

These two strands of thought, the one committed to the socialist ideals of Part 4 of Clause 4 and that associated with the more pragmatic outlook implied by Part 5, led to two broad groups forming themselves around each. Supporters of Clause 4, Part 4 became known as the left wing and those who saw it as an obstacle to progress constituted the right wing. The only occasion that a wide ranging programme of nationalisation gained the support of both of these wings was in 1945, when Labour was elected on a platform of nationalisation of transport, coal, steel and other major industries.

## Different Perceptions

Other issues which, in more modern times, have divided the right and left have been whether to abandon nuclear weapons (a policy supported by the left) and whether to join the European Community (broadly supported by the right). In addition, there has been a coolness towards NATO and a suspicion of the USA on the part of the left and a more positive attitude to both from the right as well as a greater emphasis by the left than the right on the need to increase taxes and spend more public money on public services.

Figures among the Labour Party's MPs who have been identified with the left in recent times are Michael Foot, Tony Benn and Ken Livingstone. On the right have been Jim Callaghan, John Smith and Tony Blair, while Neil Kinnock was once identified as a strong left winger but, after becoming leader, he moved steadily to the right.

## New Labour

When Tony Blair became leader in 1994, he began what became known as 'The Project', a series of initiatives which he believed would make the Labour Party more electable. Among these was a decision to refer to the party as New Labour, a term never officially adopted but so successful that it is now used as if the change of name had been made.

New Labour has seen the drift to the right by the Labour Party go further than at any time in the past. However, this is not so simple as it appears. In a desire to show a united front and succeed in getting the Party elected after losing four consecutive general elections, Blair supporters belong not only to the traditional right of the party but are also drawn from those who belonged and were recognised as belonging to the traditional left, such as John Prescott, Robin Cook and David Blunkett. Alongside traditional left wingers, who are regarded as Old Labour, stand such established right wingers as Roy Hattersley. Therefore, the terms New and Old Labour cut across traditional groupings within the Labour Party.

One important change which Blair succeeded in achieving was the adoption, in 1995, of a new Clause 4 to replace the original version. Despite the fact that this involved replacing that part of the constitution which those on the traditional left valued most, it gave Labour a declared set of aims which most party members can accept.

In his desire to modernise the Party, some supporters believe that Mr Blair has given it an ideology which encapsulates its traditional values and places these in a modern context.

## The New Clause 4
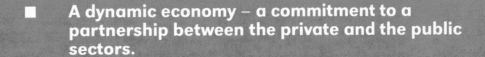

- A dynamic economy – a commitment to a partnership between the private and the public sectors.

- A just society – emphasising the need to protect the weak as well as the strong, to provide equality of opportunity and to fight against poverty and prejudice.

- An open democracy – a statement of belief in open government, the right of communities to take decisions which affect them and a guarantee of human rights.

- A healthy environment.

- A commitment to the defence and security of Britain through European institutions, the United Nations, the Commonwealth and other international organisations.

# The Liberal Democratic Party

The old Liberal Party of the 19th Century stood for individual freedom, self-reliance, free trade and a suspicion of government – ideas embraced enthusiastically by the Thatcherites of the 1980s. However, in the early 20th Century, it adopted policies which appealed to the growing working class electorate and it was responsible for the beginnings of social security in 1911. Ever since, it has projected itself as the centre party of British politics, sometimes as a radical alternative to Labour, sometimes as a moderate alternative to the Conservatives. In 1988, it merged with the Social Democratic Party – a right wing breakaway from the Labour Party – with which it had most policies in common. The new party became the Liberal Democratic Party.

In recent years, the basic principles of the Liberal Democratic Party have been commitments to electoral reform, to a federal Britain within a federal Europe and to other constitutional reforms, e.g. reform of the House of Lords, a Freedom of Information Act and the incorporation of the European Convention of Human Rights into UK law. It also believes in a mixed economy and an important role for government in liberating people from poverty, ignorance and discrimination.

# The Scottish National Party

The Scottish National Party has a simple ideology – a belief in establishing an internationally recognised sovereign state in that administrative area of the United Kingdom known as Scotland. This aim has been refined, since 1988, to Independence in Europe, i.e. an independent Scotland as a full member state of the European Union. This has done much to undermine its description by its opponents as separatist. It is also designed to demonstrate to Scots how small nations can prosper as sovereign states within the EU.

The name of the party is important – it is not Nationalist – it represents an inclusive nationalism. All residents of Scotland, regardless of race, colour, creed or country of origin would be eligible for citizenship of a newly independent Scotland. The SNP describes this as a civic nationalism (very different from the aggressive, xenophobic nationalism witnessed in the former Yugoslavia or among neo-Nazi nationalists in other European countries).

The SNP also describes itself as a moderate left of centre party and is recognised as such by its opponents. It regards itself as being part of the mainstream of European politics as represented by such parties on the continent. This development of its ideology (to focus on a particular point in the political spectrum) was a reaction to its growing electoral support and the need to define policies clearly as its supporters came to expect a more detailed response to political issues than simply the promise of future independence.

STUDY TOPIC 3

# How is party policy framed?

## The Conservative Party

The leader of the Conservative Party is at the apex of power within it and is in control of policy-making. However, in a mass party, this statement is bound to be simplistic. There are influences and interests both from outside and within the Party which the leader must consider before any policy decision is made. As a party which prides itself on its supposed lack of ideology and on its pragmatism geared towards winning elections, political considerations must be taken into account. A leader who pursues a policy which could be electorally damaging risks alienating a considerable number of MPs and members.

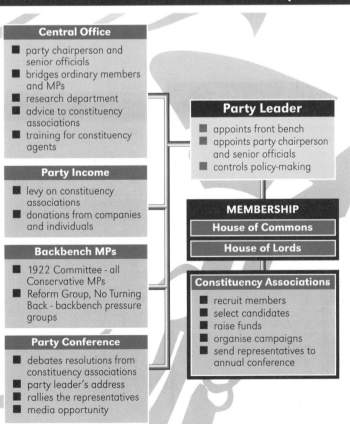

### Structure of the Conservative Party

**Central Office**
- party chairperson and senior officials
- bridges ordinary members and MPs
- research department
- advice to constituency associations
- training for constituency agents

**Party Income**
- levy on constituency associations
- donations from companies and individuals

**Backbench MPs**
- 1922 Committee - all Conservative MPs
- Reform Group, No Turning Back - backbench pressure groups

**Party Conference**
- debates resolutions from constituency associations
- party leader's address
- rallies the representatives
- media opportunity

**Party Leader**
- appoints front bench
- appoints party chairperson and senior officials
- controls policy-making

**MEMBERSHIP**
**House of Commons**
**House of Lords**

**Constituency Associations**
- recruit members
- select candidates
- raise funds
- organise campaigns
- send representatives to annual conference

- Groups of MPs, e.g. the Reform Group or the No Turning Back Group, develop their own policies which they seek to influence the leader to adopt. These groups have supporters in the Party throughout the country who will place these policies on the agenda of party meetings in order to advance their arguments to a wider audience.

- The 1922 Committee is a vehicle for backbench concerns and aspirations to be made known to the leader. There are also 24 committees of backbench MPs with responsibilities for specific areas of policy, e.g. economic affairs and foreign affairs. These committees develop policies for their areas which enter into the internal debates of the Party and can influence the leader.

- The Research Department at Central Office has officially no policy-making role. However, as a full-time, professional support group for the leader and the party as a whole, it can have a major influence on the formulation of policy.

- Leaders of the business community, although officially non-political, have always had a special relationship with the Conservatives and their views on economic and industrial matters are usually listened to.

# The Labour Party

The annual conference has, under the constitution, the responsibility for policy-making. In theory, any local branch can submit, via its CLP, a resolution to conference and, if it is passed, it becomes policy. Equally, a trade union or other affiliated organisation can do likewise. So, there is a formal vehicle within the Party for policy to be initiated from the bottom up.

Nowadays, major policy initiatives come from statements submitted to conference by the Policy Forum. The forum consists of a number of policy commissions established to recommend statements on their specific areas of responsibility, e.g. health, defence, the economy. The forum consists of representatives of CLPs, affiliated organisations, the PLP and the NEC. Since it was established by Neil Kinnock, the leadership has ensured that membership of the forum is composed of people loyal to the opinions of the leader.

The PLP, at its weekly meetings, serves as a channel of communication between the backbenchers and the leadership. In a similar way to the 1922 Committee, it can influence policy by expressing concerns to the leader. The PLP also has 14 backbench policy committees, similar to those in the Conservative Party and these allow a more formal input into policy-making from ordinary MPs.

Both inside and outside Parliament there are numerous groups of MPs and party members who have a special interest to promote and who attempt to convince the Labour Party to adopt their ideas. Examples are the Campaign Group of Labour MPs and Campaign Groups of members throughout the country, who support the policies of the traditional left and the Labour Animal Welfare Society which has campaigned, quite successfully, within the Party for animal rights.

Trade unions have still an influence on policy. Their role at conference may be diminishing but their formal links with Labour give them access to MPs and to the leadership to promote their special interests, e.g. the setting of a minimum wage.

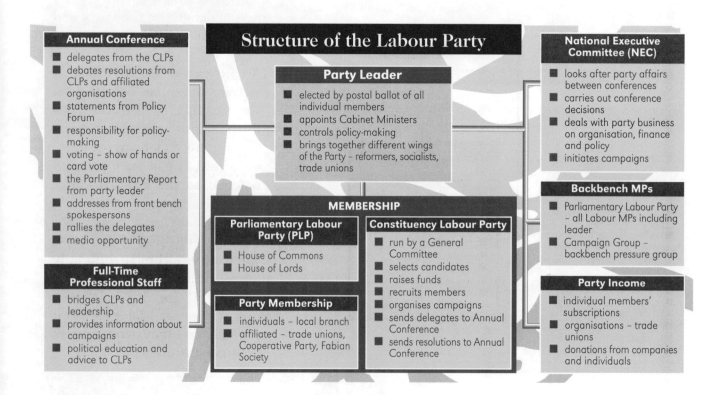

## Structure of the Labour Party

**Annual Conference**
- delegates from the CLPs
- debates resolutions from CLPs and affiliated organisations
- statements from Policy Forum
- responsibility for policy-making
- voting – show of hands or card vote
- the Parliamentary Report from party leader
- addresses from front bench spokespersons
- rallies the delegates
- media opportunity

**Full-Time Professional Staff**
- bridges CLPs and leadership
- provides information about campaigns
- political education and advice to CLPs

**Party Leader**
- elected by postal ballot of all individual members
- appoints Cabinet Ministers
- controls policy-making
- brings together different wings of the Party – reformers, socialists, trade unions

**MEMBERSHIP**

**Parliamentary Labour Party (PLP)**
- House of Commons
- House of Lords

**Party Membership**
- individuals – local branch
- affiliated – trade unions, Cooperative Party, Fabian Society

**Constituency Labour Party**
- run by a General Committee
- selects candidates
- raises funds
- recruits members
- organises campaigns
- sends delegates to Annual Conference
- sends resolutions to Annual Conference

**National Executive Committee (NEC)**
- looks after party affairs between conferences
- carries out conference decisions
- deals with party business on organisation, finance and policy
- initiates campaigns

**Backbench MPs**
- Parliamentary Labour Party – all Labour MPs including leader
- Campaign Group – backbench pressure group

**Party Income**
- individual members' subscriptions
- organisations – trade unions
- donations from companies and individuals

# The Parties in Government

When in power, the influences on policy-making in both parties increase. The main reason for this is that governments are in a position to enact policies. Similarly, the party leader has a greater say in policy-making than when in opposition, because of the position held as head of the executive branch of the government.

### The Prime Minister's Policy Unit

The Prime Minister has a policy unit at 10 Downing Street. This has eight members, drawn from professional civil servants and outside appointments from the party, universities, business and trade unions. It gives the Prime Minister advice on the whole range of government responsibilities and is very influential.

### Political Considerations

Political considerations influence prime ministers. There may be a ground swell of opinion which gains such momentum that even the government cannot resist, e.g. the call for gun control laws after the tragedy in Dunblane in 1996. The Prime Minister will keep his eye on more run of the mill concerns of the electorate and react in a manner which may represent a policy change or initiative.

### Pressure Groups

Pressure groups will attempt to influence government policy since this is their raison d'être. Their campaigns can range from petitions and advertising to lobbying Parliament.

### Full-time Lobbying Firms

There are numerous full-time lobbying firms which give advice on how to influence the government, individual ministers and MPs. In addition, they can arrange meetings. They are playing an increasing role in influencing policy.

'Think tanks', e.g. the Adam Smith Institute (right wing) and the Institute of Public Policy Research (left wing) provide detailed policies on the full range of government activities and these are examined carefully by the government and often adopted, e.g. privatisation (the Adam Smith Institute).

### The House of Commons

Select committees of the Commons often produce reports which call for government action and these are sometimes implemented, e.g. the recommendation by the Home Affairs Committee to abolish laws allowing arrest on suspicion ('sus' laws).

The opposition has a role to play in influencing policy. It may be successful in arguing that the government changes its policies, e.g. by tabling amendments to bills. It may also mount a successful campaign in the country as a whole which could lead to initiatives by the government.

Individual MPs may introduce a private Member's bill which the government, although not supporting, would find difficult to oppose, e.g. legislation on disability rights or anti-blood sports proposals. Also, Cabinet committees propose policy initiatives to the Cabinet.

### The Civil Service

Senior civil servants have a central role in advising the government on policy.

On some occasions in the past, governments have set up Royal Commissions to examine a particular issue and recommend changes. These have become the basis of future legislation, e.g. the reform of local government in the mid-1970s.

## Other Parties

Both the SNP and the Liberal Democrats have structures which allow their members to have some influence on policy-making.

The SNP has a National Council and annual conference to which branches and constituency associations send representatives. These are the SNP's policy-making bodies.

The Liberal Democrats are a federal party and have annual conferences for the four nations of the UK, as well as for the UK as a whole. Any individual member may attend these conferences which have an input into party policy.

As with the two major parties, there are other influences on the SNP and the Liberal Democrats to adopt policies on certain issues although the main targets of pressure groups and others will always be the major parties.

The leaderships of the SNP and the Liberal Democrats, as in the two major parties, have the biggest influence on their parties' policies.

## Manifestos

At election time, the party leaders choose which of their policies they wish to highlight as being their proposals for implementation if they gain power and publish these in their manifesto. These are usually regarded as commitments and, if a government does something contrary to what it promised in its manifesto, it is severely criticised by its opponents.

STUDY TOPIC 4

# What are the policies of the main political parties?

**Manifesto Commitments of the Main Parties in Selected Policy Areas at the 1997 General Election**

## The Conservative Party

 **Taxation**

- basic rate of Income Tax of 20p in the pound
- cut and eventually abolish Inheritance Tax and Capital Gains Tax
- oppose Labour's proposed Windfall Tax
- balance the nation's budget by the year 2000
- reduce public spending to 40 per cent of Gross Domestic Product in 1997-98

 **Law and Order**

- more resources for police and the other law and order agencies
- increase funding for the Scottish Prison Service
- introduce mandatory drug-testing in prisons
- expand rehabilitation programmes
- introduce new technology to help in the fight against crime
- fight drugs menace
- help victims of crime
- tougher measures against dangerous and persistent criminals
- prisoners to earn early release from prison by co-operation and good behaviour
- mandatory life sentences
- electronic tagging
- increase the sentencing powers of sheriff courts in jury cases
- DNA Sampling
- tackle teenage drinking
- make legal aid more efficient

# The Conservative Party

## Employment

keep inflation below 2.5 per cent to give stability to the economy
more flexible working practices to promote job creation
work experience for the long-term unemployed
expansion of the modern apprenticeship scheme to improve on the job
vocational training and an increase in vocational qualifications
no minimum wage which will destroy jobs
continued opt-out of the European Social Chapter
ban strikes in essential public services

## Private and Public Ownership

previous privatisations regarded as successful – a commitment to privatise
London Underground

## Health

NHS internal market to remain
continue development of GP fundholding
cut waiting lists by focusing resources where they can be used most effectively
develop a primary care led NHS, by having 'super-surgeries' to perform minor
surgery and by extending the role of pharmacists, nurses and therapists to
perform some tasks previously restricted to doctors
require local authorities to purchase residential and community care in the
private or voluntary sector unless places are inadequate or dearer than in public
sector – only elderly and incurable patients who require complex or intensive
medical or nursing care to continue to be treated by NHS
possible combination of mental and social work services to establish new
authority for mental health care
continue to increase NHS spending annually by more than rate of inflation

## Education

expand number of grant-maintained schools
guarantee school standards by intervening directly in failing schools and
education authorities
a grammar school in every town in England and Wales
allow schools to specialise, e.g. in science, languages, sport or technology
continue voucher scheme for nursery education for 4-year olds
introduce new secondary school examinations in 1998 in Scotland

# The Labour Party

## Taxation

- no return to 'penal rates' of the 1970s
- reduce starting rate for Income Tax to 10p in the pound
- no increase in Income Tax rates in first term of government
- 'loopholes' like executive share options to be closed
- cut VAT on fuel from 8 per cent to 5 per cent
- Windfall Tax to raise at least £3 billion from profits of privatised utilities like British Gas, electricity and water companies
- two-year clampdown on public spending
- accept Conservative Government's spending targets for next two years
- a 'root and branch review' of all public spending to identify economies
- continue effective pay freeze in public sector
- borrow only to invest, not to spend

## Law and Order

- tough on crime
- individual responsibility for crime
- tough penalties for serious repeat offenders
- 'zero tolerance' approach to anti-social behaviour, petty crime and crime on Scotland's streets
- review Scotland's criminal justice system to improve crime detection and conviction rates
- police to be given strong support - new technology, officers put on the beat rather than overburdened with bureaucracy
- parliamentary vote to ban all handguns
- anti-drugs supremo to coordinate battle against drugs
- encourage greater use of bye-laws to prevent under age drinking and drinking in public places
- new offence of racial harassment
- new crime of racially motivated violence
- tough on the causes of crime
- measures to relieve social deprivation

# The Labour Party

 ## Employment

inflation target of below 2.5 per cent
Windfall Tax to be used to get 250,000 under 25s off benefit and into work
tackle benefit fraud
raise skills by guaranteeing workers funds to 'learn as you earn'
offer employers £75 per week tax rebate for six months to employ someone
who has been jobless for more than two years
establish a University for Industry to provide training
introduce a statutory minimum wage at a level set by a Low Pay Commission
of trade union and employer representatives

 ## Private and Public Ownership

no reversal of Conservative privatisations
further privatisations not ruled out

 ## Health

retain purchaser/provider split of internal market but replace GP fundholding
with system of GPs jointly commissioning care from hospitals and health
authorities on an area basis
include a local councillor on boards of hospital trusts
reduce waiting lists by releasing £100 million saved from cutting bureaucracy
agree with Conservative proposals on primary care
ban all tobacco advertising
appoint a Minister for Public Health
establish a Royal Commission to make recommendations on a fair system of
funding long-term care for the elderly
halt closure of psychiatric beds until appropriate community services are
available

 ## Education

phase out Assisted Places Scheme and use savings to cut class sizes of under
7s to maximum of 30
take steps to raise standards in schools
promote lifelong learning at the workplace
abolish grant-maintained schools and no plans for new grammar schools in
England and Wales
abolish voucher schemes for nursery education and develop nursery education
for all 3-5 year olds whose parents wish this
delay new exams for secondary schools in Scotland until 1999
in Scotland, establish contracts between pupils, parents and schools
in Scotland, set targets for schools and pupils

## The Liberal Democratic Party

Liberal
Democrats

In 1997, the Liberal Democratic Party attempted to stake out a distinctive image and appear to be the one party which could make a difference. As well as its traditional commitments to constitutional reform, it introduced for the first time in Britain the idea of hypothecated taxation, i.e. taxes which would raise money to be spent on specific areas – in this case one penny on income tax to be spent on investment in education and an increase on tobacco taxes to increase spending on the NHS. Emphasis was also placed on environmental issues.

## The Scottish National Party

The SNP's overarching manifesto commitment is, of course, the establishment of Scotland as a sovereign state within the EU. Its manifesto also included specific pledges which underpinned its image as a moderate left of centre party. These included a written constitution and a Bill of Rights, a commitment to full employment, a reduction in personal and corporate taxation, investment in all sectors of education, transfer of three-quarters of housing debt from local to central government to free more revenue to be spent locally, more money for the National Health Service, environmental protection, establishment of a Scottish Defence Force and a commitment to meet the UN target for aid to the developing world.

STUDY TOPIC 5

# Have the major parties changed in recent years?

## The Conservative Party

The 1980s was a decade in which the Conservatives dominated British politics. They had won the 1979 General Election with Margaret Thatcher as leader. She began a series of policy initiatives and reforms which were very radical and affected almost every area of life. The term used to describe these reforms was Thatcherism. Mrs Thatcher led her party successfully to another general election landslide victory in 1983, when her majority in the Commons increased from 44 to 144. This was subsequently cut to 102 in her third successive victory in 1987.

## The Resolute Approach

Mrs Thatcher believed in the need to control inflation, which had reached 26 per cent in the mid-1970s, by keeping a tight control on the supply of money and on public spending. This resolute approach was a complete break from the post-war political consensus. It led to an increase in unemployment, with many firms declaring bankruptcy in the difficult financial conditions of the time which included high interest rates. This caused some concern within the Conservative Party and in the Cabinet but Mrs Thatcher insisted it was right – "there is no alternative" – since those firms closing were viewed as inefficient and those that survived would be leaner and fitter.

The Conservative Government of the early 1980s also broke with the consensus of the past by reducing the role of the state in economic and social policy. Direct taxes were cut, particularly for those on high incomes, leaving people free to choose how to spend their money. Nationalised industries like British Petroleum, British Gas and British Telecom were gradually privatised. Subsidies for loss-making nationalised industries, like coal and steel, were phased out and they, too, were eventually privatised.

## Controlling Local Authorities

Cuts in central government funding to local government and controls over council expenditure were introduced to force councils to cut their services, which the government felt were, at best, encouraging people to be dependent on the state and, at worst, wasteful and unnecessary. At the same time, councils were required to sell housing to sitting tenants at a discount. This again was designed to decrease people's reliance on the state and give them responsibility for their own property. In addition, it diminished the powers of local councils, which the government regarded in the case of many Labour councils to be experimenting with socialism at a local level. Councils were also required by law to put out to tender many of their services, resulting in lower employment levels and lower wages.

## Taking on the Trade Unions

Mrs Thatcher was also determined to confront and defeat trade unions, which she blamed for bringing about the downfall of the previous Labour Government and the last Conservative Government before that. Before her government chose its battleground, it passed into law many measures designed to weaken the unions, particularly the leaderships, which she perceived as being dominated by communists and other left wingers.

Laws were passed which:

- Allowed employers to sue unions if they did not ballot their members before strikes.

- Allowed employers to sue unions if they struck in sympathy with another union.

- Gave employers the right to sue unions if the strike was politically motivated.

- Restricted picketing.

Other measures like compulsory postal ballots for chief officials in unions were introduced as the government believed that this would weaken the grip of left wingers in the leadership.

In 1984, the national leadership of the National Union of Mineworkers called a strike to protest against the closure of dozens of collieries which the National Coal Board considered uneconomic. This was done without a national ballot and gave the government the opportunity to test its legislation against what was still regarded as the most powerful and militant trade union in the country. There were splits in the union, with some areas not responding to the strike call, and there were violent scenes between miners and police outside many collieries.

The strike lasted over a year and the government and the Coal Board did not compromise. The miners eventually marched back to work in an orderly fashion. There are still many arguments about the tactics of all protagonists in the dispute but it demonstrates just how determined Mrs Thatcher was to take on and defeat a major union.

**"Now it's time to play my tune!"**

## Ending the Dependency Culture

The Thatcher Government wanted to diminish the role of the Welfare State. It encouraged people to purchase private pension policies and although it would have been political suicide to attempt to abolish the NHS, it was determined to reform it and create an internal market for health care.

## Promoting the National Interest

In foreign affairs, Mrs Thatcher promoted British national interests aggressively. She increased defence spending and agreed with the USA that the USSR had to be confronted and outmatched in nuclear and conventional weapons. In 1982, she sent a task force to the South Atlantic to recapture the Falkland Islands from the Argentine. One action the significance of which she may not have fully realised was the passing of enabling legislation which laid the ground for closer integration with the EU – an issue which would become of crucial importance to her party.

## Loss of Party Confidence

By 1989, Mrs Thatcher had been party leader for fourteen years and Prime Minister for ten. To dominate a party, even an electorally successful one, for so long, can inevitably lead to strong opposition. One of the many members of her Cabinet who left or were replaced was Michael Heseltine, who stormed out of the Cabinet in 1986 at the height of the biggest crisis of her leadership - the Westland Affair, a bizarre disagreement in Cabinet about the future of a helicopter company. He had become the focus of discontent with Mrs Thatcher's leadership expressed by Conservative MPs. In 1989, she was challenged for the leadership by 'stalking horse' candidate, Sir Anthony Mayer, a backbencher, whom she defeated easily.

However, with Labour building a large lead in the opinion polls and many MPs fearful of losing their seats, he did gain a respectable vote.

The reasons behind the unease of MPs was the growing unpopularity of the government. It had always had a sound reputation among voters, particularly in Southern England, for good management of the economy. In May 1989, inflation had reached 8.5 per cent and, in July, the trade deficit reached £21 billion. In the same year, interest rates reached 15 per cent, making mortgages more expensive. The Chancellor resigned that October because he felt he was being ignored by the Prime Minister, who preferred the advice of her personal economics adviser, Sir Alan Walters. The government's public image was becoming tarnished.

## The Community Charge

In 1990 the effects of the introduction of the Community Charge or Poll Tax in England and Wales, a year after its introduction in Scotland, became clear. This was a flat-rate tax on all residents over 18, with even the poorest having to pay something. It replaced domestic rates, which were charged on houses. The Community Charge meant that, for example, a family of five adults, living in a four-roomed council house could pay five times what a single millionaire, living in a mansion with many rooms, would be required to pay. Clearly, this tax benefited a minority of the population at the expense of the majority and the rich at the expense of the less well off.

The Poll Tax was very unpopular leading to serious riots in Trafalgar Square in London. In small country towns throughout England and Wales, which were traditionally Conservative, anti-Poll Tax campaigns were established, as well as in large Labour supporting cities. Even the Conservative Party's natural supporters were becoming disillusioned.

Labour won a series of by-elections in 1990 and the Conservatives lost hundreds of seats at the local elections. In the opinion polls, Labour had a 24 per cent lead. Despite all this, Mrs Thatcher insisted her policies were right and refused to consider change. To many in the Conservative Party, her style of leadership was becoming presidential. As she surrounded herself with advisers who agreed with her, she seemed to be becoming more autocratic and isolated from the rest of the Party.

## The Emergence of John Major

In October 1990, Mrs Thatcher and her Foreign Secretary, Sir Geoffrey Howe, had a serious disagreement about how far Britain should integrate into the EU. Mrs Thatcher made a speech disagreeing with what Sir Geoffrey had declared previously was British policy. He resigned and made a scathing attack on the Prime Minister in the Commons.

Heseltine was urged to stand against the Prime Minister in that year's election for party leader. He did and, although she won a majority in the first ballot, it was not enough to cross the required threshold and a second ballot had to be organised.

Most of her Cabinet either advised her to step down or, while saying they still supported her, told her they thought she would lose. She decided not to run in the second ballot and John Major was elected as leader the following week. Major automatically became Prime Minister as leader of the majority party in the Commons.

## General Election Success

Major's main achievement during his first two years in power was to secure several opt-outs for Britain from the 1991 Maastricht Treaty but Europe would prove even more significant in later years. His other important decision was to decide when to hold the general election. He could have decided to go to the country after the Gulf War when his own and the government's popularity had recovered from the lows under Thatcher. In fact, he chose 9 April 1992 when, despite a severe recession and deep splits over Europe following the signing of the Maastricht Treaty, the Conservative Party surprised many pollsters by winning a fourth consecutive general election with a majority of 21.

*Margaret Thatcher and John Major*

Mirror Syndication International

## The Clouds Gather

In September 1992, Britain was forced to leave the Exchange Rate Mechanism of the European Monetary System because interest rates were being forced higher and higher. The housing market also suffered a slump and many mortgage payers were trapped by negative equity – unable to sell their house because it was now worth less than the mortgage they had borrowed. The government was again losing its reputation for good management of the economy.

Europe had been a problematic subject for the Conservative Party from 1992 to 1997. In November 1994, eight Conservative MPs defied the party whip and abstained on a vote concerning the European Communities (Finance) Bill. The whip was then taken away from the eight, and a ninth joined them by resigning the whip, despite having voted with the government. Mr Major was also seen and heard on television referring to the right-wing Eurosceptic members of his Cabinet as "bastards". Unknown to him, the cameras were still rolling after an interview. It all gave a dreadful impression of a divided Cabinet.

## Sleaze

Sleaze also haunted the Conservative Party. At the 1994 Conservative Party Conference in Blackpool, Mr Major announced a 'back to basics' campaign, i.e. a return to old standards in public and private life, emphasising family values. However, this apparently worthy strategy backfired as a continual stream of press stories regarding the private lives of Conservative MPs and ministers began to appear. Several were forced to resign. Heritage Secretary David Mellor, Tim Yeo, an environment minister, David Ashby, a Parliamentary Private Secretary (PPS) and Hartley Booth, also a PPS, all resigned over stories of alleged indiscretions in their private or family lives.

Problems concerning sleaze of a financial nature also affected the Conservative Party. Tim Smith and Neil Hamilton resigned as ministers when The

Guardian published claims that they had accepted money from Harrods' owner, Mohammed Al Fayed, to table Parliamentary questions. Jonathan Aitken also resigned as Chief Secretary to the Treasury following newspaper reports claiming that he had lied to the Cabinet over who paid his bill during a stay at the Paris Ritz.

## Other Pressures

In June 1995, Mr Major had resigned as party leader but not Prime Minister and forced a leadership election. He was facing a lot of criticism from within the Party over splits on Europe, alleged lack of leadership, by-election defeats and disastrous local election results. John Redwood, the Welsh Secretary, resigned from the Cabinet to challenge him. Major won comfortably on the first ballot, taking 66 per cent of the vote compared to Redwood's 27 per cent.

The parliamentary party also suffered from the defection of several MPs. In 1995, Alan Howarth resigned to join the Labour Party. In 1996, Emma Nicholson and Peter Thurnham joined the Liberal Democrats. In March 1997, Sir George Gardiner, who had already been deselected as the party candidate for his seat of Reigate, resigned the Conservative whip and joined the Referendum Party. Sir John Gorst also resigned the Conservative whip over the proposed closure of a hospital in his constituency.

## Major and Thatcherism

Major was the preferred choice of the Thatcherites in the Conservative Party to succeed her in 1990. However, as his premiership went on, they came to regard him as almost a traitor to their cause. Certainly, his style of leadership was less dictatorial and more conciliatory, and he tried to represent all views within his Cabinet.

He was often regarded as being too soft on Europe. This seems unfair as he did negotiate several opt-outs from the Maastricht Treaty, which did not make him look a Europhile.

As far as economic and social policy was concerned, Major did not soften his approach to the trade unions or local authorities and made no attempt to water down the internal market in the NHS. Indeed, he proceeded with privatisations which Mrs Thatcher did not attempt – coal, the railways and nuclear power.

Looked at objectively, Major did not attempt to roll back Thatcherism; he continued with the revolution. The Conservative Party under Major's leadership was as much Thatcherite in its policies as it had been previously. His big problem was almost insoluble – how to unite the two opposing Eurosceptic and Europhile tendencies behind a common policy. He was also let down in his attempt to launch his big idea of back to basics by the human frailties of some individuals in the party.

## The 1997 General Election

Mr Major called the general election for 1 May, 1997. The long six-week campaign started disastrously for the Conservatives with the resignation of Sir Michael Hirst, the Scottish Party Chairman, over newspaper reports of an alleged indiscretion in his private life. Even though the campaign got back on line again, it never looked like being a success. Labour was making no mistakes and the mood in the country was that it was time for a change. Despite a recovering economy, voters' impressions of the Conservatives and John Major were of a disunited, sleaze-ridden party, with a weak, although basically decent, leader.

The election result was a disaster for the Conservatives who had their worst electoral performance since 1945, gaining only 165 seats with 31.4 per cent of the vote. About a quarter of Conservative MPs were elected for the first time. This inexperience was compounded by the loss of many experienced senior figures. Thirty eight ministers lost their seats, including a record number of seven Cabinet ministers – Malcolm Rifkind, Foreign Secretary; Ian Lang, Trade Secretary; Tony Newton, Leader of the House; Michael Portillo, Defence Secretary; William Waldegrave, Chief Secretary to the Treasury, and Roger Freeman, Chancellor of the Duchy of Lancaster. The Scottish Secretary, Michael Forsyth, also lost his seat; in fact, not a single constituency in Scotland or Wales elected a Conservative MP.

## William Hague

The day after the election, John Major resigned as party leader, opening up the leadership battle. Five candidates, Kenneth Clarke, William Hague, Michael Howard, Peter Lilley and John Redwood, contested the first ballot in June. Howard and Lilley dropped out after this and Redwood dropped out after the second ballot. In the third round of voting, Hague beat Clarke by 92 to 70, although Clarke had won the previous rounds of voting and had the support of Conservative MEPs and constituency chairpersons.

Hague's task was a momentous one. He was only 36 but expected to unite the Party and to rebuild it. He chose the former chairman, Lord Parkinson, to advise him on reorganisation of the Party over his first two years. He set up a commission to enquire into the Party's organisation and to recommend changes. In addition, he set out his stall right away as being on the side of the Eurosceptics and totally opposed to constitutional change. Many commentators were of the opinion that he had a long time to modernise the Conservative Party due to the fact that Labour's majority of 179 looked too big to be overturned at the next general election.

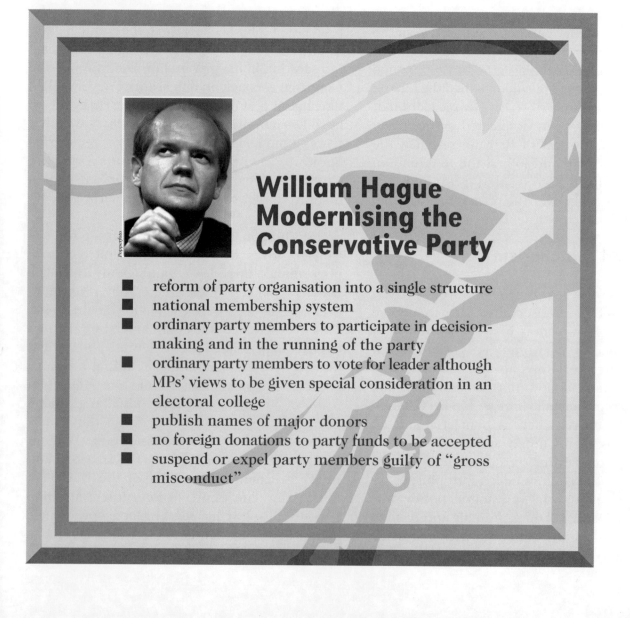

## William Hague Modernising the Conservative Party

- reform of party organisation into a single structure
- national membership system
- ordinary party members to participate in decision-making and in the running of the party
- ordinary party members to vote for leader although MPs' views to be given special consideration in an electoral college
- publish names of major donors
- no foreign donations to party funds to be accepted
- suspend or expel party members guilty of "gross misconduct"

# The Labour Party

If the 1980s was a decade of triumph for the Conservatives, the opposite could not be more true for the Labour Party. Indeed, there were serious suggestions by some commentators that the Labour Party was finished as an electoral force and could be replaced as the main opposition by a third party.

In 1980, the former Prime Minister, Jim Callaghan, resigned as leader and the PLP elected Michael Foot as leader and Denis Healey as deputy. Early in 1981, a special party conference voted to introduce two key changes – the leader and deputy leader would be elected from now on by an electoral college composed of delegates from CLPs, trade unions and the PLP; and MPs would face reselection by their CLPs before they could be candidates at the next election. Prior to this, the annual conference in 1980 had confirmed the Party's policies of unilateral nuclear disarmament, the removal of US nuclear bases from Britain, a socialist economic strategy, abolition of the House of Lords and withdrawal from the European Community.

## Lurching to the Left

This clear lurch to the left prompted leading figures on the Labour Party's right to quit. Shirley Williams, Roy Jenkins, Bill Rodgers and David Owen set up the Council for Social Democracy, initially a pressure group inside the Party, which eventually led to the creation of a new political party of the centre right, the Social Democratic Party (SDP). The new party soon formed an alliance with the Liberal Party which led to a common manifesto and candidates contesting office at local elections and at the next general election.

In 1981, left winger Tony Benn stood against Denis Healey for the post of Deputy Leader under the new electoral rules. Healey won narrowly but the campaign for that election led to public

*James Callaghan, former Labour Prime Minister*

displays of disunity and harmed the Party's image. At the same time, the SDP/Liberal Alliance was winning by-elections and riding high in the opinion polls at the expense of the unpopular Conservative Government and the clearly divided Labour Opposition.

The following year, Mrs Thatcher reversed her government's unpopularity with her leadership during the campaign to recapture the Falkland Islands from the Argentine. With falling mortgage rates and an economic boom in the South of England, the Conservatives' popularity was recovering while Labour's remained low. Mrs Thatcher decided to go to the country in 1983.

## On a Loser

Labour went into the 1983 General Election with a manifesto containing all of the left wing policies adopted by the party conference. A leading right winger in the party, Gerald Kaufman, described it famously as, "the longest suicide note in history".

The election resulted in a Conservative landslide, with a majority of 144. Labour's campaign was a shambles with no proper direction and public disagreements between leading figures. Labour polled 27.6 per cent of the vote, a post-war low, while the SDP/Liberal Alliance took 25.4 per cent.

## The Dream Ticket Modernises the Labour Party

Michael Foot resigned and the Labour Party elected the dream ticket of left winger, Neil Kinnock, as leader and right winger, Roy Hattersley, as deputy. A long slow process of rebuilding was now to take place. Kinnock began to tackle some of the causes of the Party's unpopularity.

- He persuaded conference to remove the commitment to withdrawal from the EC.

- He succeeded in having people loyal to him elected to take control of the NEC.

- He took steps to expel the Militant Tendency, a Trotskyist splinter group that had infiltrated the Party and had caused the leadership embarrassment, particularly in Liverpool where it controlled the City Council and was enacting far left policies.

- He refused to offer outright support for the miners' strike in 1984-85 in a bid to demonstrate his independence from the trade unions and to distance the Labour Party from the scenes of violence on the picket lines.

However, the commitments to unilateral nuclear disarmament, to renationalise privatised industries and to restore some of the trade union rights taken away by the Conservatives remained.

In the 1987 General Election, Labour ran a slick, professional campaign which, it was generally acknowledged, was far superior to the Conservatives. However, the Conservatives held on to their support and gained a majority of 102.

Kinnock stayed on as party leader and set up a policy review to examine, root and branch, the policies of the Party. From this, he succeeded in removing the electoral handicaps of unilateral nuclear disarmament and renationalisation in a bid to make Labour more popular with the voters.

The change of Conservative leadership in 1990 resulted in the government regaining much of its popularity lost under Thatcher. Labour went into the 1992 Election ahead in the polls and remained so throughout the campaign. With the government still struggling to deal with the problems created by a severe recession, it came as a shock to the Labour Party when it lost its fourth election in succession. It seemed that, although the Conservatives had tarnished their reputation as good managers of the economy, voters did not trust Labour to do better and still associated the Party with high taxation. Kinnock resigned as leader shortly after the election. John Smith was elected leader with Margaret Beckett as the new deputy leader.

Smith was determined to press on with Kinnock's policy of modernising the Labour Party. In 1993, he succeeded in having conference approve a rule change introducing One Member One Vote (OMOV) thus reducing the influence of the unions in voting for the leader and in the selection of parliamentary candidates. John Smith died of a massive heart attack on 12 May 1994. There was shock and genuine grief throughout all political parties and the nation as a whole.

## The Emergence of New Labour

Tony Blair was elected leader in July with John Prescott as his deputy. Under Blair, modernisation continued at an even greater pace. In April 1995, Clause 4 of the party constitution was rewritten and approved by a special conference, in which the votes for CLPs were determined by a postal ballot of all individual members. These voted for the change by a margin of 9 to 1. This removed Labour's historic commitment to nationalisation.

Blair was now referring to the Party as 'New Labour', a move designed to shed the image of a party with old-fashioned and unpopular policies and replace it with one of a party in tune with modern thinking, one that accepted the mixed economy and one which the middle classes could support, not just the traditional working class, who were becoming an ever decreasing part of the electorate.

In the months leading up to the election campaign, Blair gained the support of the Labour Party for his modernisation policies. Under the 'Road to the Manifesto' process, party members were balloted by post on party policy, leading Blair to proclaim that for the first time a political party was entering a general election with its programme for government voted on by its members.

The package approved by party members resulted in five key policy pledges.

- A reduction in class sizes.

- Fast track punishment for young offenders.

- NHS waiting lists to be cut.

- 250,000 unemployed 16-25 year olds to be taken off benefit and into work.

- The maintenance of low inflation.

Blair's modernisation of the Party caused some disquiet. In particular, the rewriting of Clause 4 prompted the departure of some left wingers, including Arthur Scargill, to form the Socialist Labour Party on 1 May 1996.

*Mirror Syndication International*

*Tony Blair, Prime Minister (left) with Gordon Brown, Chancellor*

The use of 'spin doctors' to promote policy instead of more traditional campaigning methods and the strict party discipline imposed by Blair also caused some murmurs of discontent.

As well as policies laid out in the 'Road to the Manifesto' process, Labour had been working hard in recent years to change its 'tax and spend' image. Shadow Chancellor, Gordon Brown, pledged that, if elected, he would not increase income tax for the life of the next Parliament. Blair committed the Party to low inflation and intended to leave many of the Conservatives' market reforms in place.

Labour also tried hard to project the image of being the party of law and order in the eyes of the electorate. Blair pledged to be tough on crime and tough on the causes of crime. Jack Straw, the Shadow Home Secretary, took a hard line on juvenile crime and advocated curfews for 10 year olds.

Labour approached the general election better prepared than ever before. Opinion poll ratings were consistently high and they had an impressive by-election victory in Wirral South in the early spring of 1997. Blair, mindful of the disappointment of 1992, warned the Party not to take anything for granted.

## Election Success

Even the most optimistic supporter could never have predicted the sensational outcome of the election. Labour won 44.4 per cent of the vote, giving it 419 seats in total including the Speaker's seat, up 146 on the previous Parliament. Their majority of 179 was the second biggest this century. The landslide represented a swing of 10.3 per cent from the Conservative Party to Labour, the largest since 1945. Labour had come out of its natural heartlands of the big English cities, the North, Wales and Scotland and had captured seats in areas which had never had a Labour MP before, like Wimbledon. It also regained ground in areas which had

once been Labour many years before but had returned Conservative MPs since the 1960s, like parts of Kent and East Anglia.

It was a personal triumph for Tony Blair and his principal political adviser, Peter Mandelson, whom many credit with the ideas behind the modernisation of the Labour Party.

## Blair and Socialism

Although Blair had tremendous electoral success and, in the months after the 1997 Election, his own poll ratings made him even more popular than his party which, itself, was still very popular, he does have many critics. These are both from within his own party and among his political opponents. They state that he is opportunistic and has abandoned his socialist ideals.

Certainly, the manifesto of 1997 bore little resemblance to the 1983 manifesto which was regarded as the most radical socialist manifesto ever written by the Labour Party. Labour in 1997 was committed to the EU, supported the nuclear deterrent and made no mention of nationalisation. It accepted the trade union legislation passed by the Conservatives. The promise of no income tax increases for five years and acceptance of the Conservatives' planned budget limits for the first two years represented a considerable departure from previous manifesto commitments to tax and spend.

Blair himself stresses that the socialism which he believes in is a commitment to community; the idea that we all have a responsibility to society, the reverse of what Mrs Thatcher espoused.

The new Clause 4, which Blair asked the Party to endorse, begins by stating that the Labour Party is a democratic socialist party. Most of the aims and values contained in Clause 4 are based on traditional Labour Party beliefs and, if a mixed economy was not one of these beliefs, it was what all Labour Governments practised when in power.

Therefore, some supporters argue that Blair's philosophy is not so far removed from traditional Labour values as his critics suggest.

Blair's acceptance of the Thatcherite changes is no different to how previous governments have approached changes brought about by radical predecessors, e.g. the acceptance by the Conservatives of Labour's radical post-war reforms. It is a recognition that these changes have been made and have been accepted by the mainstream of the electorate.

It is also important to consider the international context. Socialism, as it was practised in former communist countries, failed not only to meet people's wants but was, at the end, not even providing for basic needs as its economic system collapsed. Blair recognised that the Thatcherite changes were not only embedded in Britain but throughout the world, even in countries with left wing governments. He saw that any party wishing power in Britain could only accept these changes and work out its own agenda from there. Not very radical but politically astute.

Blair may have abandoned socialist ideals, if these are defined as state ownership, high taxation and public spending; but he has given his party a statement of aims and values not too far removed from Labour's traditional beliefs. What will be interesting is how he applies these values in office, while operating in a still basically Thatcherite environment.

# The Liberal Democratic Party

*The Liberal Democratic Party came into being with the merger of the Liberal Party and the Social Democratic Party in 1988. It elected Paddy Ashdown as its leader. At first, it named itself the Social and Liberal Democratic Party but a year later this was simplified to its present name.*

## A Distinctive and Radical Voice

As a centre party, the Liberal Democratic Party has always tried to project an image of being different from the two main parties. At times, this has meant taking up comparatively radical positions. For example, the former Liberal Party supported Britain's entry to the European Community while it was being established, years before the two main parties, and it has always had a raft of policies on constitutional reform – it has supported a federal UK since the beginning of the century and has called consistently for reform of the electoral system. The Party also developed distinctive policies in industrial relations with calls for workers' councils and workers' share holdings in their company.

In the 1992 General Election, the Liberal Democratic Party polled 18.3 per cent of the vote and 20 MPs were returned, with gains mainly in the South-West of England. Until 1992, the Party had always maintained that it inclined to neither of the main parties – it would assess the situation at a particular time and judge each issue on its merits. After the 1992 Election, the Liberal Democratic Party made it clear that they were no longer equidistant from the Conservatives and Labour – the Party would not support the Conservatives in the event of a 'hung

Parliament'. Paddy Ashdown also said that there would be no let up on Labour. He criticised them for being timid, uncertain and unclear as to how they will pay for their promises.

## A New Consensus?

Liberal Democrat and Labour politicians did, however, agree to co-operate on some issues, particularly on constitutional reform and the two parties agreed a joint programme promising Scottish and Welsh devolution, reform of the House of Lords, and a referendum on electoral reform. After the 1997 Election, a Cabinet committee was formed with Mr Ashdown and Mr Blair both members. The purpose of this was to discuss and develop policies over which there was broad agreement between the parties.

## Electoral Success

Between the 1992 and 1997 General Elections, the Liberal Democratic Party did have significant electoral success. In 1994, they won two seats in the European Parliament for the first time. In the same year, they won control of 55 local councils and became the second largest party in local government, beating the Conservatives into third place.

In the 1997 General Election, the Liberal Democrats won 46 seats in total, their largest number of seats since 1929 and 26 more than they won in 1992, even though their 17.2 per cent share of the vote was 0.6 per cent down. They retained their strongholds in South-West England and rural Scotland but they broke new ground in the South-East, winning from the Conservatives in Richmond Park and Sutton & Cheam. Some 29 of the Liberal Democratic intake are brand new MPs. They did, however, lose Rochdale to Labour.

Even with such a large number of seats, the scale of Labour's victory and its large

*Paddy Ashdown,*
*Leader of the Liberal Democratic Party*

majority did present problems for the Liberal Democrats. Third parties are most influential when governments have small majorities or there is a 'hung Parliament'. Labour could pass any measure it chose, including its constitutional reforms, without the cooperation of other parties. Also, if it was true that Tony Blair had shifted Labour to nearer the centre of the political spectrum, that too could prove problematic for the Liberal Democrats. Assuming that the government is seen as a successful government of the centre, it could attract support away from the Liberal Democrats. Paradoxically, if Labour becomes unpopular, why should voters switch to another centre party?

Liberal
Democrats

# The Scottish National Party

The 1980s in Scotland saw a great fall in the popularity of the Conservatives as the nation suffered an economic recession leading to factory closures and job losses in common with other former industrial areas of Britain.

At the SNP's 1988 conference, the Party adopted two campaigns of peaceful, civil disobedience – protests against the Poll Tax and the dumping of nuclear waste in Scotland. The SNP claims credit for helping to undermine Mrs Thatcher's leadership, by endorsing non-payment of the Poll Tax which she had introduced in Scotland before the rest of the UK.

At the same conference, it agreed to adopt the policy of Independence in Europe, i.e. within the EU. This was a complete change from previous policy which was to hold a referendum on membership of the EU and recommend a 'No' vote.

## Electoral Success

In 1990, after 11 years as SNP leader, Gordon Wilson decided to step down. Alex Salmond was elected leader at the 1990 party conference, having become MP for Banff & Buchan at the 1987 Election. The same year, Dick Douglas, a Labour MP, defected to the SNP, boosting the number of the Party's MPs to five. At the 1992 Election, the SNP won 21.5 per cent of the vote in Scotland (7.5 per cent more than in 1987), and three seats. Following a by-election victory in 1995, the Party had four MPs at Westminster. There are also two SNP Members of the European Parliament (MEPs).

The SNP had good results at the two Scottish by-elections between the 1992 and 1997 General Elections. In 1994, they became Scotland's second party in regional council elections, winning 27 per cent of the vote and 73 regional seats. At the 1995 local elections, the SNP won control of 3 councils in Scotland securing 182 seats in all, with a 26 per cent share of the vote - second to Labour.

At the 1997 General Election, the Scottish electorate re-elected the three SNP MPs who had been previously elected in 1992. In addition, the SNP won 3 more seats - Perth and Kinross, Tayside North and Galloway & Upper Nithsdale from the Conservatives. Overall, the SNP took 22.1 per cent of the total Scottish vote.

## The Future

The future for the SNP is closely tied in with the establishment of a Scottish Parliament. If the Parliament is a success, it could have two possible effects.

- It could satisfy the aspirations of the Scottish people for more say in running their own affairs and support for the SNP might decline.

- On the other hand, it could boost the Scottish identity and act as a springboard to total independence via the SNP.

If the Parliament is a failure and leads to wrangling with Westminster over powers or finance, it could result in disillusionment among the Scottish electorate. This might particularly affect the Labour Party, and the SNP would be beneficiaries in that situation.

STUDY TOPIC 6

# To what extent have the Liberal Democrats and SNP challenged the major parties in recent years?

## The Two-Party System

Since 1945, people in Britain have become used to what is described as a 'two-party system' where one party, obviously the larger in terms of parliamentary representation, forms the government and the party with the largest parliamentary representation after this, becomes the official opposition, a government in waiting. Both these parties would fulfil each role at different times and no other party would be in a position to be either the government or opposition.

From 1945 to 1974, the Labour and Conservative Parties between them consistently won over 90 per cent of not just seats in the Commons, but also of votes cast by the electorate. Since 1974, their combined share of votes has fallen to an average of 75 per cent, although the effects of the First Past The Post electoral system have preserved their combined total of seats at around 90 per cent.

Since 1974, other third (or fourth) parties have grown in popularity and, although this has not been reflected in the number of seats they possess, it has represented consistently 25 per cent of the vote. Therefore, in strict terms, talk of a two-party system refers only to the situation in the House of Commons. In the country as a whole, the range of parties and the considerable combined support they receive means that a multi-party system has developed in recent years.

Those who support the two-party system in the Commons argue that it provides a government which usually has a majority and can govern effectively. It is, consequently, accountable to the people for its successes and failures – because it governs alone, it alone is responsible for these. The second largest party, the official opposition, not only opposes the government but also offers alternative policies. Therefore, the people have a clear choice at the next general election between the current government or the alternative government.

## Challenges by the Liberal Party/ Liberal Democratic Party

In 1945, the Liberal Party gained only 9 per cent of the vote in the country. This slumped to 3 per cent in the 1950s. Some sensational by-election gains from the Conservatives in the early 1960s provided a degree of evidence of a revival in its fortunes and its share of the vote rose to over 10 per cent in 1964. However, it was not until February 1974 that the Liberals achieved a share of the vote approaching 20 per cent. This again followed some spectacular by-election gains from the Conservatives in 1973 and the establishment of a firm base of support in local government elections.

In the late 1970s, the Liberal Party agreed to support the minority Labour Government in Parliament in return for consultation on policy matters – the so-called 'Lib-Lab Pact'. That government was very unpopular and lost heavily in 1979. The Liberals seemed to suffer for their support of the government as their share of the vote fell to around 12 per cent.

## Realignment in the Centre

In 1981, the Social Democratic Party (SDP) was formed when a large number of Labour MPs, led by four former Cabinet Ministers and one Conservative MP, left their respective parties. The Thatcherite revolution was in full flow and the Labour Opposition was divided after having adopted controversial rule changes and having confirmed left wing policies. An unpopular Conservative Government and a divided and ineffective Labour Opposition were the conditions which gave rise in the 1960s and 70s to a series of small Liberal revivals. The strategy of the SDP leaders, the so-called 'gang of four', Roy Jenkins, David Owen, Shirley Williams and Bill Rodgers, and the Liberal leader, David Steel, was to use these conditions to engineer a realignment of British politics, combining the right wing of the Labour Party with the centre Liberals to replace the Labour Party. The Alliance was formed to try to break the mould of British politics.

The Alliance had the greatest success of third parties in the UK since 1945. It won by-elections and had successes in local government elections. In the 1983 General Election, it won 25 per cent of the vote, just narrowly behind Labour. However, the electoral system did not translate this support into seats and it won only 23 constituencies.

The Alliance became the Liberal Democrats in 1987 and, from its high of 25 per cent in 1983, its share of the vote declined and settled at 17 per cent in 1997.

Although the Alliance did not replace Labour, the shock which the 1983 result gave to Labour convinced successive leaders of the party that it needed to be modernised. The present Labour Party is one in which all the defectors to the SDP and, indeed, members of the Liberal Democratic Party, could feel comfortable. In the 1980s, the electoral system prevented the popular vote for the Alliance being translated into seats. However, the Alliance did show that third party electoral support can influence a major party to change its policies and become less extreme and more in tune with centre party ideas.

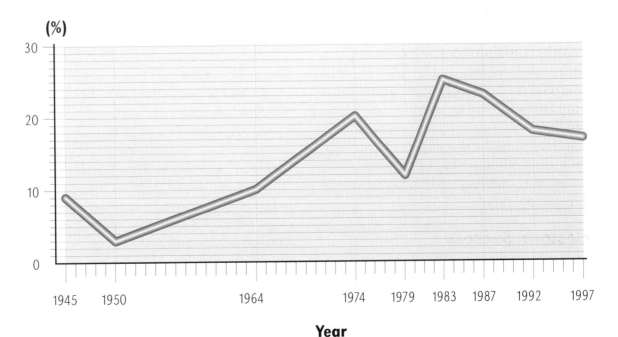

## Liberal Support at General Elections 1945 – 1997

**Year**

## Challenges by the Scottish National Party

The SNP was founded in 1934 but it was not until the late 1960s that it became a significant electoral force in Scotland. Although there is a strong national identity among Scots, the steady rise in support for independence since the 1960s owed more to economics than culture. The decline of traditional Scottish industries in the 1950s and early 60s coincided with a fall in support among Scottish voters for the Conservatives. Much hope was placed in the Labour Government of 1964-70 to generate economic growth but its failure to bring the same degree of prosperity to Scotland which Southern England was experiencing led to growing disillusionment with the ability of Westminster to deal with Scotland's economic problems. Many supporters of both main parties began considering the independence option.

In the 1970 General Election, the SNP gained 11 per cent of the Scottish vote. At the same time, exploration for North Sea oil was becoming a major economic activity in Scotland. As more oil was landed and the British Treasury benefited from the revenues paid to it by oil companies, the SNP seized the opportunity to try to convince the Scottish electorate that Scotland could be a wealthy independent state and not a depressed region of the UK. It used international law to show that the oil fields would belong to an independent Scotland which would receive the revenues, not Britain. Using the slogan, "It's Scotland's Oil", the SNP was able to remove many voters' fear that independence might lead to more poverty.

## Electoral Success

In the February 1974 General Election, the SNP won 22 per cent of the Scottish

*Alex Salmond, Leader of SNP*

vote and 7 seats. Four months earlier, the Kilbrandon Commission had recommended the establishment of a Scottish Assembly within the UK. The Labour Party used this opportunity to revert to what had been the 'home rule' policy of the Party at the time it was founded in 1900, i.e. devolution for Scotland and Wales. This appeared in its manifesto for the second general election of 1974 which was held in October. It hoped that this would stem the tide of nationalism. The Labour Party feared an independent Scotland because the country returned a majority of Labour MPs to Westminster. In fact, the SNP's share of the vote rose to 30 per cent (5 per cent more than the Conservatives and only 5 per cent less than Labour). The First Past The Post electoral system meant, however, that the SNP won only 11 seats.

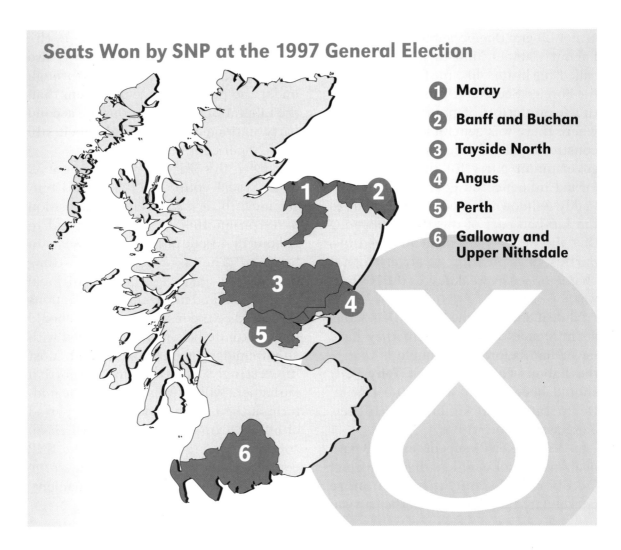

## Seats Won by SNP at the 1997 General Election

1. Moray
2. Banff and Buchan
3. Tayside North
4. Angus
5. Perth
6. Galloway and Upper Nithsdale

In the 1979 General Election, the SNP's vote almost halved and they lost 9 of their 11 MPs. Labour argued that this was the Scottish people punishing the SNP for voting with the Conservatives in a motion of confidence and bringing down the Labour Government. It was more likely due to a weariness with constitutional matters after a long campaign for devolution, which resulted in a poor turnout for a referendum and there being insufficient 'Yes' votes to allow an assembly to be established. The SNP's electoral appeal diminished further to around 12 per cent in 1983, when the Alliance was successful in Scotland as in the rest of Great Britain.

During the 1980s, the SNP became involved in campaigns against closures in the Talbot car plant in Linwood, the British Leyland truck plant at Bathgate and the steel strip mill at Gartcosh. Their profile was highest, however, after the 1987 General Election when they began their campaign against the Poll Tax. This recovery continued right through to 1992, when they won 21.5 per cent of the vote and to 1997 when they gained 22.1 per cent, winning 6 seats.

## Future Successes?

Both parties are handicapped by the electoral system. The Liberal Democrats have traditionally fared best when a Conservative Government is in office and it can benefit from protest votes from disaffected Conservatives. After the 1997 Election, it agreed to form a special Cabinet committee with the Labour Government, consisting of the Prime Minister as Chairman, along with five senior Liberal Democrats and another five Labour Cabinet Ministers including so-called 'big hitters' like the Chancellor and the Foreign Secretary. This was to discuss the formulation of policy on matters where there was general agreement, e.g. constitutional reform. This gave a non-government party for the first time a formal influence on government policy. Paddy Ashdown denied it was similar to the Lib-Lab pact of the 1970s, claiming that the new arrangement involved two parties in a position of strength, not characterised by weakness as the 70s pact was.

While it does give the Liberal Democrats an influence on government they have never had before, the gamble is that, if the Labour Government of Tony Blair should become unpopular, the Liberal Democrats might suffer through their close association with it.

In 1997, the SNP's support may still have been over 8 per cent less than its high of October 1974 but it was a more consolidated support and left the Party in

a strong position to advance if the conditions were right. The SNP was also better placed to make a breakthrough under the present electoral system than the Liberal Democrats. It was the second party nationally in Scotland, albeit still over 20 per cent behind Labour.

In 1997, the SNP controlled 3 out of 32 of the local councils in Scotland but, significantly, it was the largest opposition party on another 11. It was second to Labour in 43 out of Labour's 56 seats in Scotland. Therefore, it was in a strong position to challenge Labour in local government and in Westminster elections and could be the main beneficiary should the electorate become disillusioned with an unpopular Labour Government. Most interestingly, elections for a Scottish Parliament will take place during the mid-term of the Labour Government's period of office, a time, traditionally, when all governments are less popular. The SNP could be well placed to secure a strong presence in the new Scottish Parliament.

# Decision Making in Central Government

STUDY TOPIC 1

## To what extent can pressure groups and public opinion influence decision making?

### Introduction

There are many thousands of pressure groups. Some groups, which have sophisticated organisations and multi-million pound funding, receive national coverage and have obvious influence. Other smaller, local groups often have to survive on a shoestring budget and are concerned with a single issue of relevance to only a small number of people. However, despite this diversity, all pressure groups have in common the fact that they are formed to bring influence to bear on decision-makers in accordance with the views of their members.

In contrast to political parties, pressure groups do not seek to govern the country. Instead, they often seek to influence the government to take their views into account when formulating policy and enacting legislation.

# Pressure Groups Defined

In general terms, pressure groups can be divided into two categories: cause groups and interest groups.

*Cause groups* pursue objectives that are not directly related to the advancement of the economic or professional interests of group members. Instead, members are united by the fact that they have a shared view of the way in which society could be improved. There are two main types of cause group – sectional cause groups and attitude cause groups.

■ Sectional cause groups exist to promote the interests of a disadvantaged group in society. For example, members of the Child Poverty Action Group are united in their concern regarding the detrimental effects of poverty on young people. Shelter seeks to improve the lot of the homeless.

■ Attitude cause groups aim to influence public opinion and ultimately to shape attitudes on a particular issue. For example, the Campaign for Nuclear Disarmament (CND) seeks to convince the public that the abolition of nuclear weapons would benefit the whole of mankind. The Electoral Reform Society is intent on drawing attention to what it considers to be fundamental weaknesses in the British electoral system and presenting the case for proportional representation.

*Interest groups* exist to advance the economic or professional interests of their members. Within this category, trade unions and employers' associations constitute significant influences on decision-making. It is a feature of such groups that they are concerned with a particular section of society and will strive to ensure that they attract as many eligible members as possible. Professional associations such as the British Medical Association for doctors and the Law Society for solicitors can exert significant influence on the basis that they can claim to be the 'voice' of their respective professions.

However, the distinction between interest groups and cause groups is not as clear-cut as the explanations given above would suggest. For example, although trade unions are interest groups they have made an important contribution to the advancement of particular causes. In recent years, trade unions have been active in opposing apartheid, supporting equal opportunities and attempting to advance the position of disadvantaged groups such as the unemployed and the disabled.

*A typical sectional cause group*

# Pressure Group Influence

The influence of pressure groups and the strategies which they employ to promote their particular viewpoints is to a great extent dependent on whether they are insider groups or outsider groups.

## Insider Groups

Insider groups are those which the government regards as potentially helpful, possibly due to their perceived influence or expert knowledge of an issue. As a result, those groups are given access to policy makers such as government ministers and civil servants.

Some of the insider groups referred to are closely linked to the operation of the state. For example, the Police Federation, which represents the interests of police officers throughout the country, is well placed to comment on policy matters relating to the service.

Other insider groups owe their privileged status to the position of power and influence that they occupy. For example, the National Farmers' Union and the Road Transport Federation have been able to successfully lobby the Department of Agriculture and the Department of Transport respectively on the basis that they represent powerful commercial interests.

Insider groups have the advantage that they will be consulted by the government automatically and at an early stage in the policy making process. This is prior to the time when government proposals will be made public and the prospects of effecting significant change begin to recede.

However, insider groups often have to endure restrictions on their activities as a result of their close relationship with the government. They will be expected to observe confidentiality conditions at key stages in policy development and their capacity to mount aggressive public campaigns to drum up support for their views will certainly be undermined as such action would jeopardise their valued relationship with the government.

DIAGRAM 1

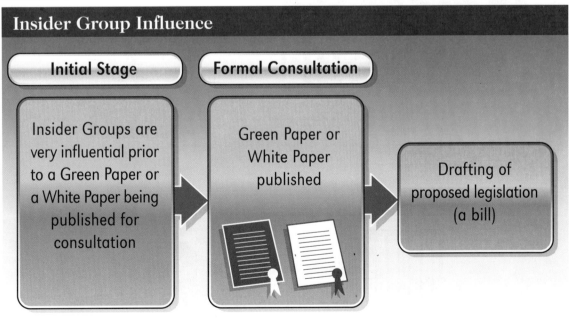

Insider Group Influence

| Initial Stage | Formal Consultation | |
|---|---|---|
| Insider Groups are very influential prior to a Green Paper or a White Paper being published for consultation | Green Paper or White Paper published | Drafting of proposed legislation (a bill) |

# The Nature of Insider Groups

Typical insider groups are powerful economic interest groups which, in terms of their organisation and finance, are well placed to ensure that their views are listened to in government circles. However, some cause groups do occupy positions of influence on the basis that they are renowned experts in their chosen field; their area of concern is perceived to be of high political importance or their views correspond closely to those of the government on particular issues. Insider groups tend to share some of the following characteristics which cause the government to recognise their concerns about a given policy area as legitimate.

## Information and Analysis

Government policy makers depend on access to information and analysis which will guide their decisions and help to ensure that the policies developed are likely to prove successful. For this reason, the input of certain pressure groups who are acknowledged experts in a particular field can be viewed by the government as invaluable.

Pressure groups may be able to identify defects in a proposed policy direction and suggest necessary improvements. Such co-operation at this early stage can prove sufficient to allow the groups concerned to express support for the policy when it enters the public domain. For example, the Howard League for Penal Reform has proved an important influence on policy development within the Home Office in relation to prison reform as a direct result of its recognised expertise in this area.

DIAGRAM 2

## Howard League for Penal Reform – Influence on Policy Development

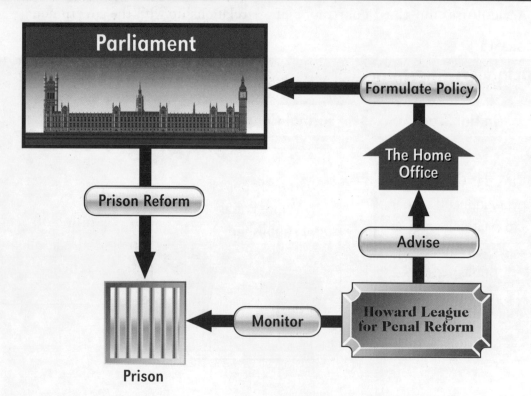

## Membership, Leadership and Organisation

The capacity of a pressure group to speak with authority on a certain issue is related to the size and composition of its membership and the ability of its leaders to develop clear strategies and unite members behind them. If an interest group can demonstrate that it has managed to attract almost all of those eligible to join and its leaders are seen to command the support and confidence of the great majority of members, its authority will be greatly enhanced.

The social class structure of the membership is also important. Groups which consist largely of articulate, middle class members will have more influence than those whose leadership is largely made up of less advantaged individuals.

Organisational matters are also of some significance. To function effectively, an organisation will often require an efficient administrative structure which is well resourced in terms of high quality staff and finance.

## Compatibility

There can be little doubt that those pressure groups whose principles and aspirations broadly correspond to those of the government will enjoy a degree of influence on the policy process. In recent times, the strong relationship which existed between the 'New Right' Thatcher Government and like-minded pressure groups such as the Adam Smith Institute and the Centre for Policy Studies elevated their status, in terms of having a say in policy development, to a considerable extent. Also, those groups whose area of activity is considered by the government to be of potential political advantage in winning the support of voters will have greater influence. Therefore, pressure groups such as Age Concern, which seek to improve conditions for elderly people, will command a considerable degree of respect on the basis that policy development in this area will be relevant to the needs of many millions of voters.

## Sanctions and Leverage

Certain pressure groups are powerful due to the fact that they have political leverage. For example, the sanctions which trade unions are able to apply in terms of restrictive practices and strike action can deny society vital goods and services and this will quickly lead to demands for action being made to the government by the general public and business leaders.

Similarly, powerful business interests can have a determining influence on levels of investment and employment. This ensures that the collective voice of business, as expressed by their representative organisations including the Confederation of British Industry and the Institute of Directors, is listened to by the government.

*Farmers demonstrate outside the House of Commons*

# Outsider Groups

It is a feature of many outsider groups that the limited nature of their organisation or the fact that considerable divergence exists between their views and those of the government has led to them being largely excluded from the policy making process.

However, a number of groups consciously reject insider status as they believe that restrictions relating to campaigning combined with requirements of confidentiality and the need to compromise would undermine their work. Such groups often favour highly co-ordinated public campaigns and will seek to mobilise public opinion in order to influence government decision-making.

Examples of groups favouring such direct action in recent times have included CND, Greenpeace, Compassion in World Farming and the Anti-Poll Tax Federation. The activities of such pressure groups may include elements of civil disobedience and lead to a level of media coverage which alerts the general public to an issue and generates a level of expectation that a government response will be required.

For example, media coverage of demonstrations against the exportation of live animals in conditions viewed by campaigners as unacceptable led to this issue being brought to the forefront of national consciousness.

*Demonstrators against the exportation of live animals block access to Dover docks*

Popperfoto

DIAGRAM 3

## Pressure Group Activities

Pressure groups exist to promote the interests of a particular group within society or to advance a cause about which members hold a shared conviction. To an important extent, the activities in which pressure groups become involved depend on whether they can be described as insider or outsider groups.

Insider groups tend to operate within existing political decision-making processes secure in the knowledge that they will be consulted in due course. They seek to influence the government by means of consultation.

Outsider groups are more reliant on direct action and the oxygen of publicity which it is hoped will generate a groundswell of supportive public opinion forcing the government to act.

### The Media and Direct Action

Most pressure groups attempt to obtain favourable media coverage and, in this way, improve their standing in the eyes of the public. Such support can enhance campaigns involving direct action by encouraging the public to exert economic pressure by boycotting products or to add their voice to a wave of public opinion intended to place political pressure on the government.

Television, radio and the press are often willing to report the activities of pressure groups as they are a valuable source of stories which involve the public and thereby capture their attention. The direct measures taken by some pressure groups are often highly newsworthy as they may involve mass action. In particular, those pressure groups which have little prospect of, or interest in, being able to influence political decision-making at the consultation stage depend on their ability to attract publicity and mobilise the support of their members and the general public.

Their activities include mass action such as sit-ins, marches, meetings, demonstrations, petitions, strikes and lobbying Parliament. However, this will often be complemented by newspaper advertising, mailshots and the generation of promotional materials such as posters.

The capacity of pressure groups to function effectively is based on their ability to organise short term campaigns which capture public attention at a point in time and to develop medium to long term education campaigns designed to shift public attitudes and generate a steady supply of new members.

# Pressure Groups and Direct Action

The role of the media in securing the objectives of pressure group campaigns is vital. The media can often facilitate the work of pressure groups by providing national coverage of campaign activities and educating the public about the issues involved. The attention arising from media activities may lead to an increase in membership and donations for the group affected.

However, no pressure group could afford to become solely dependent on media coverage as such attention is transient and another news item or issue will quickly emerge to dominate headlines and broadcasts. Indeed, pressure group activity is often adversely affected by the so-called issue-attention cycle whereby deep public concern about an issue is followed by a period of relative disinterest and a low level of media coverage. Nevertheless, environmental groups such as Greenpeace have been able to secure remarkable growth in membership (see page 113) as a result of sustained public interest in environmental issues and the attendant media coverage.

# Professional Lobbying

A feature of modern British political life has been the significant increase in the number of professional lobbyists who, in return for an appropriate payment, offer to assist their clients in the presentation of a well-structured case to decision-makers. Many interest groups use their economic power to purchase the services of lobbying organisations. However, some of the wealthier cause groups such as the Royal Society for the Prevention of Cruelty to Animals have also taken this step.

Professional lobbyists often have considerable experience of the political decision making process and can provide those pressure groups (which can afford to pay) with valuable insight into current political thinking on relevant issues, ensure that decision-makers are made aware of the arguments which the pressure group would wish to present and provide advice regarding the strategies which are most likely to result in success.

## Direct Lobbying

Many pressure groups cannot afford or would not choose to employ a professional lobbying organisation. Such groups often depend on lobbying MPs and leading politicians directly.

- Members can be mobilised to write letters to their MP.

- Petitions may be presented to decision-makers.

- A mass lobby of Parliament involving activists may be organised.

All of the activities referred to above will have the effect of ensuring that the issue concerned is prominent in the minds of politicians. In particular, pressure groups may target those MPs who have been successful in the ballot to present a private Member's bill or those who are members of influential parliamentary committees.

*A WPC speaks to an animal protestor outside London's High Court*

## Bridging the Information Gap

In recognition of the fact that many politicians lead very busy lives, a number of pressure groups dedicate a considerable amount of funding to the production of well-researched reports on issues which are of concern to them. Such reports normally incorporate a wide range of sources and contain reasoned recommendations for action. In this way, the groups involved hope to become recognised as having expert knowledge of their field. This is based on a wide-ranging examination of available evidence and a respect for objectivity. Should they succeed in this aim, they are likely to attain their goal of insider status.

## Financial Contributions

Some interest groups make substantial donations to political party funds. The Conservative Party is a major beneficiary of such donations as it has traditionally attracted a substantial element of its funding from commercial interests. In making a donation to a political party, interest groups are often signalling their approval of party policies and they may also hope to enlist a wider and more influential audience for their particular point of view. In this regard, some concern was voiced regarding the proposed operation of the Conservative Party's 'Premier Club' which had two levels of membership and was developed to augment party funds. According to reports published during 1996, the sum of £10,000 per annum secured the opportunity to meet Cabinet ministers at special events. The top tier of membership cost £100,000 per annum and provided the opportunity to attend two dinners at which John Major, who was then Prime Minister, would be present.

# Pressure Groups and Democracy

A number of commentators subscribe to the essentially pluralist view that pressure groups are good for democracy. According to this perspective, representative democracy is undermined when voters consider their main, and possibly only, role within the political process to be that of electing a government every four or five years when a general election is called.

It is argued that healthy, modern democracies require a high level of participation to ensure that the views of the people are communicated throughout the life of a government, thereby allowing them to have some influence on government decisions between elections. Indeed, some observers have claimed that the very existence of pressure groups is a reflection of the democratic freedoms, such as freedom of speech, which citizens living in liberal democracies enjoy.

The view that pressure groups are good for democracy is based on a number of related points. These are as stated below.

- Pressure groups provide detailed information and recommendations and some are involved in the consultation process which can guide policy development.

- They have a valuable contribution to make to open and effective government. Policies which are the product of consultation and compromise are more likely to command public support and this will promote social stability.

- Pressure group activity can act as a brake on any government policies which may take insufficient account of the opinions of those people most affected by the proposed changes.

- The major political parties are often most responsive to majority viewpoints with the result that party manifestos may hold little appeal for some minorities. The existence of pressure groups ensures that minority opinions can be expressed in a structured way with the result that they are likely to prove more influential.

- Pressure groups are a means by which participation in the political process can be enhanced. Members of the public are often interested in the work of one or more cause groups as evidenced by the fact that, by 1992, the Royal Society for the Protection of Birds (RSPB) had attracted over 880,000 members. Furthermore, the interests of more than ten million workers are represented by trade unions.

- Pressure groups can make a further contribution to political stability by providing a legitimate opportunity for ordinary citizens to express grievances and attempt to bring about change which will improve their circumstances.

- Pressure groups can subject government activities to detailed scrutiny and identify elements of inefficiency. This is considered to be a further contribution that they make to effective government.

*A delegation from Dunblane meet with Tony Blair, George Robertson (far left) and Jack Straw (far right)*

However, despite the strong arguments which exist in favour of pressure group activities, the pluralist view has been criticised for suggesting that a balance of power will prevail among competing interests.

Those who are sceptical about this interpretation note that insider groups often have the capacity to influence the government prior to formal proposals being made to the general public. This is significant as insider status is often linked to political leverage and the resources available to an organisation. Therefore, it is argued that those groups which are well-resourced and represent the privileged in society are often better placed to influence government decisions than others which attempt to protect the interests of the disadvantaged.

On a similar note, some critics consider the claim that pressure groups have a major contribution to make to open government to be deeply flawed. In this regard, they point out that some of the most important steps in the consultative process involving insider groups and the government take place behind closed doors. The confidentiality of such discussions is maintained with the compliance of the pressure groups involved.

With regard to statements made concerning pressure groups and political stability, it has often been asserted that the actions of such groups in pressing their own particular claims can heighten conflict in society. According to this view, the success of pressure groups in this regard can undermine democracy as the government may be required to compromise its programme in order to accommodate the views of a section of society when these may not be shared by the great majority of citizens.

Also, some reservations have been expressed about the quality of democratic processes existent within pressure group organisations. It is pointed out that procedures for appointing the leadership and other senior staff are often deficient.

In addition, it is claimed that

inadequacies in canvassing the views of members often result in pressure groups pursuing strategies favoured by the leadership rather than those which reflect the collective views of members.

Recently, there was some controversy over whether the leadership of the 'Snowdrop Campaign', the anti-gun carrying pressure group formed after the Dunblane tragedy, spoke with a collective voice and whether or not some leaders were speaking for the organisation or for themselves.

Accordingly, an analysis of the contribution that pressure groups make to democracy is more complex than would first appear. Pressure group activity certainly provides a wide range of opportunities for people to participate in society and exert some influence on decision-making. However, there can be little doubt that the capacity of pressure groups to influence decision-making is very varied. The pressure groups with most influence are those which represent powerful economic and professional interests, are well-resourced and hold views which correspond closely to those of the government.

# Pressure Group Effectiveness

It is often contended that the influence of pressure groups has declined in recent years. This analysis is based, to an important extent, on the decline in corporatism after the Conservative Government gained office in 1979.

Corporatism was at its height in Britain during the 1960s and 1970s. It involved government decision-makers meeting with the CBI (Confederation of British Industry) and the TUC (Trades Union Congress) representing the interests of employers and trade unions respectively. The aim of these frequent meetings was to forge agreement on major issues of concern to all three groups including prices and incomes, investment, employment and training.

However, the widespread industrial unrest which became known as the 'Winter of Discontent' in 1978-79, signalled the final collapse of such arrangements and the incoming Conservative Government, led by Mrs Thatcher, was elected with a mandate to take tough action to reduce the power of trade unions. As an initial step, the Conservative Government took steps to exclude trade unions from decision-making processes and thereby dismantle the corporatist structure. Mrs Thatcher's administration took office in 1979 with a radical 'New Right' agenda and this made it less tolerant of interest groups which might seek to deflect or delay the government in its attempts to implement key elements of its programme.

It was a feature of the Thatcher years (1979-90), in particular, that only very short formal consultation periods on proposed measures were allowed. The net effect of this was to make it very difficult for groups which no longer had insider status such as the trade union movement and local authorities to operate effectively. Furthermore, the Conservative Government also reduced the consultative role of the CBI and it found itself at odds with a range of professional bodies representing doctors, lawyers and teachers, who questioned the appropriateness of new policies affecting their areas of concern.

In contrast, those groups which shared the government's perspective on policy direction found their influence increasing with little consideration given to such issues as membership.

The developments outlined above served to emphasise the point that the capacity of pressure groups to influence decision-making is dependent, to a great extent, on the Government's willingness to enter into a process of meaningful consultation.

During the 1980s, a number of pressure groups which found themselves excluded from formal consultation, concentrated their efforts on lobbying to press their case. For example, the solicitors' campaign of opposition to changes in conveyancing law was fought with the support of professional lobbyists.

Nevertheless, despite the fact that some pressure groups had difficulty maintaining a position of influence during the 1980s, this period witnessed a substantial growth in the membership of many cause groups with environmental groups being among the major beneficiaries. Both Greenpeace and Friends of the Earth recorded prodigious increases in membership levels during that decade.

Early indications of the approach being taken by the new Labour Government suggest that it is likely to be more inclusive and allow diverse pressure groups to present their arguments to decision-makers. However, the comments of Mr Blair and other leading Labour politicians have served to stress that there is little prospect of any return to the failed corporatist model of the 1970s.

## Summary: Effective Pressure Groups

The pressure groups which are most effective in exerting influence are those whose views correspond closely to those of the elected government. Such groups will often attain insider status with ease. Other groups which are likely to be able to establish a close working relationship with the government are those which possess some or all of the following characteristics.

- Pressure groups which represent powerful economic and professional interests.

- Pressure groups which are well-resourced, with sound leadership, administration and finances.

- Pressure groups which have been successful in attracting members and much of the membership is drawn from the middle class.

- Pressure groups which have a high level of expertise in their chosen field.

Such groups are likely to command a degree of respect and be included in the consultation process at an early stage. However, the capacity of outsider groups which are more dependent on direct action to influence the government should not be underestimated. A successful publicity campaign can generate a shift in public opinion and the government may be obliged to take action even if this involves changing its policy direction.

The effectiveness of pressure groups depends on a range of factors and the influence of any particular group may vary with changing circumstances. However, the work of pressure groups in general is significant. Pressure groups allow ordinary citizens to participate in the political process and feel empowered. Democracy is strengthened when people believe that their efforts can help bring about the improvement of society.

STUDY TOPIC 2

# How effective is Parliament?

## Introduction

The United Kingdom Parliament consists of three elements – the House of Commons, the House of Lords and the monarchy. All three elements work together to carry out the work of Parliament although the House of Commons, the main legislative chamber, enjoys the primary role. The House of Commons, House of Lords and monarchy all have to approve any new law which is passed. However, the major role in law-making is taken by the House of Commons, the democratically-elected assembly. The House of Lords, which is unelected, amends and delays the passage of some laws but it is now unknown for the Queen to interfere with the legislative process. In recent years, the role of the House of Lords within the legislative process has come under increasing scrutiny and demands for changes to the Lords have been aired by politicians as part of a package of greater reforms to the UK constitution.

DIAGRAM 4

## The Layout of the House of Commons

1.   Civil Servants

2.   Clerks

3.   Government Front Bench

4.   Government Backbenches

5.   Prime Minister

6.   Dispatch Box

7.   Ayes Lobby

8.   Government Backbenches

9.   Opposition Front Bench

10.   Opposition Backbenches

11.   Leader of the Opposition

12.   Mace

13.   Noes Lobby

14.   Other Opposition Parties

DIAGRAM 5

## The Work of the House of Commons

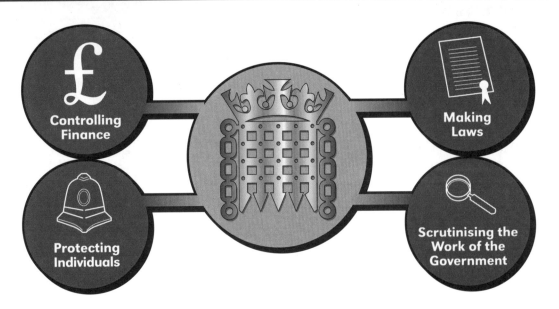

The House of Commons is made up of 659 Members of Parliament, each representing a single constituency and elected by the First Past the Post or Simple Majority system. The physical layout of the House of Commons emphasises the fact that the UK has an adversarial chamber, with Government MPs sitting on one side of the House and Opposition MPs on the other. This is quite unlike many other European countries which have chambers where MPs sit in a semi-circle or horseshoe pattern.

Government ministers occupy the government 'front bench', with the Shadow Cabinet directly opposite them. The Prime Minister and the Leader of the Opposition face each other over the dispatch box. The business of the House of Commons is controlled by the Speaker. The Speaker acts as a chairperson for debates and at Question Time and applies the rules of the House. Many of these rules are very old and reflect the long traditions of the House of Commons. Today, some people would argue that the rules and operation of the House should be modernised, while others claim that the ancient traditions generate greater respect for democracy.

## Controlling Finance

The Commons has absolute responsibility for financial matters. Each year the Chancellor of the Exchequer presents his Budget statement to the House of Commons. In this, the Chancellor outlines how the government intends to raise the money that it needs to run the country in the next financial year. The Chancellor will also outline the government's spending plans – the Estimates. The two sides – income and spending – should tally, so that the Budget is balanced. The House of Commons debates the Budget statement, the Finance Bill as it is properly called, and must approve it before the government can make changes to taxation.

The House of Commons can check on the spending of any government department through the Public Accounts Committee. This committee can examine cases of overspending by a department, can demand to see any accounts or documents which it considers necessary and can hold meetings in order to question witnesses.

# Scrutinising the Work of Government

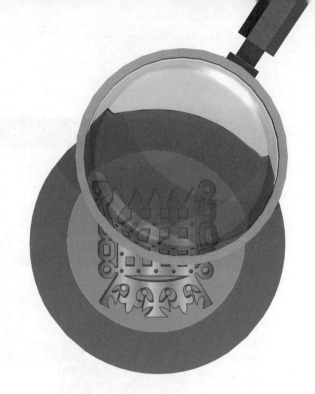

Scrutinising the work of Government is a further function of the House of Commons. The government is made to explain its policies and there are opportunities for criticising the government. Scrutiny is carried out by Select Committees, at Question Time, during Adjournment debates and on Opposition days.

For each government department, there exists a Parliamentary select committee. Like the Public Accounts Committee, select committees have the power to see written evidence and to examine witnesses. Select committees usually have eleven backbench members. Different parties are represented in proportion to the number of MPs that they have in the House of Commons – this means that the government will usually have a majority on each select committee. These committees should not be confused with the standing committees which deal with the detail of legislation.

All government ministers are responsible to Parliament for the work of their department. They are obliged to answer questions concerning their area of responsibility. Most of the questions receive written answers, but some are dealt with at Question Time. This takes place in the middle of the afternoon in the House of Commons from Monday to Thursday – ministers take it in turn to face questions.

For example, shortly after the General Election in 1997, Dr Jack Cunningham, the newly appointed Minister of Agriculture, Fisheries and Food addressed the concerns of James Wallace MP (Orkney and Shetland) regarding licensing of crews and quota hopping. The Minister said that, to qualify for a licence, a combination of several criteria had to be met: 50 per cent of catch should be landed at UK ports; a majority of the crew should be resident in the UK and a majority of fishing trips should start from a UK port.

The Prime Minister is always 'on the spot' each Wednesday for 30 minutes and other Ministers can expect to be involved approximately once every three weeks. Civil servants help ministers to develop replies to the questions which are published in the House of Commons Order Paper.

Adjournment debates take place each day for the last half hour of business in the House of Commons – regardless of how late the sitting goes on. Individual MPs have the chance to raise matters of special concern to their constituents, e.g. electricity pylons being built across an area of great beauty in the constituency. Adjournment debates allow MPs to bring the matter to the attention of the House and the minister concerned.

For twenty days in the Parliamentary year, the topic for debate in the House of Commons is chosen by one of the Opposition parties – seventeen by the Official Opposition – at present the Conservatives – and three by the second largest Opposition party – the Liberal Democrats. These days are known as Opposition Days although they are sometimes still referred to by their former name – Supply Days. On the first allotted Opposition Day of Tony Blair's Government, there was a debate about the future of the London Underground. This was followed by a debate on charging for NHS services.

## Protecting Individuals

The House of Commons also has a responsibility for the protection of individuals. Any citizens of the United Kingdom are entitled to petition the House of Commons. Traditionally, written petitions would be placed in the Petition Bag which hangs behind the Speaker's chair. Individual MPs must also make themselves available for consultation with constituents who lobby them at the House of Commons.

# Making Laws

There is no one single process for making laws in the UK. Sometimes, the people as a whole are consulted on a piece of legislation before it becomes law. In the autumn of 1997, for example, the people of Scotland and Wales were asked for their opinions in a referendum, before legislation was enacted, about whether to create Scottish and Welsh assemblies. However, the use of a referendum is unusual in the British system of law-making and has been restricted to constitutional matters. Normally, the British people delegate the business of law-making to their elected representatives – their Members of Parliament. This is the basis of representative democracy, when constituents elect one representative, the MP, to make decisions on their behalf.

New laws begin life as bills. The two main types of bill are private bills and public bills.

The government needs to plan its programme of legislation very carefully because there is a shortage of Parliamentary time. The government would not wish to lose a particularly important piece of legislation through lack of time in the Parliamentary calendar. Each bill is steered through Parliament by a minister. Government bills usually manage to pass through the House of Commons successfully because most governments of recent times have held an overall majority. Unless some of their own MPs choose to vote against them, a government with an overall majority should not lose votes in the Commons.

The process of the passage of a bill begins before the legislation even reaches the House of Commons. The government department responsible for the new piece of legislation produces draft proposals. Sometimes, these are published for public consultation in a 'Green Paper', which may set out various policy options,

DIAGRAM 6

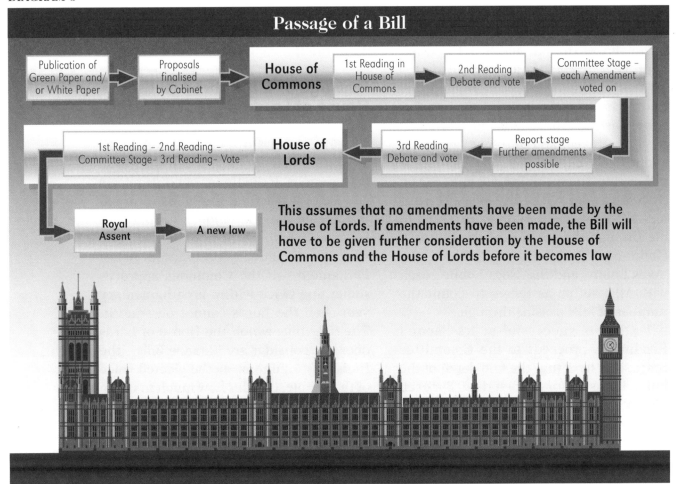

Passage of a Bill

This assumes that no amendments have been made by the House of Lords. If amendments have been made, the Bill will have to be given further consideration by the House of Commons and the House of Lords before it becomes law

or in a 'White Paper' which is really a draft form of the bill. It is not necessary to publish either a Green or a White Paper for every item of legislation. Cabinet is responsible for finalising government bills to be presented to the House of Commons. Bills are drafted by a team of civil servants who have legal expertise and who try to ensure that there are no loopholes. They work in conjunction with ministers from the department involved and the Cabinet or Cabinet committee concerned. Once the Cabinet is happy with a bill, it is ready to be presented to the House of Commons.

The First Reading of a bill is really just a way of letting MPs know that the bill exists. There is no debate at this stage – the minister concerned simply announces to the House that a bill has been published.

The Second Reading often takes place a few months later. The minister explains the importance of the bill, outlines its main contents and answers general questions about it. At this stage, the House of Commons will vote on the general principles of the bill and, if MPs do not approve it, the legislation will fail.

Votes in the House of Commons are known as divisions. Initially, the Speaker simply asks all those in favour of the bill to shout "Aye", and all those against to shout "No". If there is a clear victory for either side, the result is final. If, however, there is any doubt, the division bell is rung and MPs have eight minutes in which to file through the 'lobbies' of the House of Commons. There are two lobbies, the 'Ayes Lobby' and the 'Noes Lobby', each with MPs acting as tellers to count the number of MPs passing through.

If a bill is successful at its Second Reading, it proceeds to the Committee Stage. It is here that the fine detail of the bill is discussed for the first time. For each bill, a standing committee is set up, usually made up of around twenty MPs. If the government has an overall majority in the Commons, it can also expect to have a majority on the standing

committees. The MPs to serve on a committee are chosen by the Committee of Selection and will include the minister and shadow minister involved as well as MPs with a specific interest in the content of the bill. At the Committee Stage, the aim is to make amendments to the bill rather than to change its general purpose. The amendments discussed and voted on by the committee are often simply intended to make the legislation clearer or less ambiguous.

After the Committee Stage, the whole House of Commons must be told what happened at the Committee Stage. If amendments have been made, a new version of the bill will be printed for the Report Stage, when MPs are advised of the deliberations of the committee.

The Third Reading is the final stage of the passage of a bill through the Commons. At this stage, no major changes can be made but the general principles of the bill are again given consideration. There is a vote at the end of the Third Reading and, if successful, the bill passes on to the House of Lords.

## Passage of a Bill through the House of Lords

The House of Lords must review all legislation that comes through the House of Commons. If the House of Lords rejects a piece of legislation, the bill is returned to the House of Commons. If a bill goes back to the House of Lords within one year, it automatically becomes an Act of Parliament – if the Commons approves something twice within a parliamentary year then the Lords cannot obstruct it. The only bills which the House of Lords does not consider are Finance Bills – the House of Commons, as the elected voice of the people, decides how much taxation the people should be subject to.

The House of Lords applies the same stages to a bill as the House of Commons – First Reading, Second Reading, Committee Stage, Report Stage and Third

## Private Members' Bills, Private Bills and Public Bills

A private Member's bill is introduced by an individual MP rather than by the government. Such bills often deal with controversial topics and, because they do not have the support of the government, frequently do not succeed in becoming law. Private Members' bills can be introduced by either MPs or members of the House of Lords. In 1997, private Members' bills included: the Employment of Children Bill (Chris Pond MP); Cold Weather Payments, Wind Chill Factor Bill (Nigel Evans MP); Fireworks Bill (Linda Gilroy MP) and the Co-ordinated Universal Time Bill (Lord Tanlaw).

■ Private bills only affect one particular area or organisation and are now quite unusual. In the nineteenth century they were common when a private bill was necessary before building a new railway line or canal. Examples of contemporary private bills are the Channel Tunnel Rail Link (Stratford Station and Subsidiary Works) and the Greater Manchester (Light Rapid Transport System – Airport Extension).

■ Public bills affect the whole country rather than just one group of people. Most public bills are generated by the government, which uses a series of bills to bring its policies into effect. For example, the Local Government (Contracts) Bill and the Social Security Bill were sponsored by John Prescott and by Harriet Harman, respectively, for the government.

Reading. The only major difference is that the Committee Stage takes place in the House of Lords itself, not in a small committee so that all Lords have the opportunity to contribute.

If the House of Lords makes any amendments to the bill at the Committee Stage, these must go back to the House of Commons for consideration. Usually, they will be accepted by the Commons or a compromise will be reached but, failing this, the House of Commons may have to present the bill again within a year to over-rule the Lords' amendments.

This role of the House of Lords in reviewing proposed new legislation is a crucial one according to its supporters. The House of Lords has much more time available than the Commons to scrutinise new bills and to identify possible defects, ambiguities or loopholes. This 'revising' role of the Lords is often described as being essential to our democracy and, if it did not exist, it is likely that there would be more instances of defective legislation being passed.

## The Royal Assent

Once the two Houses of Parliament have passed a bill, it has to go to the monarch for the Royal Assent. In the late twentieth century, the monarch would never obstruct a bill which has been passed by the House of Commons. The Royal Assent is now simply a ceremonial formality. A number of bills are normally taken together and the Queen signs what are known as Letters Patent to signify her assent.

## Parliamentary Debates

Apart from committee work, the House of Commons conducts much of its business in the form of debates. These are controlled by the Speaker who has to apply a host of traditional rules and conventions. Debates in the House of Commons are based on motions which can either deal with the passage of a bill through the House or with a more general issue. The most serious type of motion in the House of Commons is a 'confidence motion' which, after a full debate, leads to a vote being taken on whether or not the House has confidence in the government. If a government loses a confidence motion, it will resign and a general election will be held.

In parliamentary debates, the principal speaker for the motion speaks first. Since most motions are proposed by the government, a minister will usually speak first, followed by the principal speaker for the Opposition, usually a front bench shadow spokesperson. Other MPs will then have the opportunity to contribute to the debate. The Speaker will have been informed in advance of which MPs particularly want to speak in a debate. However, individual MPs will still jump to their feet and try to 'catch the speaker's eye' in order to make a contribution. Sometimes, they will try to interrupt an MP who is speaking by standing up but, if the person speaking refuses to 'give way', they must sit down again. The Speaker can have a difficult job at times to maintain order and debates can sometimes appear to be chaotic. In the last hour of any debate, 'winding-up' speeches are usually made by front benchers from the government and Opposition summing up the main points of the debate.

Most debates have a time limit on them – up to two or even three days in length. If the government has a majority in the House of Commons, they can pass a 'timetable motion', or 'guillotine' as it is sometimes called, which strictly limits the amount of time given to a debate. This can mean that discussion about a bill can be greatly reduced. The Opposition can attempt to delay a bill by 'filibustering' –

this is a tactic in which they talk for so long that time runs out and the bill cannot make further progress. The government can ask for a 'closure motion' and, if the House and the Speaker agree, the debate will end there and then and a vote will take place.

## The Whip System

Each political party needs to maintain good discipline within the ranks of its MPs. Government MPs are expected to support their party in pushing through its legislative programme and Opposition MPs are expected to put pressure on the government by attempting to delay and disrupt this process. The task of maintaining discipline amongst MPs falls to the party Whips. Within each party, there is a chief Whip and a number of assistant Whips, depending on the number of MPs in the party.

Each week, the Whips send MPs a notice giving the order of business for the following week. Each matter to be discussed will be underlined once, twice or three times according to its importance. If something is underlined once, it is not that important and the attendance of the MP is simply requested. Items that are underlined twice are more important and attendance is particularly requested. Three-line whips mean that attendance is essential and MPs are expected to be there regardless of other plans and engagements, at home or abroad.

Government MPs may have a 'pair' with an Opposition MP whereby they both agree to stay away from divisions. However, when the government has a huge overall majority, as is the case with the Labour administration after the 1997 General Election, the government Whips organise teams of MPs called 'bisques' that can be excused on any given day without affecting the overall majority.

It is not in the interests of MPs to defy their Whips who are the link between the

*State Opening of Parliament (1989) when television cameras were allowed in to record the ceremony*

front bench and the back benches and can pass on information to senior party members about the attitudes and opinions of MPs. Whips make recommendations as to who would make good junior ministers. If an MP defies the Whips, he or she will be warned or can have the whip withdrawn. This means that the MP no longer receives normal party support. In the short term, such MPs will lose all the back-up and support of their party organisation and, in the long term, they are unlikely to hold on to their seat in the House of Commons if they are required to stand as independent candidates.

The chief Whips from both government and opposition, along with the Leader of the House, work out the programme of legislation for the House of Commons. They have to plan well ahead and have a good idea of how long particular items of business will take.

## The Ombudsman

The Parliamentary Commissioner for Administration (the Parliamentary Ombudsman) is independent of government and is an officer of Parliament. The Ombudsman is responsible for investigating complaints referred by MPs from members of the public who claim to have been the victims of incompetence or unfair treatment by a government department. An example of this, in 1997, related to the Child Support Agency (CSA). The Ombudsman received, and investigated, many complaints that the CSA was not always acting in people's best interests.

# Reforming the Parliamentary System

## Changing Role of Select Committees

Select committees, which monitor the work of government, represent one of the most important developments in parliamentary procedure of recent times. MPs usually have a particular interest in and expertise for the committee that they serve on so that they are well placed to make criticisms and comments. Select committees can actually increase the power of backbench MPs to exercise some control over government.

However, when these committees are too critical or attempt to exert too much influence, they may find that their membership is changed. The members of the committees are appointed by government – the very group that they should be monitoring! Consequently, they can be weakened by changes to their make-up.

Nicholas Winterton chaired the Health Select Committee from 1990 to 1992 but was replaced when the committee was deemed to be too vigorous in its scrutiny of the workings of the Department of Health. His replacement, Marion Roe, was regarded as a party loyalist who would cause fewer problems for the government.

Select committees have often had problems getting the information that they require to carry out their work properly. Ministers cannot be compelled to attend unless the House of Commons orders them to do so but, even if they do attend, it can sometimes prove difficult to obtain comprehensive answers from ministers, civil servants or other witnesses.

## Increasing Effectiveness and Efficiency

During the 1997 General Election campaign, the Labour Party voiced concern about democracy in the United Kingdom. Immediately after Labour's victory, the Queen's Speech outlined the sort of measures they would take to improve democracy. Devolved assemblies were proposed for Scotland and Wales and these were approved by the Scottish and Welsh people when they voted in referendums during the autumn of 1997. The government also proposed to set up a new select committee of the House of Commons to look at ways of making Parliamentary procedure more effective and efficient.

## Increasing Independence of MPs

There is some evidence to suggest that MPs are now more likely to defy their Whips than was the case in the past. The division of the Conservative Party over its policy towards the European Union brought this into sharp focus in the mid-1990s when a number of Conservative MPs had the party whip withdrawn.

Sometimes, MPs feel very strongly about an issue and are prepared to argue against their own party's stance. If this happens too frequently, they are unlikely to be considered for important posts within the party structure. If the MP involved is a veteran of the House of Commons, the party may accept this and tolerate them in the knowledge that everyone is aware of the individual's 'maverick' views. Tam Dalyell, Labour MP for West Lothian and a long-time opponent of devolution, or Edward Heath, former Conservative Prime Minister and long-standing supporter of Europe, are good examples of this scenario.

# Are MPs Representive of British Society?

DIAGRAM 7

| MPs Elected in 1992: Social Class Background (percentage) | | |
|---|---|---|
| Background | Conservative | Labour |
| Social Class 1 + 2 | 90 | 66 |
| Public School | 68 | 14 |
| Further Education | 82 | 79 |
| University | 70 | 56 |
| Oxbridge | 44 | 15 |
| Women | 5 | 9 |
| Ethnic Minorities | 0 | 2 |

*Adapted from Crewe, 1993*

Members of Parliament are supposed to represent the British public in Parliament. However, it would be false to think that MPs are truly a representative cross-section of the population of the country.

In terms of social class, MPs tend to belong to the middle and upper classes. Conservative MPs are often bankers, barristers or company directors. Some come from families who own large areas of land and estates around the country. The Labour Party has many middle class MPs drawn from the ranks of teachers and lecturers, doctors and lawyers. Only a small minority of MPs, mostly Labour, come from working class backgrounds. Liberal Democrat MPs tend to have similar backgrounds to Labour members.

In terms of education, the majority of Conservative MPs attended university, most of them Oxford or Cambridge. Most Conservative MPs were educated at private schools and a substantial number attended 'top' schools such as Eton, Harrow and Rugby. Futhermore, the majority of Labour MPs were also university graduates although very few attended private schools.

The age profile of MPs shows that the majority are middle aged. This reflects the fact that to reach the level of MP in politics usually requires considerable political experience. Many MPs will have had previous involvement in local government or in trade unions. Being a Member of Parliament is a massive commitment and, by the time people reach comparative old age, they tend to stand down as MPs, or the electorate make the decision for them.

Women have consistently been under-represented in the House of Commons. The Conservative Party has had the poorest record for female representation although even Labour and the Liberal Democrats have struggled at times to find successful female candidates. Various explanations have been put forward for the under-representation of women in the House of Commons. It may be that the electorate do not view women candidates in a positive light and vote for men instead. However, a more significant factor is the fact that many women are reluctant to become involved in national politics in the first place. The Parliamentary calendar and timetable make it difficult for a woman with a family to take on the responsibilities of being a Member of

Parliament. Given that most MPs are in the 30–50 age group, when family responsibilities are important, prospective candidates may be faced with a choice between family life and parliamentary life. Until now, society has deemed that it is more acceptable for men than women to 'opt out' of family life. In addition, some women may feel intimidated by the male-dominated atmosphere in the House of Commons.

Ethnic minorities have also been poorly represented in the House of Commons. As with women candidates, the view is sometimes taken that prejudice will result in ethnic minority candidates losing votes. The size of UK constituencies means that there are few where constituents from an ethnic minority background constitute a majority of the electorate.

## Breakthrough at the 1997 General Election

The 1997 General Election saw a breakthrough in the representation of women, ethnic minorities and other under-represented groups. While the 165 Conservative members of the new Parliament continue to reflect the traditional image of the party – educated at public school, predominantly male and from a middle or upper class background – the new intake of Labour MPs contained more women than ever before, more MPs from ethnic minority backgrounds, the first openly homosexual MPs (including Chris Smith, a Cabinet minister) and several disabled MPs including Anne Begg (Aberdeen South) and David Blunkett, the Minister for Education and Employment, who is blind. Clearly, the 1997 Parliament represents a much closer reflection of the real composition of the British population and it is hard to argue against the view that this is a positive step for democracy.

*Women Labour MPs with Tony Blair*

Mirror Syndication International

# Standards in Public Life

In 1994, the Sunday Times newspaper revealed that two backbench Conservative MPs had accepted £1000 each in return for tabling written questions to government ministers. The newspaper set up an undercover operation asking twenty MPs, ten each from Labour and Conservative, to ask questions in Parliament. Four Conservatives agreed to ask questions – one asked for no payment, one asked for money to be donated to a charity and two others asked for payment to be made to their home address.

Further revelations involved claims that two junior ministers in the Conservative Government, Neil Hamilton and Tim Smith, had also accepted cash for questions. Smith resigned from the government immediately although Hamilton continued in office.

The Commons Select Committee on Privileges and the Conservative Government set up an enquiry into standards in public life under Lord Justice Nolan. The Nolan Committee made various recommendations about the standards that should apply in public life. It concluded that there should be seven principles followed by those in public life.

*Lord Justice Nolan*

- **Selflessness**
  Holders of public office should take decisions solely in terms of the public interest and should not do so in order to gain financial or other benefits for themselves, their family or friends.

- **Integrity**
  Holders of public office should not place themselves under any financial or other obligation to outside individuals or organisations that might influence them in the performance of their official duties.

- **Objectivity**
  In carrying out public business, including making public appointments, awarding contracts or recommending individuals for rewards and benefits, holders of public office should make choices on merit.

- **Accountability**
  Holders of public office are accountable for their decisions and actions to the public and must submit themselves to whatever scrutiny is appropriate to their office.

- **Openness**
  Holders of public office should be as open as possible about all decisions and actions that they take and should give reasons for their decisions and restrict information only when the wider public interest clearly demands it.

- **Honesty**
  Holders of public office have a duty to declare any private interests relating to their public duties and to take steps to resolve any conflicts which arise in a way that protects the public interest.

- **Leadership**
  Holders of public office should promote and support these principles by leadership and by example.

*Martin Bell, MP for Tatton*

# Labour and Allegations of Sleaze

The Labour Party have been quick to take action when allegations of sleaze have been made against them. They are conscious of the effect that allegations of this nature had on the Conservatives, contributing to their massive defeat at the 1997 General Election. Labour, in the months following the election, were determined to be seen as being hard on sleaze.

Labour were delighted when their candidate, Mohammed Sarwar, was elected as MP for Glasgow Govan at the 1997 Election. However, the campaign had been dogged with difficulties, including a very messy selection process involving allegations of impropriety between Sarwar and his rival Mike Watson, the former MP for Glasgow Central. Sarwar's selection and subsequent election gave Labour their first Muslim MP.

Allegations quickly arose that Sarwar had been involved in making payment to another Asian candidate at the election. The claim was that he had been paid to run an ineffective campaign to

The allegations concerning Neil Hamilton dogged the Conservative Party in the run up to the 1997 General Election. By this time, the media had applied the term 'sleaze' to accusations of improper behaviour by politicians. The leadership of the Conservative Party wanted Mr Hamilton to stand down as candidate for his Tatton constituency in Cheshire. However, he stood his ground and pointed out that his constituency party had supported his continuing candidacy by voting for him at a constituency meeting and therefore wanted him as their MP. The Labour, Liberal Democrat and other candidates stood down to allow one independent candidate to stand against Hamilton. Former television news reporter, Martin Bell, took up the challenge, standing as an 'independent anti-sleaze' candidate, and defeated Hamilton to take his place in the House of Commons.

*Mohammed Sarwar*

allow Sarwar to take the bulk of the Asian vote. Sarwar vigorously denied the allegations stating that the payment was simply a personal loan, a common enough procedure amongst Glasgow's Asian community. Labour's National Executive and the police set up an enquiry into the affair and Sarwar was suspended from the party.

Also, in Glasgow, Labour were forced to investigate the activities of various local councillors, including the leader of the Labour Group on Glasgow City Council. Allegations that favouritism had been shown in sending councillors on foreign trips in return for supporting certain motions were just what Labour did not want. Once again, the party set up an enquiry and eight councillors were suspended from the party.

The death of Paisley MP, Gordon McMaster, in the summer of 1997, brought fresh controversies into the open. McMaster left a suicide note in which he named various individuals in the Labour Party who, he said, had conducted a smear campaign against him. Labour was forced to set up yet another enquiry into its internal affairs.

Under Tony Blair's leadership, Labour appears determined to root out any suggestions about sleaze or corruption. The difficulties are not confined to Scotland – another investigation took place into the affairs of councillors in Doncaster. It seemed that Labour were determined to apply the findings of the Nolan Committee to their own affairs and to present a 'clean image' to the electorate.

# The British Parliament and Europe

The relationship between Westminster and the European Union (EU) has never been easy. Significant elements within the Conservative Party have always opposed European integration and, even within the Labour Party, there has been considerable scepticism about the benefits of closer ties with Europe.

However, the Labour Party was elected as Government in 1997 stating that it would take Britain closer to Europe. This will have various effects on the life of the country but will also bring into sharper focus the issue of legislation. Britain's membership of the EU has raised important questions about the limitations of the powers of the UK Parliament. EU law takes precedence over law in individual parliaments and, when Britain signed up as a member of the EU in 1973, it accepted this.

Britain was able to negotiate special exemption from certain aspects of the Maastricht Treaty in 1992. The Conservative Government at that time was unhappy about the implications of the 'Social Chapter' of the Treaty, which enforced such provisions as health and safety regulations, minimum wage levels and an agreed maximum number of working hours.

The Conservative Government claimed that this would reduce the competitiveness of British industry and would lead to unemployment. In order to save the Treaty as a whole, the other EU members allowed Britain to opt out of this section. The reality was that the provisions of the Social Chapter went against Conservative ideology but the episode did serve to prove that Britain could negotiate out of specific European legislation. Labour introduced the Social Chapter to the UK in the aftermath of their 1997 General Election victory. There is little doubt that the wheels of European integration are moving rather more quickly now. Equally, it is likely that there will be further conflicts in future between Westminster and the EU, not least regarding whether or not, and on what time scale, Britain should adopt the single currency.

# Reforming the House of Lords

Although the House of Lords has an important part to play in the UK legislative process, it also has a wider function. The House of Lords helps to examine the work of the government, by setting down questions which ministers must answer. Each day, about half-an-hour of Lords' business is given over to starred questions, which often result in ministers providing general statements about their policies and progress.

The Lords also hold general debates on important issues. The Commons, because of its crowded schedule, does not have time for debates like these, and the atmosphere in the Lords tends to be less adversarial, leading to more detailed debate. The House of Lords is also the highest court of appeal in the land, with cases heard by the top legal brains of the country, known as the law lords.

Membership of the House of Lords is divided into several categories.

■ The Lords Spiritual are the 26 Bishops of the Church of England, the official state church.

■ There are almost 800 hereditary peers who can pass their titles on to their children. Some hereditary peers claim titles going back to the thirteenth century but most were created in the last hundred years or so. Nowadays, very few new hereditary peerages are created.

■ Life peers are given a seat in the Lords for their own lifetime. More than six hundred of these have been created since the late 1950s. Although their titles are officially conferred by the monarch, they are chosen by the Prime Minister, and include many former politicians, MPs, business people or legal experts. Other party leaders are also asked to nominate people for life peerages to maintain some political balance in the House of Lords.

■ The final group of Lords are the law lords, usually around 30 in number, including several with special knowledge of the Scottish legal system.

■ Before 1958, there were no women in the House of Lords. Since the creation of life peers, this has changed and there are now a number of women in the Lords, although representation is poorer than that in the House of Commons.

DIAGRAM 8

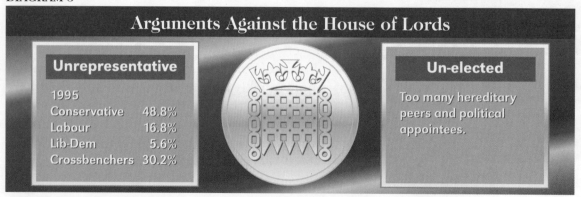

## Arguments Against the House of Lords

### Unrepresentative

1995
Conservative    48.8%
Labour          16.8%
Lib-Dem          5.6%
Crossbenchers   30.2%

### Un-elected

Too many hereditary peers and political appointees.

DIAGRAM 9

## House of Lords: Membership (1st October, 1997) and by Peerage Type

| | | |
|---|---|---|
| Archbishops and bishops | 26 | |
| Peers by succession | 752 | (16 women) |
| Hereditary peers of first creation | 9 | |
| Life peers under the Appellate Jurisdiction Act 1876 | 26 | |
| Life peers under the Life Peerages Act 1958 | 425 | (74 women) |
| **TOTAL.** | **1,238** | |
| *Of whom:* Lords without Writs of Summons. | 71 | (3 minors) |
| Peers on leave of absence from the House. | 56 | |

*11 persons who had inherited peerages have disclaimed them for life (2 of these now sit in the House by virtue of other titles).*

DIAGRAM 10

## Composition of the House of Lords by Rank

| | |
|---|---|
| Prince (of the Blood Royal) | 1 |
| Archbishops | 2 |
| Dukes + Dukes of Blood Royal | 25+3 |
| Marquesses | 35 |
| Earls + Countesses | 169+5 |
| Viscounts | 103 |
| Bishops | 24 |
| Barons + Baronesses + Ladies | 786+82+3 |
| **TOTAL** | **1,238** |

DIAGRAM 11

## Party Strengths in the House of Lords

| Party | Life Peers | Hereditary Peers | Lords Spiritual | TOTAL |
|---|---|---|---|---|
| Conservative | 157 | 4 | 322 | - | 483 |
| Labour | 111 | 1 | 14 | - | 126 |
| Liberal Dem. | 32 | 0 | 23 | - | 55 |
| Cross Bencher | 120 | 4 | 200 | - | 324 |
| Other | 25 | 0 | 73 | 25 | 123 |
| TOTAL | 445 | 9 | 632 | 25 | 1,111 |

*N.B: These totals exclude peers without Writs of Summons or on leave of absence.*

*Adapted from House of Lords Information Office*

# Why Is There a Need for Reform?

There are various arguments put forward to suggest that the House of Lords should be abolished, or at least reformed. The main argument against the House of Lords is that it is an unelected body and, as such, should have no part in the law-making process. Furthermore, because of the large number of hereditary peers, the Lords has an inbuilt Conservative bias. Despite the creation of many more life peers, these hereditary peers are still numerous enough to swing the balance. Normally, it is the life peers who conduct most of the work of the Lords. Most hereditary peers, or 'backwoodsmen' as they are sometimes called, seldom attend the House. However, on occasions, the Conservative Party has requested that they attend in order to ensure the passage of particular pieces of legislation which the life peers might have rejected.

Opponents of the House of Lords divide into those who feel it should be abolished totally and those who feel it should be reformed.

Reformers believe that a second chamber is desirable but that it should also be an elected body. Many countries, notably the United States and Germany, have a two-chamber (bi-cameral) system, where both chambers are elected. Americans vote for senators for their upper chamber and representatives for the lower chamber. Such a system allows the upper chamber to continue its work of scrutinising and examining the work of government. The less partisan atmosphere of the Lords allows for a more relaxed and detailed examination of legislation, and often the amendments suggested by the Lords make a genuine improvement to proposed legislation.

Supporters of the House of Lords argue that the present British system works well, and if it isn't broken then there is no need to fix it. The introduction of greater numbers of life peers, representing a better cross-section of the country as a whole, has modernised the House of Lords and made it more suitable for carrying out its legislative function. The same people would argue that if the Lords was elected, it would lead to the sort of party political bickering which is associated with the House of Commons, and that the quality of the work done in the Lords would suffer as a result.

The Labour Party have committed themselves to reform of the House of Lords. In particular, they have focused on the voting rights of hereditary peers, which they believe should be removed. This would mean that the Lords would be composed of appointed life peers, with inbuilt safeguards to ensure that a cross-section of views is represented. The Liberal Democrats believe that the House of Lords should be an elected body, chosen by proportional representation.

STUDY TOPIC 3

# What is the Executive and how does it function?

Tony Blair led the Labour Party into the general election on 1st May 1997 knowing that his party was well in front in most opinion polls. As leader of the Labour Party, he would become Prime Minister if the result turned out as predicted. As the polls closed at 10 pm and the first results were announced a few hours later, it became clear that Blair's greatest dream was going to come true. The results gave Labour a huge overall majority in the House of Commons as they swept to power for the first time since 1979.

The United Kingdom is a constitutional monarchy, meaning that the monarch retains some constitutional powers, although these are largely ceremonial. Accordingly, before Tony Blair could be declared Prime Minister, he had to be formally invited to Buckingham Palace where the Queen asked him to form a Government. As leader of the party of government, Blair was then able to settle into his new job as Prime Minister of the country.

*Mirror Syndication International*

***Tony and Cherie Blair on the doorstep of 10 Downing Street***

# The Role of the Prime Minister

The powers of the Prime Minister in the United Kingdom can be divided into various categories.

## Power of Appointment

The first, and arguably most important, is the power to appoint Cabinet ministers. The Cabinet is the group of around twenty political appointees who head the various government departments. The Prime Minister appoints them, can dismiss them or organise a reshuffle of the appointments. As well as Cabinet appointments, there are also many other jobs that the Prime Minister must fill – including the junior ministerial posts. Often these go to people who are regarded as promising politicians who might be considered for a Cabinet post in future years. The fact that the Prime Minister is responsible for all of these appointments gives him considerable influence over MPs. Most of them will try to impress the Prime Minister in the hope of gaining a place in the Cabinet. Within the Cabinet itself, there is a clear hierarchy of posts. Jobs such as Chancellor of the Exchequer, Home Secretary and Foreign Secretary carry the highest status, whereas posts such as Minister for Transport or the Secretary of State for Wales are seen as being more junior.

The Prime Minister has other powers of appointment. Top civil servants, ambassadors, bishops and judges are included in posts to be appointed from number 10 Downing Street. The Prime Minister has a responsibility to appoint people from different backgrounds and perspectives to these posts, without political bias.

A further power of appointment is the ability to create peers and distribute honours, known as the power of patronage. The Prime Minister's honours list includes people who will be appointed to the House of Lords, usually as life peers. It is the monarch who actually confers peerages although the appointments are made on the recommendation of the Prime Minister.

## Controlling Government Business

The Prime Minister also has considerable power to control government business. For example, the Prime Minister is responsible for compiling the agenda for Cabinet meetings. The Prime Minister also chairs Cabinet meetings which means that he or she can influence what is discussed and who is given the opportunity to contribute. Issues which the Prime Minister considers to be important can be given a prominent place on the agenda, while others which the Prime Minister would prefer not to be discussed can be relegated to the end of the agenda. Time constraints may mean that they are never actually discussed in full. Prime Ministers can also set up Cabinet sub-committees to deal with specific topics. Sometimes Prime Ministers have used this device to exclude from key decisions those Cabinet members with whom they do not agree. The Prime Minister also controls the circulation of minutes from Cabinet and Cabinet committee meetings.

## Policy Development and Presentation

The Cabinet is the major policy-making body in the UK political system. As its head, the Prime Minister has a major input into deciding government policies on all issues. Within the House of Commons, the Prime Minister is the leader of the party of government. As such, the Prime Minister has certain ceremonial functions and duties but must also work for his or her own party as the main spokesperson

*John Major on the general election campaign trail, April 1997*

and a leading figure in debates. The party of government will look to its leader for inspiration and ideas and the leader will rely on party MPs for support.

## Representing Britain

The Prime Minister also has certain powers and duties when representing Britain in international relations. This may involve attending summit meetings or head-to-head discussions with the leaders of other nations. In addition, the Prime Minister also receives heads of Government from other countries when they visit the United Kingdom such as at the Commonwealth Heads of Government Meeting in Edinburgh in October, 1997.

## Calling a General Election

Finally, the Prime Minister has the power to ask for a dissolution of Parliament and call a general election. When the Prime Minister feels that the time is right for a general election, he or she must ask the Queen to dissolve Parliament. The Prime

Minister can then announce the date of the election. Often, a Government will run its full five-year term before a general election is called. However, sometimes – as in 1983 – the Prime Minister can call an early general election to take advantage of increased popularity. Margaret Thatcher did this to capitalise on high public opinion poll ratings achieved as a result of the Falklands War and economic successes.

In March 1997, John Major launched the general election by telling the nation: "I'd like to confirm that I've seen Her Majesty the Queen this morning and sought her permission for a dissolution of Parliament and a General Election on the 1st of May."

## Constraints on the Prime Minister

In theory, the Prime Minister has enormous powers which would allow the occupier of this position control over virtually every aspect of government. However, in reality, there are various

*Tony Blair, Prime Minister, with Donald Dewar, Secretary of State for Scotland*

constraints on the power of the Prime Minister which mean that he or she cannot be involved in all aspects of running the country.

The first of these dictates who can be appointed to the Cabinet. Most Prime Ministers have taken care to appoint a range of people, representing different shades of opinion within the governing party. Normally, they must do this in order to retain the confidence and trust of the party and the country as a whole. The notable exception to this was Margaret Thatcher in the early and mid 1980s – with her huge overall majority, she enjoyed considerable freedom of action in making Cabinet appointments.

Secondly, the media may exert influence on the Prime Minister to appoint or dismiss certain individuals. Cabinet members who have been guilty of some indiscretion can face a campaign from the media calling for their dismissal and the Prime Minister may feel obliged to respond.

Thirdly, the Prime Minister does not always have the time to play a major part in the initiation of policy. As party leader, the Prime Minister will have been closely involved in drawing up the manifesto upon which he or she was elected but, once in government, the expertise for policy initiation lies mainly within each department. Thus, Tony Blair entrusted Donald Dewar, Secretary of State for Scotland, with the task of steering Scotland's constitutional changes.

Finally, the Prime Minister will be unable to control the agenda of all Cabinet meetings and committees through constraints of time. The nature of the work undertaken by the Prime Minister means that many of the day-to-day functions of government must be delegated to others. It would simply not be possible for the Prime Minister to approve every minute prior to release.

Overall, the most important constraint on the Prime Minister is the need to retain popularity. This is not easy – there are many different groups to please. Within Parliament, Prime Ministers must retain the support of their own party's MPs. Outside of Parliament, the Prime Minister needs to ensure that the confidence of their party at grass-roots level is maintained while also retaining the approval of the general public. Increasingly, Prime Ministers also have to ensure that they enjoy the confidence and approval of the media, who could otherwise destroy their career through a campaign to undermine their position. Some commentators consider that this was a factor in John Major's defeat in the 1997 General Election.

# Prime Ministerial Styles

Although the basic powers and duties of the Prime Minister are identical whoever holds the position, different people have adopted particular styles while occupying 10 Downing Street. Every Prime Minister has their own individual strengths and personality which they bring to bear on the way that they carry out the job.

## Margaret Thatcher

Margaret Thatcher was Prime Minister from 1979 until 1990. She had a very strong personality and translated that into action as Prime Minister. She earned a justifiable reputation as a dominant figure within the government. She used her powers to hire and fire ministers to maintain control. Cabinet ministers who disagreed with her policies or argued against her were not tolerated for long.

*Margaret Thatcher, former leader of the Conservative Party (1975-90) and Prime Minister (1979-90)*

She tended to fill the Cabinet with individuals, albeit very able politicians such as Norman Tebbit and Michael Forsyth, who actively supported her ideas and policies. Thatcher adopted a 'hands-on' approach to the job of Prime Minister and wished to be actively involved in and able to influence all decisions. This approach was successful when things were going well for the Conservative Party. However, when divisions began to appear, Mrs Thatcher was portrayed as a domineering and intolerant leader who was single-minded to the point of stubbornness. This was articulated most publicly in Sir Geoffrey Howe's resignation speech in the House of Commons shortly before Mrs Thatcher's demise as leader. When developments favoured the Conservatives, Mrs Thatcher was able to take the credit. However, adverse circumstances would often result in ministers being sacked to satisfy public and media attention. She was prepared to take risks and, at times, to make provocative statements. The public came to expect this of her and, for years, they admired her blunt style, her 'resolute approach', her 'no turning back' philosophy. However, towards the end of her tenure as Prime Minister, some people began to tire of her abrasiveness and reluctance to back down in the face of overwhelming opposition.

## John Major

Mrs Thatcher's successor as leader of the Conservative Party and as Prime Minister was John Major. If the party of government choose to change their leader during their term in office, then the new party leader will automatically become Prime Minister. Under such circumstances, there is no need to hold a general election.

John Major adopted quite a different approach to the job of Prime Minister. He was a more tolerant and conciliatory figure, willing to listen to different views from within the Conservative Party. One of his first actions as Prime Minister was to bring Michael Heseltine back into government – he had walked out of the Cabinet under Mrs Thatcher's leadership.

John Major's ability to bring about consensus helped him to hold on to power until 1997 when divisions about policy towards Europe ripped the Conservative Party apart. Had it not been for his skills of diplomacy and conciliation, then his government might not have survived as long as it did. Part of the reason for John Major's approach to the role of Prime Minister was the fact that his government did not have the massive overall majority enjoyed by Mrs Thatcher. After their surprise win in the 1992 General Election, the Conservatives saw their majority gradually whittled away to nothing as they failed to win one by-election after another. The Conservatives were also under mounting pressure from the media as allegations of sleaze and misconduct grew.

## Tony Blair

Tony Blair may offer yet another perspective on the role of Prime Minister. Some observers have suggested that he is turning the job into something akin to that of the American president. Although Blair owes his status to his position as Labour Party leader, he has adopted a role that almost takes him above party politics.

Norton (1987) identified four categories of Prime Minister based on how they performed in office. The first two categories describe how Prime Ministers initiate policy.

Innovators have a personal agenda to follow which does not necessarily match up to that of their party. They want to stamp their own individual mark on policy and are prepared to risk upsetting people to do so. Margaret Thatcher was clearly an innovator in the sense that she brought a whole new ideology to bear on the Conservative Party. What had begun as the beliefs and policies of the 'New Right'

within the party became full-blown 'Thatcherism', and dominated the policy-making agenda throughout the early and mid 1980s.

Reformers, on the other hand, adopt policies and goals that have been established by others and change them to meet their own needs. John Major could be described as a 'reformer' – he accepted many of the major policy targets and goals of the Thatcher years, but adapted them to suit his own needs in the 1990s. He adopted a more pragmatic approach to policy than Thatcher, who was guided by her own ideology.

The other two categories describe the individual style of Prime Ministers. Egoists are concerned mainly with their own image and the desire to hold on to power. They exercise power and, for them, this is the purpose of being Prime Minister. In the middle years of the twentieth century, it is clear that Winston Churchill came into this category, and more recently Margaret Thatcher was also an egoist.

Balancers have a quite different aim – they try to keep various factions content and see themselves as providing the best compromise. Sometimes, they are virtually forced into office as compromise candidates, but others seek office as 'middle of the road' candidates, convinced that moderate policies will be best for their party. John Major emerged as the compromise candidate for the leadership of the Conservative Party in 1990. In the aftermath of the 1997 General Election, the Conservatives were left to find a new leader. Many of the likely candidates had lost their seats in the election defeat, but once again they opted for compromise. Kenneth Clarke and John Redwood represented the two wings, left and right respectively, within the Conservative Party, but William Hague came through as a compromise candidate. However, some observers predict that his period as leader of the party will be short, and that a true egoist will emerge again as a balance to Tony Blair.

## A Presidential Role

During the 1997 General Election, it was suggested that Blair was treating the campaign more like an American presidential election. As an individual, he deliberately courted public popularity. Consequently, he emphasised his own personal qualities and goals as much as the policies of his party. The campaign became a head-to-head between the two individuals – Tony Blair and John Major. This trend had become more marked since the 1970s with each passing general election being fought as a contest between two party leaders, with the detail of policy relegated to secondary importance. In the mid 1980s, Margaret Thatcher was masterly in her ability to manipulate audiences and situations to her own personal ends. Her rival, Labour leader Neil Kinnock, was responsible for introducing party political broadcasts which focused more on personal qualities rather than the policies of his party. Kinnock's wife, Glenys, and his 'deputy', Roy Hattersley, were also introduced to the campaign broadcasts. This was the first real evidence of voting for a 'ticket' of Prime Minister, deputy Prime Minister and 'first lady' in the American style.

Despite the fact that election campaigns were fought on presidential lines, there was little impact on the way that the functions of the Prime Minister were carried out. Margaret Thatcher and John Major, despite having very different styles and approaches to the job, still saw themselves in the traditional mould of Prime Ministers, welding together their government role and that of party leader. The early signs during Tony Blair's tenure as Prime Minister suggest that he may be different. He has adopted policies and made statements which indicate there may be limited policy differences between the Labour and Conservative parties. His reputation as Prime Minister will in part depend on how he handles different circumstances and individuals. He has shown considerable ability to maximise positive publicity arising from initiatives.

Blair has adopted many of the characteristics of an American president. He can be described as a populist – one who seeks popularity with the public rather than having a fixed agenda of policies which might not be popular. He has also brought his wife and family into the public eye, although he states that his children should be protected from the limelight. His statements about looking for a 'better Britain' have elements of a personal crusade rather than a specific party policy. Blair's individual popularity cut across party lines in 1997 and suggested that, if he was attempting to achieve presidential status, he was meeting with some success.

# Reforming the Post of Prime Minister

In the 1980s, the post of deputy Prime Minister was filled by William Whitelaw and then by Geoffrey Howe. At that time, the position was relatively unimportant. In her autobiography, Margaret Thatcher states:

*"This is a title with no constitutional significance ... In practical terms it just meant that Geoffrey sat on my immediate left at Cabinet meetings."*
(Margaret Thatcher, The Downing Street Years, p 757)

John Prescott was appointed to the post of deputy Prime Minister within hours of Labour's victory in the May 1997 General Election. His appointment indicated that Blair saw the post of deputy as more important than his Conservative predecessors. Prescott is one of the few survivors from 'Old Labour' and his inclusion at such a senior level shows Blair

acting as a 'balancer' to accommodate different shades of opinion within his Cabinet. Blair also gave Mr Prescott special responsibility for environment, transport and regional policy to add meat to a post which had become little more than a reward for long service.

Within weeks of taking office, Blair also announced changes to the way in which he would function as Prime Minister. In particular, he announced changes to Prime Minister's Question Time. The two fifteen minute sessions on Tuesday and Thursday were to be replaced by one half-hour session on Wednesday. The practice of MPs asking the Prime Minister to list his earlier engagements was also scrapped. Blair argued that the changes made Question Time more meaningful and less of a circus but opponents claimed that the Prime Minister was now less accountable to Parliament as a result of these developments.

*The appointment of John Prescott as deputy Prime Minister provided balance between the traditional and New Labour Party factions when formulating policy*

---

# The Prime Minister's Office

Prime ministers require staff and advisers to help them with their work. Cabinet ministers often have the support of huge departments to assist them with their work. In contrast, in 1995, only 35 people were employed in the Prime Minister's office, which is divided into four departments.

The Prime Minister's private office is headed by a principal private secretary. The work of this office is to deal with the Prime Minister's official engagements, and to liaise with other government departments. The civil servants who work in this office also filter the vast amount of information that is delivered to the Prime Minister each day. It is their job to make sure that the Prime Minister is provided with all important information at an early stage and is not troubled with irrelevant or unimportant information.

Secondly, there is the political office. The Prime Minister is a constituency MP, just like any other Member of Parliament. Tony Blair, for example, is the MP for Sedgefield in County Durham. The political office is usually staffed by young politicians keen to impress the Prime Minister. They deal with constituency matters and, at times, they can advise on the Prime Minister's speeches and other political activities.

The press office handles all relations between the Prime Minister and the media. The civil servants who work there can influence the way in which information is presented to the media but should not have any input to policy-making. Nevertheless, the press secretary can become a well-known figure as was the case with Sir Bernard Ingham during Margaret Thatcher's spell as Prime Minister.

The fourth department is the policy unit. Its job is to advise the Prime Minister on policy matters – particularly to look at the medium and long-term implications of

DIAGRAM 12

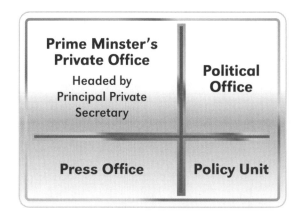

different policy options. Those who work in the policy unit are appointed by the Prime Minister. Sometimes, they can be asked to comment on proposed policies which have been generated by the Prime Minister or the Cabinet. At other times, the policy unit proposes ideas of its own – it has been documented that when John Redwood was head of the policy unit in the late 1980s, he suggested the idea of the 'NHS internal market', based on observations of what had happened in the United States. Redwood took the idea to Prime Minister Thatcher who adopted it as policy.

The Prime Minister may also appoint advisers on specific issues. Margaret Thatcher made Professor Alan Walters her economic adviser, sometimes taking his advice in preference to that of the Chancellor of the Exchequer. This led to the resignation of the Chancellor, Nigel Lawson, in 1989.

Tony Blair appointed Peter Mandelson to the post of Minister without Portfolio in his first round of Cabinet appointments after the 1997 General Election. Mandelson acts as an adviser to the Prime Minister, in addition to the more formal appointees within the Prime Minister's office.

# The Cabinet

According to an official publication:

*"The functions of the Cabinet are policy-making, the supreme control of Government and the coordination of Government departments."*
(HMSO, 1994, p39)

The Cabinet is the group of top politicians from the governing party who meet regularly to discuss and debate policy and to supervise its implementation. Full Cabinet meetings take place once or twice a week, lasting for a couple of hours each time. It is not possible for the Cabinet to debate every single issue in full, nor to approve every individual decision, so, at times, the Cabinet tends to 'rubber stamp' the recommendations made elsewhere.

Since the middle of the twentieth century, the Cabinet has tended to consist of around twenty members, chaired by the Prime Minister. Most Cabinet ministers are responsible for an individual government department. As a result of the need to defend policies and decisions in Parliament, they are usually Members of Parliament, although a few may be members of the House of Lords. It is not unknown for outsiders to be brought into the Cabinet – in 1997, Sir David Simon, head of British Petroleum, was co-opted to the Cabinet as Minister for Trade and Competitiveness in Europe, taking a pay cut of nearly one million pounds per year to do so!

# Functions of the Cabinet

Once a party is in government, the Cabinet becomes the major policy-making group. Debate within the Cabinet is often intense and decisions may be taken on the basis of a vote. However, the most influential members of the Cabinet, including the Prime Minister, may have a disproportionate influence. As noted earlier, when Margaret Thatcher was Prime Minister, she tended to appoint ministers who would agree with her, and as a result the Cabinet was not really a forum for debate. Instead, ministers tended to endorse decisions that had already been taken by Mrs Thatcher and her immediate colleagues and advisers. Traditionally, however, the Cabinet has been appointed to reflect different views and attitudes from throughout the party of government. On that basis, the Cabinet should enjoy the confidence of the party and the country as a whole. John Major appointed Ministers in this way, and Tony Blair's first Labour Cabinet for almost twenty years also reflected a spectrum of views. Although policy-making is one of the functions of the Cabinet, it is important to realise that pressure of time often leads to detailed decisions being made elsewhere, with Cabinet only providing endorsement for them.

The Cabinet also plans the business of Parliament. Each government has a programme of legislation which it intends to progress through Parliament. Cabinet is involved in prioritising the policy areas and deciding the timescale for putting legislation before Parliament. This is an important function and divides into two scales.

DIAGRAM 13

## Functions of the Cabinet

ensures government departments follow policies

policy making

settles disputes between government departments

reviews and evaluates work of the government

plans business of parliament

- On a macro-scale, the Cabinet must decide when to implement major policy decisions which may affect the popularity of the government. For example, the Scottish and Welsh Devolution Bills had to be pushed through quickly by the new Labour administration in order to keep promises made at the 1997 Election. Not surprisingly, potentially unpopular policies involving increased taxation would not be planned for the last year of a government's term of office.

- On a micro-scale, for each session of Parliament, the Cabinet must decide which issues are the most important and need to be placed at the head of the legislative calendar, thus increasing their chances of being passed through the various stages necessary to expedite implementation. The Cabinet also decides how much time to allocate to individual pieces of legislation in Parliament. The Conser-vatives were angered at the limited period of time set aside for debate of the devolution proposals, claiming that such a fundamental change merited closer scrutiny.

- The Cabinet also arbitrates in disputes between government departments. The Chancellor of the Exchequer, who controls the finances of government, frequently comes into dispute with other ministers. Since the Chancellor can dictate expenditure plans, ministers may not be able to implement the policies that they want. Such disputes should be settled in Cabinet rather than being brought out into the open.

- The Cabinet ensures that all government departments and ministers follow the same basic agenda when implementing policy. Margaret Thatcher was particularly effective at introducing the free-market ethos to all areas of government policy, and any dissenters would have been dealt with in Cabinet.

- The Cabinet also serves as a mechanism for reviewing and evaluating the work of government. Ministers who have been responsible for failures or indiscretions will have to justify themselves to their colleagues.

DIAGRAM 14

## Cabinet Table Layout

1. Prime Minister
2. Depute Prime Minister
3. Cabinet Secretary
4. Chancellor of the Exchequer
5. Home Secretary
6. Foreign Secretary
7. Junior Cabinet Ministers
8. Middle Ranking Cabinet Ministers

The physical lay-out of the Cabinet room influences discussion. The Cabinet meets around a long table, with the Prime Minister sitting at the middle of one of the long sides. The most senior ministers sit close to the Prime Minister or directly opposite. More junior ministers are relegated to the ends of the table from where they cannot so easily become involved in discussions. Cabinet meets as a formal committee and contributions must be made through the chair, making meaningful debate more difficult.

To the general public, members of the Cabinet symbolise the highest level of government. Along with the Prime Minister they form the executive branch of government, and would wish to be seen as honest, hard-working and honourable servants of the country.

## Where Does Power Lie?

The traditional view is that the Cabinet is all-powerful in the British political decision-making process. Policies should be thrashed out in private by the Cabinet and then publicly supported by all members. However, the burden of work which would fall on the Cabinet if it were to make all decisions would be enormous and consequently some of the power is delegated to Cabinet committees.

### Cabinet Committees

These are sub-committees of the Cabinet, composed of ministers. Some Cabinet committees only contain full Cabinet members, while others also contain junior ministers. Civil servants also assist the work of the Cabinet. Civil servants, who are non-political employees, have 'official committees' which shadow the work of Cabinet committees. There are two types of Cabinet committee – 'standing' and 'ad hoc'.

- Standing committees are more or less permanent and deal with a particular policy area – transport, defence, foreign policy etc.

- Ad hoc committees are established for a particular purpose and have a limited life span.

The Prime Minister chairs the most important Cabinet committees. It has become common practice for many important decisions to be taken by committees and for these not to be debated further at full Cabinet meetings. Indeed, in some cases the decisions of Cabinet committees may not even be reported to the full Cabinet. However, although Cabinet committees may make major decisions about the implementation of policy, they tend not to initiate policy itself – this is done either by the full Cabinet, or through the policy unit.

In addition to the formal meetings of the full Cabinet or the Cabinet committees, government also makes use of informal meetings between senior politicians and officials. These can range from a casual chat in a corridor outside the House of Commons, to regular social meetings between influential politicians. Informal groups which include the Prime Minister are particularly significant. It is here that policy ideas and options may be discussed and 'bounced off' other government officials before they are taken to Cabinet for more formal consideration.

One explanation for the increasing importance of informal groups in formulating policy is concern over possible leaks. The Prime Minister and senior Cabinet members are anxious to maintain secrecy about policies until the appropriate moment and the less that is discussed outwith the 'inner sanctum' of people, the less chance there is of information becoming public at an inopportune moment.

## Collective Responsibility

Within Cabinet, ministers are free to express their own opinions. Cabinet meetings can turn into heated debates but, at the end of the meeting, an agreed policy must be reached. Ministers are then expected to publicly support the decision of the Cabinet whether they personally agree with it or not. This principle is known as 'collective responsibility'. Any minister who cannot publicly support an agreed Cabinet decision is expected to resign their post in government.

The concept of collective responsibility originally applied only to Cabinet ministers. However, in recent years, it has become clear that it applies also to junior ministers and parliamentary private secretaries.

Depending on the nature and personality of the Prime Minister, other ministers may be pressured into agreeing with and supporting policies that they do not like. Under Margaret Thatcher, for example, ministers realised that, if they argued against her policies in Cabinet, they would be sacked at the next reshuffle. This meant that the Cabinet approved decisions which individual members privately disagreed with, such as the Poll Tax. However, once agreed by the Cabinet, even if debate had been restricted, the ministers had to publicly support the policy.

The idea of collective responsibility was shattered in John Major's Conservative Government of the early 1990s by divisions over Europe. John Major's style

*John Major, leaves 10 Downing Street (May 2nd 1997)*

of leadership as a 'balancer' meant that he had to accept different viewpoints and, although he asked that differences should not be aired in public, no minister resigned on the grounds of collective responsibility while he was Prime Minister.

## The Cabinet Office

The Cabinet office is headed by the Cabinet secretary, one of the major posts in the civil service. Within the Cabinet office, the Cabinet secretariat arranges the times of meetings, and in conjunction with the chairperson of the Cabinet and the main committees, usually the Prime Minister, sets the agenda. The secretariat also publishes and circulates minutes of Cabinet meetings.

Controversy has grown over the role of the Cabinet office in dealing with policy. In theory, its role should be simply to support the work of the government and to ensure the smooth running of the decision-making process. However, critics of the system have pointed out that the Cabinet office could influence the decision-making process. The Cabinet

secretary sits in on all Cabinet and Cabinet committee meetings and is responsible for taking minutes of the meetings. The Cabinet office advises the government on the implementation of policy and, at times, the advice provided could be designed to obstruct particular policies.

The Prime Minister, Tony Blair, caused some controversy when he appointed Peter Mandelson as Minister without Portfolio, to work from the Cabinet office. Mandelson is the leading Labour 'spin doctor', and he is responsible for presenting government policies to the public. Critics of the role say that Mandelson is little more than a propagandist. The term spin doctor evolved during the early 1990s to describe politicians working behind the scenes to spread information, highlight personalities and generally try to manipulate information to generate maximum advantage for their political masters.

*Peter Mandelson, Minister Without Portfolio*

# The Shadow Cabinet

In Britain's constitutional monarchy, a special role is reserved for 'Her Majesty's Opposition', usually the second largest party in the House of Commons. From 1979 until 1997, Labour were in Opposition but after the 1997 Election it was the Conservatives who took on that mantle. The Opposition party has spokespersons for each key area of policy who are sometimes known as the 'Shadow Cabinet'. Their role is to shadow the work of government departments, to question and challenge them, and to lead the Opposition's contribution to debates in the House of Commons on the topics assigned to them. Shadow ministers can be regarded as 'ministers in waiting'. Although they formulate policies, they have no opportunity to put them into practice and they do not have the support of the civil service for their work.

**DIAGRAM 15**

## The Promotion Route

# Climbing the Ministerial Ladder

Ministers combine their job in government with their constituency role as a Member of Parliament. The commitment required is enormous and this can have a telling effect on the personal life and health of some ministers.

The top ministerial job is that of Chancellor of the Exchequer, the minister responsible for the Treasury. The Prime Minister has the power to amalgamate various government departments or to create new departments. This can lead to the loss of Cabinet posts or the creation of new ones. In June 1997, the Department of the Environment and the Department of Transport were amalgamated to form the Department of the Environment, Transport and the Regions, but more than one minister was appointed to this enormous office.

At the lowest level, the route to promotion starts with appointment as a Parliamentary Private Secretary (PPS). This is an unpaid but important job, acting as a general parliamentary assistant to a minister. This can involve helping them with constituency matters, and acting as their 'eyes and ears' in Parliament. The effective PPS will be able to report back information to their minister which will help the minister concerned to judge the mood of the party. The PPS must also find a 'pair' for their minister – this is an Opposition MP who agrees to abstain from votes when the minister is absent on government business. Tom Clarke, currently Labour MP for Coatbridge and Chryston, was 'paired' with George Younger when the latter was Secretary of State for Scotland and Defence Secretary.

From PPS, ambitious MPs would hope to progress to become a Parliamentary Under Secretary of State and then a minister of State. Neither of these posts has Cabinet status, but the incumbents work under the guidance of a Cabinet minister. Parliamentary Under Secretaries and ministers of State do much of the donkey work of Government, but they get little of the credit. Much of their work involves attending meetings and reading briefing papers. Civil servants provide them with vast quantities of documents and reports which the junior ministers read, initial and return. Having done so, the junior minister concerned can be held responsible if something goes wrong!

These junior minister posts are regarded as 'up or out' posts. The people who hold them either make quite rapid progress and are promoted to Cabinet level or, if they are deemed to have been inadequate, they are quickly replaced from the ranks of backbench MPs. When the government has a huge majority, as was the case with Labour after the 1997 General Election, the Prime Minister has a wide choice of candidates to take on junior ministerial responsibility although many MPs may have little or no experience of Westminster, let alone of government.

## Ministerial Roles and Individual Responsibility

Ministers are responsible for policy initiated in their departments. This is known as the 'doctrine of individual responsibility'. Ministers may take advice from Cabinet meetings or the Prime Minister and go back to their departments to initiate policy designed to meet the government's objectives. They will test out ideas on their senior civil servants and will listen carefully to the advice that they give. However, in the final analysis, the decisions made and actions taken are the minister's responsibility and he or she, alone, is held accountable.

Some decisions are made on ideological grounds. During the long period of Conservative Government from 1979 to 1997, ideology was a very important factor

in determining policy as the free-market ethos was brought into all aspects of government. Financial factors may also help determine decisions. Even within a department, it would be impossible for a minister to keep in touch with all decisions that are being made and all of the policies that are being implemented. An effective minister delegates responsibility to junior ministers but expects to be kept informed of any developments or problems that may arise. Ministers are adept at taking the credit when their department enjoys successes and at passing the buck when they have failures to account for.

The role of civil servants within a government department is to implement policy and to advise. Civil servants are just that – servants of the government. Their jobs are not political and they should be able to serve governments of any political persuasion with equal efficiency. Senior civil servants are motivated by their desire to serve the country and to maintain the process of democracy which has elected the government of the day.

Ministers are expected to demonstrate responsibility, both in their personal lives and in their professional duties. Several ministers have been forced to resign their posts because of revelations concerning their personal lives. Most prominently, Conservative minister Cecil Parkinson was forced to resign following an affair with his secretary in 1983 and, more recently in 1994, junior minister Tim Yeo resigned after an extra-marital affair. The publicity which accompanies such disclosures undermines public confidence in the minister concerned and, in some cases, there may also be security implications. If a minister's private life could leave him or her open to being blackmailed, resignation will almost inevitably follow.

Like other MPs, ministers are also expected to declare any business interests or connections which might influence their role in decision-making. Ministers are further expected to take responsibility for decisions made in their department. If a minister is thought to have been negligent or to have made a wrong decision, that individual will come under pressure to resign. Eventually, it may prove necessary for the Prime Minister to become involved if the minister concerned appears reluctant to give up his or her post.

The United Kingdom has no written constitution which means that there are no clearly set down rules against which to judge the performance of ministers. However, centuries of precedent have established the sort of circumstances in which a minister has to resign. Nevertheless, it is a feature of the late twentieth century that these precedents are being undermined with the media playing an increasing role in influencing public opinion for or against an individual.

## What is the Role of the Civil Service?

In theory, the role of the civil service is simply to implement government policy and to offer advice when asked. Civil servants in the UK, unlike many other countries, are not appointed on political grounds. However, it is clear that their role involves more than simply professional advice and policy implementation.

Civil servants must remain totally impartial. They cannot become involved in any form of political activity and they must not express opinions publicly. They are well advised not to express opinions in private either, as these are liable to be leaked. They sign the Official Secrets Act when they take on their appointment and must not divulge any information related to their job.

On occasions, the neutrality of the civil service has been called into question. In 1992, the 'Arms for Iraq' affair hit the headlines. Civil servants were accused of helping government ministers circumvent a ban on selling arms to Iraq and of deliberately misleading Parliament and the public. The Scott Inquiry into the affair concluded that civil servants were guilty of providing bad advice and colluding in a cover-up although it was claimed that the government had also been involved in deliberately misleading Parliament through withholding important information.

Civil servants face a difficult moral dilemma. They are asked to serve the country on a neutral and impartial basis yet they work for political masters who are far from neutral and impartial.

*Saddam Hussein, President of Iraq, waves to supporters in Baghdad*

# Models of the Relationship between Ministers and Civil Servants

Theakston (1992) described four different models of the relationship between ministers and the civil service.

- The constitutional model – civil servants are truly neutral and impartial, they offer advice when asked and implement policies dictated by their political masters without question.

- The adversarial model – ministers and civil servants are in conflict, ministers want to implement change but civil servants prefer to maintain the status quo.

- The village life in Whitehall community model/the cohabitation model – ministers and civil servants co-exist and work together in harmony: civil servants have the expertise and ministers provide the ideas.

- The bureaucratic expansion model – civil servants are empire builders interested only in expanding their own power.

The reality of the situation in the late 1990s is that the relationship between ministers and civil servants is in a state of flux. After almost 20 years of Conservative government, many civil servants have known no other political masters and have had to adjust to the needs of the new Labour government. Some observers claim that certain top civil servants will have difficulty in adjusting due to the fact that they owe their status to the former Conservative administration as government ministers have to approve such appointments. It is certainly true that ministers can enhance the promotion prospects of particular civil servants who share their ideological goals. Civil servants who are seen as obstructive will often be passed over as appointments are made to the most senior positions.

The neutrality of the civil service has frequently been questioned. Top civil servants tend to share an educational and social background with Conservative ministers so it might be thought that they would be sympathetic to Conservative goals. However, the Conservative Party has consistently argued that 'good government is less government', attempting to reduce the influence of centralised government machinery. The traditional Labour view that government should provide a wide range of centrally-organised and funded services would be more likely to satisfy any lust for power and influence on the part of the civil service. However, New Labour policies are far removed from traditional Labour and the role of the civil service could be in for further change under Tony Blair's administration.

# Central and Local Government in Scotland

## STUDY TOPIC 1

# What is the place of Scotland within the United Kingdom?

## Historical Background

In 1603, King James VI of Scotland also became James I of England, following the death of Queen Elizabeth of England, of whom he was the closest successor. Although this gave Scotland and England the same monarch, each country retained its own parliament and, in effect, remained separate countries. In 1707, the parliaments of both countries voted to dissolve themselves and be replaced by the Parliament of the United Kingdom of Great Britain.

Although there are still disagreements about how much coercion or bribery of the Scottish Parliament took place to reach this decision, this meant that Scotland was entering voluntarily into a union with England, unlike Wales or Ireland, which had been forcibly united with their larger neighbour. Consequently, Scotland was in a position to negotiate the terms of the Union. There were to be perpetual safeguards for the Presbyterian established Church of Scotland, the Scottish universities, the Scottish legal system and the rights of royal burghs.

Within these safeguards lie the roots of the present realities of a separate established church, a separate legal system and special arrangements for legislation applying solely to Scotland, a separate education system – both at higher education level and at school level also, since schools were the responsibility of the Church of Scotland at the time – and a separate system of local government.

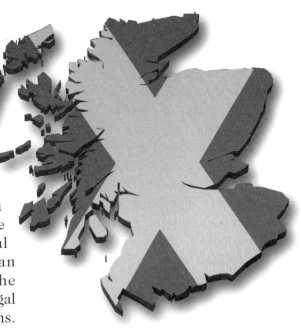

DIAGRAM 1

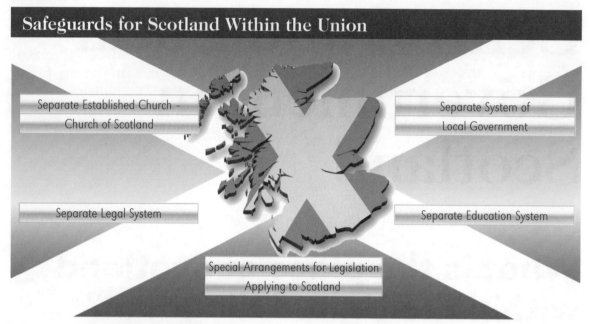

**Safeguards for Scotland Within the Union**

- Separate Established Church – Church of Scotland
- Separate System of Local Government
- Separate Legal System
- Separate Education System
- Special Arrangements for Legislation Applying to Scotland

# The Secretary of State for Scotland

The post of Secretary of State for Scotland was also established at the time to administer government in Scotland. However, this post disappeared for almost a century and a half after 1746 and the post of Scottish Secretary, with cabinet rank, was only re-established in 1885. The Secretary was made responsible for the Scottish Office in London, which was also established at the same time, for administering Scotland's legal system, for introducing Scottish legislation and for Scottish Boards which administered education, agriculture, local government and health – responsibilities which the Scottish Office retains today.

In 1926, the name of the post was changed to the original version of Secretary of State. In 1928, the Scottish Boards became departments of the Scottish Office. In 1939, the main headquarters of the Scottish Office moved to St Andrew's House in Edinburgh. The responsibilities of the Scottish Office continued to grow after the Second World War to the present day.

Also negotiated at the time of the Union was the right of Scotland to specified

*Donald Dewar (right), Secretary of State for Scotland, with Tony Blair*

membership of both Houses of Parliament. Any change in Scotland's allocation requires new legislation. This is particularly important in the context of the debate on a devolved Scottish Parliament and the number of Scottish MPs in the House of Commons.

# A National Identity

Scotland is a nation but not a state. A state is a sovereign political entity – in more everyday terms, a country with total control of its own affairs, free to legislate on all matters within its frontiers and to enter voluntarily into agreements with other countries – recognised in international law as such an entity. At present, Scotland does not meet those criteria.

Other political entities which are part of a greater entity, such as the fifty states of the USA, have the guaranteed right to legislate for matters concerning their own state, a right which, in 1997, Scotland still did not have. Yet, these American states are not nations as Scotland is. However, like these states, Scotland does have its own political system, where political parties define distinct issues related to Scotland and seek the support of the Scottish electorate to implement policies which address these distinct issues.

Most important of all, the vast majority of Scots feel that they are part of a Scottish nation. What then makes Scotland a nation and causes Scots to have their own national identity? The reasons range from what can be described as serious to the trivial, although these trivial reasons can seem very important to people and be as equally enforcing of a Scottish identity as the more serious reasons.

# National Institutions

Firstly, a nation has to have national institutions. The separate Scottish legal system is such an institution. The fact that there are areas of law which are different in Scotland to England and a different courts administration to interpret and enforce these laws demonstrates to Scots that there exists a distinct national institution and reinforces their national identity.

Scotland's distinct educational system is another national institution which has an effect on those who experience it and makes them feel distinctly Scottish. Scottish History, in addition to British History, is taught in schools, particularly in the primary sector. From an early age, this causes Scots to identify national heroes, such as Wallace or Bruce, and to realise that, up to 1707, Scotland was a separate state, as well as a nation. In secondary schools, students are presented for different examinations, run by a separate Scottish Qualifications Authority. The curriculum in Scottish schools is different and there are subjects which are simply not taught in the rest of the UK, such as Modern Studies. The structure of Scottish university degrees is different from the rest of the UK, with longer and more broadly based courses.

The separate established Church of Scotland is a focus for national identity. It distinguishes Scotland from England. The Roman Catholic Church has a separate Scottish hierarchy, which reinforces a Scottish identity among Scots Catholics. There are other Christian churches which have adherents solely in Scotland – the Scottish Episcopal Church, the Free Church of Scotland and the United Free Church of Scotland being examples. Other non-Christian religions, such as Judaism, Islam, Hinduism and Sikhism are also keen to project themselves as part of a Scottish community. Although religious observance is declining, it is still relatively strong in Scotland and the separate Scottish identities of these religions serve to reinforce the overall Scottish identity.

# A Political Identity

The role of the Secretary of State and the Scottish Office, together with the Scottish committees in Parliament, demonstrate to Scots the separate identity of Scotland within the United Kingdom. The distinct Scottish political system which this has caused to develop means that the political parties must also take account of the special circumstances of Scotland within the UK government. The three main UK parties now all describe themselves as 'Scottish' before their name and, of course, there is a party which organises only in Scotland and whose purpose is to persuade a majority of the Scottish electorate to vote for independence from the UK – the Scottish National Party (SNP). The decision of the UK parties to adopt Scottish names in Scotland and the development of the SNP demonstrate the distinctiveness of the Scottish political system within the UK and this reinforces the Scottish identity among voters.

The separate system of local government in Scotland has helped to develop and reinforce the Scottish national identity. It is responsible for the distinct Scottish schools system and sometimes the same services are described differently in Scotland and England, e.g. social work in Scotland is social services in England. However, it is when the UK government legislates differently for the Scottish local government system that its distinctiveness becomes important. In some cases, this can lead to resentment and increase the feeling of Scottishness among Scots. Examples of this were when the Conservative Government introduced the Community Charge (Poll Tax) one year earlier in Scotland in the 1980s than elsewhere and when the same government changed the system of local government in Scotland in the 1990s, without consultation or an independent commission as was the case in England. Both of these actions caused great resentment, particularly the former, which intensified the feeling of national identity in Scotland.

# A Distinctive Scottish Media

The media in Scotland are either distinct from the rest of the UK or, if part of a British company or group, attempt to project a peculiarly Scottish image. The BBC has separate programme making facilities and studios in Scotland. Between programmes, even those of no specific Scottish relevance, BBC 1 and BBC2 TV channels identify themselves as BBC 1 Scotland and BBC 2 Scotland. BBC Radio Scotland is almost entirely Scottish in terms of programme origin and interest. Scottish Television, Grampian and Border are all part of the ITV network and take many programmes from this but the terms of their lease demand production of programmes which reflect local, in effect Scottish, interest. Independent local radio stations, like Radio Clyde or Forth, by their very nature, have programmes which reflect and enhance the Scottish national identity. The largest selling popular evening newspaper, the Evening Times, and the largest selling quality daily, The Herald, are both part of the Scottish Media Group, which also has interests in Scottish Television. The Scotsman and the only Scottish quality Sunday newspaper, Scotland on Sunday, are part of the Edinburgh-based Scotsman Newspapers Limited. The Daily Record, owned by Mirror Group Newspapers, has always been independent of influence from its English counterpart, the Daily Mirror. Other newspapers describe themselves as Scottish for their editions North of the Border, e.g. the Scottish Sun, the Scottish Daily Express, the Scottish Daily Mail. The most overtly Scottish newspaper, in a traditional sense, the Sunday Post, is owned by DC Thomson of Dundee and is also the newspaper with the highest saturation circulation in the world. Again, the Scottish media not only reflect but promote a Scottish national identity.

# The People's Perspective

There are also perhaps more trivial factors contributing to national identity in Scotland but, since these impinge on people's everyday experiences, they are no less important.

Separate Scottish banks and their different banknotes reinforce a national identity, particularly when Scottish money is not accepted in England. Many companies in Scotland have 'Scottish' as part of their name, even though they may be entirely owned by non-Scots. This could be good commercial practice since they are recognising the importance of the national identity in Scotland and hope to attract customers in this way. It also reinforces the Scottish identity among customers. The employers' organisation, the Confederation of British Industry (CBI), has a distinct Scottish organisation. Most trade unions have Scottish areas and there is a separate Scottish Trades Union Congress (STUC).

Sport and culture play an important part in developing and strengthening the Scottish identity. Most sports have separate Scottish national teams. The two most popular spectator sports, football and rugby, play a particularly significant role in this. Anyone, Scots or otherwise, who has witnessed the national fervour among Scottish rugby fans in their annual contest with England or Scottish football supporters when their team was playing England in Euro '96 could hardly have failed to be impressed at these displays of pride in the national identity. There is a separate Scottish Arts Council and separate Scottish Ballet and Scottish Opera companies. These also engender a similar, if more genteel, feeling of national identity.

Popular culture also should not be forgotten for its contribution to the Scottish identity. Such icons as 'the Broons', 'Oor Wullie' and 'Irn Bru' go a long way towards initiating the feeling of

*Scottish football supporters celebrate*

Scottishness among children. Other distinctly Scottish items, goods or customs, like haggis, tartan, shortbread and Hogmanay may be trivial but, in their insidious influence on people's way of looking at themselves and perceiving differences between themselves and other peoples in the British Isles and further afield, are important in the development and reinforcement of a Scottish identity.

Evidence that Scots actually feel Scottish has been identified in many opinion polls over the years. One by MORI in 1995 showed that 64 per cent of Scots felt more Scottish than British – one of two countries in Great Britain (the other, Northern Ireland) where a majority chose the option of the home nation against Britain. However, only 30 per cent of Scots did not feel British at all. This means that a majority of Scots, while feeling Scottish and, presumably, proud of it, still feel themselves part of a larger multi-national state, viz. the United Kingdom. Most Scots can feel equally happy supporting vociferously their national team against England at football or rugby and still feel part of a larger British nation, for example during the Olympic Games or on occasions like the funeral of Diana, Princess of Wales.

STUDY TOPIC 2

# How is Scotland governed at present?

## The Secretary of State

The United Kingdom is a unitary state. This means that it has one legislature, the Westminster Parliament, making laws and one executive, the UK Cabinet, in charge of the day-to-day running of the country. Sometimes, laws are passed which affect the whole of the UK; sometimes, laws are passed which affect either England, Scotland, Wales or Northern Ireland alone; but all laws are made by the procedure of debate, scrutiny and voting in the House of Commons and the House of Lords.

The Secretary of State for Scotland is a member of the Cabinet. As such, he or she is a member of the party with the majority of seats in the Commons. This is not necessarily the party with a majority of seats in Scotland. So, it is not uncommon for a Secretary of State to be of a different party to the majority party in Scotland. This was the case from 1979 until 1997, when the Conservatives had a majority at Westminster, but a minority of seats in Scotland. Indeed, there is no constitutional convention which implies that the Secretary of State need be an MP for a Scottish constituency. Before the 1997 General Election, the Welsh Secretary was William Hague, an English MP representing Richmond, an English constituency. Since direct rule from Westminster was introduced in Northern Ireland in the 1970s, the Secretary of State has never been a Northern Irish MP. In 1997, the Conservatives did not win a single seat in Scotland. Had they won that election throughout the UK, the Secretary of State would have been a Conservative MP representing a non-Scottish constituency.

DIAGRAM 2

## The Secretary of State for Scotland

'The Government's Representative in Scotland'

- Administers the Scottish Office – Victoria Quay and Old St Andrew's House (Edinburgh) and Dover House (London)

- Accountable to Parliament for the actions of the Scottish Office at Scottish question time

- Spokesperson for government policy in Scotland

- Introduces Scottish bills in the Commons

The Secretary of State is responsible for introducing Scottish bills into the Commons, administering the Scottish Office, and is accountable to Parliament for the actions of the Scottish Office at Scottish question time. The Secretary of State is also expected to be a spokesperson for all aspects of government policy in Scotland, whether these are the specific responsibility of the Scottish Office or not. The Secretary of State is often described as "Scotland's representative in the government" although a more accurate description is "the government's representative in Scotland". After the 1997 General Election, Tony Blair appointed Donald Dewar to be the Secretary of State. There are two Ministers of State and three Under-Secretaries of State to assist the Secretary of State in running the Scottish Office. There is a Permanent Under-Secretary of State (a professional civil servant) who has the same role as Permanent Under-Secretaries in other departments. Until February 1998, this post was occupied by Sir Russell Hillhouse who has since been succeeded by Muir Russell.

# The Scottish Office

The Scottish Office is one of the largest departments of government. It has responsibility for functions which, in England, are shared by eleven different government departments. Its head-quarters, in Leith, has over 8,000 civil servants, second only to the Home Office. In 1997-98, its budget was £14.5 billion, over £130 per week for every family in Scotland, about £30 per week more than the equivalent figure for England.

The Scottish Office is divided into five main departments responsible for the administration of legislation specific to Scotland.

## The Agriculture, Environment and Fisheries Department

This department brings together responsibility for agriculture, environmental protection, water and sewerage services, sustainable development, rural affairs, natural heritage and fisheries. In pursuit of its aims, the department administers UK-wide market support schemes for agriculture, supports agricultural and fisheries research and enforces fisheries legislation in Scottish waters through the Scottish Fisheries Protection Agency. The department is responsible for the Scottish Environment Protection Agency, which took over responsibility for most aspects of pollution control and environmental protection on 1 April 1996, for Scottish Natural Heritage, and for the three new water and sewerage authorities.

## The Scottish Office Home Department

This department is responsible for policy on police, fire and social work services, criminal justice policy and civil law matters. The Scottish Prison Service is an executive agency within the department.

## The Scottish Office Education and Industry Department

This department is responsible for policy and aspects of funding for education and training in Scotland, from pre-school nursery provision through primary and secondary schools to further and higher education and vocational training. On the industry side of its responsibility, the department also supports business development and inward investment in Scotland, promotes exports and sponsors the work of public bodies involved in enterprise and tourism. It also administers the financial support arrangements for the arts and sport.

## The Scottish Office Health Department

This department has overall responsibility for the administration of the National Health Service in Scotland, including the setting of targets for health boards and the promotion of health education.

## The Scottish Office Development Department

This department is responsible for relations between central and local government, including grants, permission to borrow money and planning. It is also responsible for a range of other matters, including housing and building control, roads and transport and ancient monuments and historic buildings.

The Secretary of State also appoints members of 'quangos' – public bodies with functions related to the departments of the Scottish Office, e.g. the Scottish Fisheries Protection Agency, the Scottish Qualifications Authority, the Scottish Tourist Board, Scottish Homes, the Water Authorities and the Scottish Prison Service as well as other bodies such as health boards and NHS trusts.

DIAGRAM 3

### The Departments of the Scottish Office

The Scottish Office Agriculture, Environment and Fisheries Department

The Scottish Office Home Department

The Scottish Office Education and Industry Department

The Scottish Office Health Department

The Scottish Office Development Department

*The Rt Hon Donald Dewar*
Secretary of State for Scotland

*Henry McLeish MP*
Minister of State at The Scottish Office with responsibility for Home Affairs, Devolution and Transport

*Brian Wilson MP*
Minister of State at The Scottish Office, with responsibility for Education and Industry

*Calum MacDonald MP*
Parliamentary Under Secretary of State at The Scottish Office, with responsibility for Local Government, Housing, Planning, Area Regeneration, European Affairs and Natural Heritage. House of Commons Spokesman on Agriculture, the Environment, Fisheries and Forestry matters

*Sam Galbraith MP*
Parliamentary Under Secretary of State at The Scottish Office, with responsibility for Health, Social Work, the Arts and Sport

*Lord Sewel*
Parliamentary Under Secretary of State at The Scottish Office, with responsibility for The Scottish Office, Agriculture, Environment and Fisheries Department and for the Forestry Commission. House of Lords Spokesman on all Scottish Affairs

# Scotland in Parliament

## Scottish Questions

Each month, there is time devoted in the Commons to Scottish questions. This is when the Secretary of State and junior ministers are held to account by MPs for the functions of the Scottish Office and also government policy in general, as it relates to Scotland. All MPs can attend and ask questions. By custom, there has always been an opposition spokesperson with responsibility for Scottish affairs in the Commons – the Shadow Secretary of State – with junior shadow ministers to assist. However, after 1997, when the Conservatives had no Scottish MPs, it was felt inappropriate by the Conservative leadership to have a Shadow Scottish Secretary representing a non-Scottish seat. Consequently, a spokesman for constitutional affairs, Michael Ancram, was appointed, only part of whose remit was to act as shadow to the Scottish Secretary. It used to be the case that any non-Scottish MP who asked a question would be regarded as having broken a parliamentary convention. However, during the period 1979-97, when the Conservatives were in power at Westminster, but with a comparatively small number of Scottish MPs, more and more English Conservative MPs attended and asked questions. This action was taken in order to increase the amount of support for the Conservative Government. Eventually, such practice became accepted and was no longer regarded as unusual. Indeed, after the 1997 General Election, the only way the official opposition could take part in Scottish questions was to have non-Scottish MPs present.

There is always a junior Scottish minister in the House of Lords to introduce Scottish bills there and to promote the policies of the government. The opposition parties also have Scottish spokespersons in the Lords.

## Scottish Committees

There are distinct Scottish committees of the House of Commons which have different responsibilities, ranging from debate and legislation to scrutiny of the work of the Scottish Office.

## The Grand Committee

The Scottish Grand Committee consists of all 72 MPs for Scottish constituencies. It debates purely Scottish bills at the Second Reading although the vote is taken by the whole House, i.e. all MPs, not just those representing Scottish constituencies.

This committee has other functions as well as legislative. It debates the Scottish Estimates – the proposed government spending plans on areas of responsibility

DIAGRAM 4

## Opposition Spokespersons for Scotland (December 1997)

*Spokesman on Constitutional Affairs*
Rt Hon Michael Ancram MP (with overall responsibility for Scottish & Welsh Affairs)

*Commons Front Bench Spokesman*
Dr Liam Fox MP (Scotland)

*Spokesmen in Lords*
Rt Hon Lord Mackay of Drumadoon
Lord Mackay of Ardbrecknish

of the Scottish Office. Although the Grand Committee cannot reject these, it allows the opposition parties and backbench MPs the opportunity to gain publicity about any concerns they may have. It also holds 'Matter day' debates. There are about six of these a year and, as the name suggests, they are about matters of concern to Scotland. In the past, the government chose the subjects for debate. As part of its 'Taking Stock' exercise between 1992 and 1997, the Conservative Government allowed the opposition parties to choose some topics. Another innovation was to hold the Committee's meetings in Scotland and to rotate the venue around the country, allowing all parties the opportunity to choose its meeting place. These events are televised and have become the focus for demonstrations and lobbying of both the government and individual MPs.

## Scottish Standing Committees

These deal with the Committee Stage of Scottish bills. Like all standing committees, these must reflect the composition of the whole House, not the party strengths among Scottish MPs. This means that, when the whole House is of a different composition to that of Scottish MPs, the government of the day has to draft in non-Scottish MPs to ensure the committee's membership by party reflects the whole House. These MPs vote on Scottish legislation, even though the legislation will not affect their constituencies. This situation occurred throughout the term of office of the Conservatives from 1979 to 1997.

The Report Stage and Third Reading of Scottish bills can also be taken in the Grand Committee, although this has never happened. So, it is theoretically possible for a Scottish bill to pass through all stages, except the formal First Reading, in Scottish committees, although all meaningful voting will be done by the whole House, not just Scottish MPs.

## The Select Committee on Scottish Affairs

This committee was established in 1969. Its remit is an investigatory one, defined as examining the expenditure, administration and policy of the Scottish Office and associated public bodies. It consists of backbench MPs and, again, must reflect the composition of the whole House. It has the power to examine witnesses, including ministers and civil servants, and to scrutinise documents relevant to its enquiries. The Select Committee used these powers to great effect during the 1980s, when the Conservatives were in power. The majority of the Committee was Conservative – to reflect the whole House – and the Chairman was Labour – a concession to the political composition of Scottish MPs – although, as backbenchers, they often acted in a manner which was not party political but more in line with the independence required for their investigative role. Many Committee reports criticised the government over a number of issues, not just those related to the Scottish Office, e.g. the closure of the Gartcosh Steelworks in 1986. This led some backbench Scottish Conservatives to leave the Committee, with the result that the government could not find sufficient numbers to reflect the whole House. As a result, there were long spells when there was no Scottish Select Committee, leaving the Scottish Office as the only government department without a formal process of scrutiny. After 1997, this was not a problem since there were large numbers of Labour MPs to fill the government positions. It was uncertain, however, if enough non-Scottish Conservatives could be persuaded to be members to allow the Committee to reflect the composition of the whole House.

STUDY TOPIC 3

# Why was there a demand for change?

## Administrative Devolution or a Scottish Parliament?

The rise of the SNP, and its influence on Labour's decision to adopt the setting up of a Scottish Parliament as one of its policies, is discussed elsewhere. However, there are other concerns about the way Scotland has been governed which have been identified as reasons for the devolution of power to an elected Scottish legislature.

There is already administrative devolution to the Scottish Office, with all its functions and responsibilities. It has been argued that proper accountability cannot be delivered by six ministers who, by necessity, must split their time between Scotland and London, as well as five of the six having to look after their constituency business as MPs. A Scottish Parliament would divide responsibility for the functions of the Scottish Office among several ministers and their assistants, accountable to the Parliament and the Scottish people. It has been argued also that such accountability would detect waste and inefficiency and actually save money to be spent elsewhere or used in reducing taxes.

A Scottish Parliament would also bring under its control the many 'quangos' which have been created over the years, ranging from the White Fish Authority and health boards to the Scottish Consumers' Council and the Scottish Qualifications Authority. Appointments to these have been made in the past by the Secretary of State, without reference to any other body. Some commentators claim that, often, these have been people of the same political persuasion as the Secretary of State. During the 1980s and 1990s, this was seen as an affront to the Scottish electorate, among whom Conservatives were a small minority. It is argued that bringing these under the control of, and making them accountable to, a Scottish Parliament would make them more efficient and would also ensure that their members were representative of the electorate as a whole.

# The 'Democratic Deficit'

The distinct process for Scottish legislation at Westminster recognises the different conditions in, as well as the needs of, Scotland. However, in most cases, this usually means that the passing of this legislation depends on disinterested non-Scottish MPs being dragooned by their whips into the Commons. If this is done sensitively, then it will cause few concerns or problems, although there will be the normal political disagreements. However, there was a feeling, particularly in the 1980s, that the separate Scottish legislative process at Westminster was being used to experiment with new legislation in Scotland, before applying it to the rest of Britain. This feeling was strongest in the case of the Community Charge or Poll Tax, which is discussed elsewhere. To many, this showed what they called the 'democratic deficit' in the way in which Scotland was governed. A government which had only a minority of Scottish seats was using its non-Scottish MPs to impose a new system of local government finance, through the distinct Scottish legislative process, on a nation which had rejected such an idea through the majority of MPs for whom it had voted. A Scottish Parliament would make such a situation less likely.

A Scottish Parliament would remove the anomaly of Scotland being the only nation

in the world with a distinct legal system and body of law without a legislature.

Other people believe that a Scottish Parliament would be a focus for the national identity of Scotland, leading to a flourishing of art and culture. This cannot be proved, obviously, but it would give a nation with a strong identity a vehicle to promote art and culture which would be more responsive to their needs than a legislature 400 miles away.

Many supporters of a Scottish Parliament also see it as the engine by which constitutional reform for the whole UK can be brought about. They see it as the first step towards 'rolling devolution', where other areas of the UK would see the benefits of devolution and press for their own parliaments or assemblies – similar to what has happened in Spain over the past twenty years. Also, such an atmosphere of change could lead further – to the reform of the House of Lords, a Freedom of Information Act, a Bill of Rights and proportional representation.

DIAGRAM 5

| Party Representation in Scotland 1983-1997 (No. of MPs) | | | | |
| --- | --- | --- | --- | --- |
| | 1983 | 1987 | 1992 | 1997 |
| Conservative | 21 | 10 | 11 | 0 |
| Labour | 41 | 50 | 49 | 56 |
| Liberal Democrat | 8 | 9 | 9 | 10 |
| SNP | 2 | 3 | 3 | 6 |

# The 'Doomsday Scenario'

The attitude of the various political parties after the 1997 Election to the way that Scotland is governed was formed in the period of Conservative rule from 1979 to 1997.

The Conservatives won four consecutive general elections, sometimes with huge majorities in the UK as a whole, but were always in a minority in Scotland. Within the unitary UK state, this meant Scotland being governed from the Scottish Office by a succession of Conservative Secretaries of State, implementing policies in Scotland for which the majority of Scots had not voted.

This came at the same time as the economic and financial policies of Conservative Governments were causing a 'shake out' of old, declining industries like heavy engineering, iron and steel and shipbuilding. This had a disproportionate effect on Scotland, where unemployment began to rise rapidly and remained high during the 1980s. Meanwhile, the areas of Southern England (at least outside London) were experiencing a boom in new 'sunrise' industries. There was a buoyant housing market and people there felt prosperous. Although the 'North', in this 'North-South divide', included declining areas in the North of England too, there was a feeling in Scotland of being dominated by a prosperous and uncaring England.

By the 1987 General Election, commentators were speaking of the 'Doomsday Scenario' where, if the Conservatives won again in the UK and continued to decline in Scotland, there would be such a revulsion in Scotland that a constitutional crisis would follow. There was talk of Scottish MPs walking out of Westminster, of there being a surge in support for the SNP and independence and even of the possibility of riots in the streets. However, this did not materialise. The only mass action in Scotland was against the Community Charge and this was mainly peaceful and ceased being an issue when Mrs Thatcher resigned in 1990 and the Community Charge was replaced by the Council Tax.

# The Scottish Constitutional Convention

In 1988, the Scottish Constitutional Convention was formed. Membership was open to all political parties, to the churches, to trade unions, to representatives of local government and to other national organisations. The Labour, Liberal Democratic, Green and Communist parties all agreed to take part, as did the churches, local councils and trade unions. However, the Conservative Party and, soon after, the Scottish National Party declined to take part and nor did the Confederation of British Industry in Scotland. The remit of the Convention was to draw up a scheme of self-government for Scotland. With the absence of the SNP, the only organisation supporting independence was the small Scottish Green Party. Inevitably, this meant that any scheme would be one of devolution of power to a Scottish Parliament within the UK. Some principles for a Parliament were drawn up before the 1992 Election, but a full scheme was not agreed by then. The Convention continued its work after the Conservatives' victory at that election.

*John Major, former Prime Minister, with Ian Lang, former Secretary of State for Scotland*

## 'Taking Stock'

After 1992, the Conservative Government promised a 'Taking Stock' exercise in Scotland to review and improve the way government was conducted in Scotland. Since the Prime Minister, John Major, had made the Union of Scotland and England a key issue during the election and, since Scotland was the only UK region to swing to the Conservatives at the election, any great change in the status quo was unlikely. A White Paper, 'Scotland in the Union: a Partnership for Good' was published in 1993. Changes proposed were the right of the Grand Committee to debate the Third Reading of Scottish bills and the rotation of the venue around Scotland. The Prime Minister would also be allowed to address and be questioned by the Committee. The Secretary of State would also make more regular appearances before the Scottish Select Committee. Other changes strengthened the Scottish Office, e.g. the control of European Union funds for training was devolved from the Department of Trade and Industry to the Scottish Office. As far as their opponents were concerned, these changes did not tackle the key problem in the government of Scotland – a Scottish Office controlled by a Secretary of State without majority support in Scotland, who could use Westminster to impose policies for which the majority of Scots had not voted.

# 'Scotland's Parliament – Scotland's Right'

Meanwhile, the Scottish Constitutional Convention had published a blueprint for a Scottish Parliament – 'Scotland's Parliament – Scotland's Right' – on St Andrew's Day, 1995. This was agreed by all members and proposed a devolved Scottish Parliament within the UK. Westminster would be responsible for the economy, social security, foreign affairs and defence. Scotland would still send MPs to Westminster. The Scottish Parliament would be responsible for all the functions of the Scottish Office. There would be a total of 129 Members of the Scottish Parliament (MSPs) – 73 elected by the current Westminster constituencies (Orkney and Shetland would have one MSP each) and 56 elected by proportional representation using the Additional Member System. The Convention expressed the desire to have equal numbers of men and women in the Parliament but did not specify how this

could be achieved. The Parliament would elect a First Scottish Minister who would appoint a team of Scottish ministers – in effect, a Scottish Prime Minister and Cabinet. These would take over most of the functions of the Secretary of State and junior ministers. The Secretary of State would remain as a member of the UK Cabinet. Finally, the Parliament would be financed by a block grant (equivalent to £14.5 billion in 1997) from the UK Treasury and would be able to raise or lower income tax in Scotland by a maximum of 3p in the pound (£).

These proposals were included in both the Labour and Liberal Democrat manifestos at the 1997 Election, with the very important addition by Labour that there would be a referendum with two questions, one on the principle of establishing the Parliament and the second on whether it should have the proposed tax-varying powers.

DIAGRAM 6

## Scotland's Parliament – Scotland's Right

- A devolved Scottish Parliament within the UK
- Westminster responsible for the Economy, Social Security, Foreign Affairs and Defence
- Scotland to continue to send MPs to Westminster although numbers reduced
- Scottish Parliament responsible for all functions of the Scottish Office
- 129 Members of the Scottish Parliament (MSPs)
     73 elected from Westminster constituencies
     56 elected by Proportional Representation
- Desire for equal numbers of men and women
- Parliament to elect a First Scottish Minister
- First Scottish Minister to appoint Cabinet
- Secretary of State to remain member of UK Cabinet
- Financed by block grant from UK Treasury
- Raise or lower income tax in Scotland by a maximum of 3p in the £

## SNP and Unionist Opposition

Critics of the scheme came from the opposite ends of the debate on Scotland's future. The SNP criticised it because it would not make Scotland a sovereign state – the SNP's long-term objective – and left control of Scotland's oil resources and the revenues from these with the UK Government. Conservatives and other Unionist opponents, like Tam Dalyell, the Labour MP for Linlithgow, pointed to what they saw as weaknesses and dangers in the scheme.

The tax-varying powers were depicted as tax-raising ones and were attacked as being dangerous in that Scots would be taxed at a higher rate than other people in Britain. Also, control of local government would give the Parliament the right to change the way that businesses pay rates to councils. Both of these were seen as being disincentives to new industries being attracted to Scotland and even to established industries staying in Scotland.

## The West Lothian Question

During the 1979 referendum campaign for a Scottish Parliament, Tam Dalyell, at that time MP for West Lothian, used the following question to demonstrate what he saw as the dangers and illogicalities of devolution: "Why should I be able to ask questions and vote on matters concerning education in Blackburn, Lancashire, but not be able to do the same for Blackburn, West Lothian?" This became known as the 'West Lothian Question'. It drew attention to the fact that, after devolution, Scottish MPs at Westminster would still be able to vote on English legislation pertaining to matters which, in Scotland, would be the responsibility of the Scottish Parliament. Therefore, English MPs and, indeed, Scottish MPs, at Westminster would, by definition, be denied a vote on parallel Scottish legislation. He and other anti-devolutionists repeated this question in 1997. They saw in it a possible source of resentment among English MPs and the English people and feared it could lead to tensions between the Scottish Parliament and Westminster, eventually leading to a break-up of the UK.

### The West Lothian Question

*"Why should I be able to ask questions and vote on matters concerning education in Blackburn, Lancashire, but not be able to do the same for Blackburn, West Lothian?"*

TAM DALYELL, MP

## The Block Grant

Another source of possible tension identified by anti-devolutionists was the block grant of £14.5 billion (in 1997 terms) which would be negotiated every year. Traditionally, this had meant a higher level of spending per head of the population in Scotland than in England, based on the so-called 'Barnett Formula', particularly in the Health Service and in local government. Those opposed to devolution argued that the UK Treasury would come under pressure from non-Scottish MPs to lower this amount, since Scotland would be seen as having preferential treatment, having both its own Parliament and a higher level of funding from the Treasury than England. The Scottish Parliament would, of course, resist any reduction in the block grant. The anti-devolutionists argued that such disagreements would cause the Scottish Parliament to consider breaking away from the rest of the UK and bring an end to the Union. The fear, then, for those opposed to a Scottish Parliament, was that devolution would put Scotland on the 'slippery slope' to independence.

## Independence in Europe

To the SNP, of course, this was no fear at all, since their policy was Independence in Europe. This entails Scotland becoming a sovereign state within the European Union (EU), with its own representation on the institutions of the EU. This has attractions for many Scots, as it removes the tag of 'separatist' from the SNP and it has the capacity to give Scotland the opportunity to become one of the successful small independent states already members of the EU, e.g. Ireland, Denmark, Luxembourg.

It was with this policy that the SNP fought the 1997 Election. It gained an impressive 22.1 per cent of the vote albeit that this constituted only a small increase on their 1992 vote. After the election and

Labour's landslide victory with a commitment to legislate for a Scottish Parliament within a year, the SNP embarked on the process of re-evaluating its position on the government's devolution proposals.

## Diminishing Influence at Westminster?

Anti-devolutionists also saw the possibility of Scotland's influence at Westminster diminishing if a Parliament was established. They argued that the office of Secretary of State would disappear as most of its functions would be taken over by the new Parliament. Scotland would then lose its voice in the UK Cabinet. There was no proposal by the government to abolish the office of Secretary of State but many pro-devolutionists do concede quietly that the post may eventually 'wither away'.

Also, Scotland, traditionally, has had more MPs at Westminster than its size of population would justify in proportional terms. This was some recognition of its status as a distinct nation, of the fact that it joined voluntarily the Union with England in 1707 and that more Scottish MPs were needed to deal with Scottish legislation at Westminster, as well as playing their full part in the usual work of the Commons. However, the fact remains that if Scottish constituencies were the same average size as those in England, the number of Scottish MPs at Westminster would be around 60, rather than the 1997 total of 72. Anti-devolutionists argued that, if Scotland had its own Parliament, there was no strong case for continuing with this 'over-representation' at Westminster. This would diminish further Scotland's influence there.

It is worthy of note that, after the 1997 Election, the government conceded that legislation would be introduced to enable the Boundary Commission to make such a reduction.

# The 1997 Devolution Referendum

After the 1997 Election, Tony Blair appointed Donald Dewar, Secretary of State for Scotland, to chair a Cabinet Committee whose job was to draw up a White Paper outlining the Government's proposals for a Scottish Parliament. The White Paper, 'Scotland's Parliament', was published in July 1997. Its first print run sold out inside a day, becoming a best-seller which topped the charts for book sales in Scotland up to the day of the referendum. The proposals which it contained were largely in line with the scheme of the Constitutional Convention apart from the Labour manifesto commitment to hold a two-question referendum on the proposals. Dewar was also given responsibility to introduce a bill into Parliament to approve the referendum. The bill was duly passed and the date for the referendum was set for 11th September, 1997 – the 700th anniversary of William (Braveheart) Wallace's victory over the English at Stirling Bridge.

## 'Yes Yes' or 'Think Twice'

The Liberal Democrats, partners with Labour in the Constitutional Convention, immediately agreed to support the White Paper. The SNP, although having reservations, decided that they, too, could support a proposal to give Scotland a measure of self-government. They all agreed to support the 'Yes Yes' campaign of 'Scotland FORward', a pro-devolution organisation. They also agreed to campaign jointly and as individual parties for a double 'Yes' vote in the referendum.

An anti-devolution group, 'Think Twice', was set up to campaign for a double 'No' vote. The Conservatives decided not to join this group but did campaign for the same result. Some of the leaders of the 'Think Twice' group were also individual Conservative Party members.

## The Campaign

The campaign started badly for the pro-devolutionists when Gordon McMaster, a Paisley Labour MP, was found dead in his garage, having committed suicide. His farewell note accused fellow party members, including a neighbouring MP, Tommy Graham, of a smear campaign against him. This focused attention again on Labour Party activities in Paisley where, two years previously, allegations of corruption and criminal activity had emerged. Another Labour MP, Mohammed Sarwar of Govan, had also been suspended over allegations of bribery during the 1997 General Election campaign. A continuing inquiry into the behaviour of Glasgow City Labour Group, along with these more recent revelations, gave the anti-devolutionists a weapon to argue against the Parliament, saying that these were examples of the type of politics you could expect in a Scottish Parliament.

However, the campaign did get back on track again over the summer and the real issues relating to the Parliament came to

*Tony Blair campaigning in Scotland for the 'Yes, Yes' Vote*

the fore. Normal campaigning was suspended in early September, to show respect for the death of Diana, Princess of Wales. The following week, the week of the referendum, normal campaigning resumed. Tony Blair, still popular and even more so, following his statesmanlike conduct of affairs during the week of mourning for Diana, visited Scotland and this gave a boost to the 'Yes Yes' campaign. William Hague also visited that week but his impact was reduced by the simultaneous visit of Baroness (Margaret) Thatcher who spoke against the Parliament. The pro-devolutionists thought her intervention would actually help their cause, because she had been a very unpopular Prime Minister in Scotland and was responsible for introducing the Poll Tax in Scotland a year earlier than in England and Wales – an issue which crystallised, from the 'Yes Yes' point of view, the argument for a Parliament.

As the week wore on, opinion polls suggested a big majority for the first question – the principle of establishing the Parliament and a slightly smaller one for the tax-varying powers. One worry for the pro-devolution side was that the turnout of voters might be small, casting doubt on the legitimacy of the result.

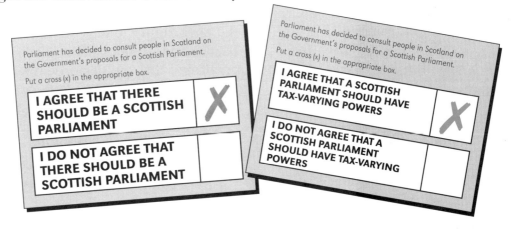

DIAGRAM 7

| The 1997 Devolution Referendum |
| --- |
| **Approval for the Parliament in Principle** |
| 74.29% Yes |
| 25.71% No |
| **Granting of Tax-varying Powers** |
| 63.48% Yes |
| 36.52% No |
| **Turnout 60.16%** |

## The People Speak

The actual results, shown above, were even better than the strongest devolution supporter was predicting, at least in private. The turnout was less than at a general election but much higher than for council or European Parliament elections. All 32 electoral areas voted 'Yes' for the first question and only two, Orkney and Dumfries and Galloway, failed to do so for the second question. Probably, the most pleasing aspect for the 'Yes Yes' campaign was that both questions were supported by more than 40% of those entitled to vote. This was the controversial barrier which caused the devolution vote in 1979 to fail.

## Future Implications

Since the referendum was Labour's idea, the result can be regarded by Labour as a great success. In particular, it showed Tony Blair to be a popular Prime Minister. He identified with the campaign and urged the Scottish electorate to "trust itself". Some commentators suggested that, even allowing for proportional representation, Labour could look forward to being the largest grouping in the Scottish Parliament after the first elections on 6 May, 1999. However, it is worthy of note that a repeat of its huge 46 per cent share of the Scottish vote gained in the 1997 General Election would still prove insufficient to secure a majority in the Scottish Parliament.

There could be several outcomes arising from this. The co-operation between Labour, Liberal Democrats and SNP during the referendum campaign could be maintained in the Parliament. However, a three-way coalition like this seems most unlikely, given that the aim of the SNP is independence while that shared by the other two parties would be the status quo (at that time) of the devolved Scottish Parliament within the UK. To some, a formal coalition between Labour and Liberal Democrats is possible, given the continuing cooperation between the two over constitutional reform. However, the most likely scenario would be a minority Labour administration seeking the support of other parties to pass legislation on particular matters as they arose – co-operation without formal coalition.

The implications for the Conservatives were very interesting. They no longer controlled any local councils in Scotland. They had no Euro-MPs in Scotland. They lost all of their Scottish Westminster seats at the 1997 General Election but still won almost a fifth of the popular vote. The irony was that, under the system of proportional representation to be used in elections to the Parliament, they would gain a percentage of seats which was closely linked to the percentage vote obtained. Therefore, the very body whose creation they had opposed since 1979 may prove to be the one which gives them the opportunity to have a 'fresh start' in Scotland. Indications after the referendum confirmed that the Conservatives would contest elections to the Parliament and there were expressions by some Scottish Conservatives of their desire to play a full part in the Parliament and make sure that the many thousands of Conservative supporters in Scotland were fully represented.

STUDY TOPIC 4

# How is Scottish local government organised?

## Democratic Accountability and Responsiveness to Local People

Central government makes a whole variety of decisions on issues such as taxation, defence and social welfare. If it is perceived as desirable that central government should make laws concerning education, e.g. the school-leaving age, then it is equally self-evident that decisions about where a school should be built should be taken by local people who know the area in which they live.

However, should decisions of this nature be taken by government appointed bodies such as health boards or by local councillors as the elected representatives of the people?

Councillors are elected to represent a ward (the equivalent of a parliamentary constituency). The councillor will be accountable to the people of that ward. This accountability is evident in a number of ways, e.g. by constituents visiting surgeries, by lobbying their councillor or presenting petitions. The councillor is ultimately accountable to constituents at the next council elections when they can continue to vote for their sitting councillor or choose an alternative. The fact that councillors are elected means that the provision of services by the council can be regarded as an expression of the democratic will of the people in that area.

It is also argued that, in a democracy, alternative sources of power to central government are intrinsically good. Often parties will be voted in to take control of their councils which are different to the ruling party in central government.

*Renfrewshire Council Headquarters, Paisley*

# How is Local Government Established and from Where Does It Derive Its Powers and Responsibilities?

## The Powers of Local Government

Local government does not exist as of its own right. Its powers are granted by central government and central government can take these powers away. The way that local government is organised is also decided by central government and can be changed by central government. In the past thirty years, for example, there have been two local government reorganisations in Scotland, as a result of two Local Government (Scotland) Acts in 1973 and 1994. There have also been numerous other Acts of Parliament which define, increase or limit the powers and obligations of local councils, e.g. the Education (Scotland) Act, 1996.

The powers of local government can be divided into three broad categories.

- Mandatory powers, i.e. those that councils must provide by law and in which they have no choice. For example, the provision of education in primary and secondary schools.

- Permissive powers, i.e. those that councils are permitted to provide, but do not have to. An example of this is sports centres.

- Discretionary powers, i.e. the power to spend limited funds in the interests of their area and its inhabitants. For example, some councils pay a Christmas bonus to pensioners in their area.

## Regions, Districts and Island Councils

Until 1995, these powers and responsibilities were divided between 9 regional and 53 district councils, a 'two-tier' system, on the Scottish mainland, while the Western Isles, Orkney and Shetland had 'all-purpose' island councils responsible for all local government functions. The regions were responsible for services which it was considered could be more efficiently and effectively delivered on a large scale, i.e. the strategic services. Usually, but not always, these were also services with large budgets. They included education, social work, police and fire, strategic planning, economic development, roads and transport, water, consumer protection, protection of coasts and registration of births, deaths, marriages and voters. Districts were responsible for housing, local planning, leisure and recreation, environmental health, parks, cemeteries, libraries and licensing of public houses and betting shops. These were usually the services which required a greater degree of local knowledge.

The 1975 reorganisation also required district or island councils to establish community councils. As their name suggests, these served an identifiable community – a housing estate in a town or city, a small village or a town which had been previously a burgh with its own burgh council. Community councils had no powers, but were to be the means whereby a community could make its feelings known to local councils serving their people on matters like planning, street lighting or school catchment areas. They were also designed to be vehicles for a community to express concerns to other public bodies, e.g. health boards.

# Local Government Reform

In 1995, new councils were elected. Under the terms of the Local Government (Scotland) Act, 1994, regions and districts were abolished and 29 new all-purpose councils were formed. The island councils remained unchanged and community councils were retained. The reasons which the Conservative Government gave for this reorganisation were that the system would be simplified and made easier for people to understand. The argument was also put forward that the removal of one tier would reduce costs and be more efficient.

However, opponents of the change pointed to the economies of scale that the larger regions could produce, e.g. by using their purchasing power to negotiate lower prices for supplies to schools than would be otherwise possible. They also argued that some of the new authorities, although smaller than the former regions, were larger than the former districts, thus making the delivery of services like housing repairs more remote from the people than before. This perception of increased remoteness was amplified by the establishment of joint boards for police, fire and water services. Previously, these had been functions of the regions but were now made up of appointees of the Secretary of State, with no guarantee of elected councillors being allocated places.

DIAGRAM 8

## The New Local Authorities in Scotland

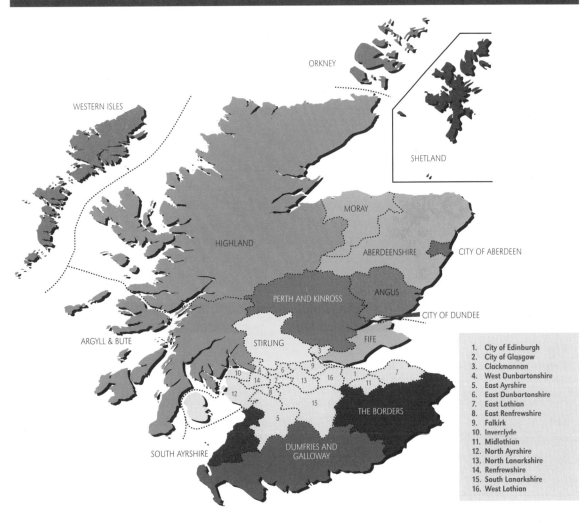

1. City of Edinburgh
2. City of Glasgow
3. Clackmannan
4. West Dunbartonshire
5. East Ayrshire
6. East Dunbartonshire
7. East Lothian
8. East Renfrewshire
9. Falkirk
10. Inverclyde
11. Midlothian
12. North Ayrshire
13. North Lanarkshire
14. Renfrewshire
15. South Lanarkshire
16. West Lothian

More controversial was the assertion by these same opponents that the changes were politically inspired, designed to reduce the influence of the Labour Party, particularly in the huge Strathclyde Region, which served half the population of Scotland. They also pointed to the fact that the reforms were not the result of an independent commission, as in England, but drawn up by government ministers. They highlighted how paragraphs of the Act were devoted to minute descriptions of the boundaries of the proposed East Renfrewshire Council, an authority coterminous with the parliamentary constituency of Eastwood, whose MP was Allan Stewart, the Minister responsible for drawing up the Bill.

Whatever the objections, the new councils came into being in 1996, one year after the elections. The Conservatives failed to win control of any of the new councils and some opponents saw this as a reaction by the Scottish people to the alleged 'gerrymandering' of the boundaries.

It is more likely that the Conservatives locally were simply suffering from the unpopularity of the Conservative Government at the time. With the election of the Labour Government in 1997, it is highly unlikely that any further changes will be made to the organisation of Scottish councils until the Scottish Parliament has had the opportunity to examine the issue, local government being one of the responsibilities devolved to it.

# How is Local Government Financed?

There are three types of expenditure which councils undertake and which have different sources of income.

## Capital Expenditure

Capital expenditure is when a council is using money to finance the building of a major new asset, such as a school or a leisure centre. Clearly payment for this type of project, costing many millions of pounds, could not be done in one financial year. Thus, a council borrows money from financial institutions and repays it over many years, like a family buying a car or a house. Sometimes, this will be done in a partnership with other bodies who will partly finance the project, e.g. with a house-building firm, a housing association or even the European Union. Permission to borrow must be received from central government.

Increasingly, councils are also looking towards Public-Private Partnerships (formerly known as the Private Finance Initiative) to finance major new capital projects. In such an arrangement, the private partners, such as banks or builders, would finance, design, build and maintain a new asset like a school and the council would lease the building from them and manage the school.

DIAGRAM 9

## Sources of Local Government Income

| For Capital Expenditure | For Revenue Expenditure | For Housing Expenditure |
|---|---|---|
| Borrowing from Banks | Grants from Central Government | Council House Rents |
| Public/Private Partnerships | Non-Domestic/Business Rates | Central Government Grants |
| European Union | Council Tax | |
| | Charges for Selected Services | |

## Revenue Expenditure

Revenue expenditure consists of the annual running costs of a council. These include the wages of employees, telephone and heating bills, photocopying and stationery as well as repaying loans for capital expenditure.

There are four main sources of income for revenue expenditure.

Grants from central government make up about 66 per cent of this income. This is to take account of the mandatory functions which central government requires of councils but there are also elements of needs to be taken into account, e.g. deprivation and poverty in urban areas and the special problems of sparsely populated, far flung, rural areas.

Non-domestic/business rates are paid by owners of shops, offices and factories. Since 1991, central government has set the level of these (this applies throughout Scotland) and distributes the income among local authorities. This means that the non-domestic/business rates have become almost like another grant from central government. They amount to 19 per cent of local government income. The implication of this is that councils have control of only 15 per cent of their total income.

Most of this remaining element of income is raised through the Council Tax, paid by the owners or tenants of residential property. There are eight bands of this tax. A house is valued at what the council assessor estimates it would have cost in April 1991. The higher the band the estimate falls into, the more is charged in Council Tax.

Councils also raise a small proportion of their income from charges for certain services, e.g. entrance to swimming pools, school meals and the hire of skips.

## Housing Expenditure

Most of the income for housing comes from council house rents, some 98 per cent. The other 2 per cent comes in the form of central government grants.

By law, the income and expenditure relating to council houses must be kept as a separate account. Expenditure is mainly on loan repayments, repair and maintenance and supervision and management.

# Political Groupings

Nowadays, all the political parties contest local government elections in all parts of Scotland. It was only in the 1980s that the Conservatives decided to participate in elections in rural Scotland. There is a strong tradition of candidates standing as 'Independents' in these areas and, even in 1995, 'Independents' were the biggest groups in Argyll and Bute, the Borders, Dumfries and Galloway, Highland and on the existing three island councils.

Parties organise themselves into 'groups' and behave in much the same way as their parliamentary counterparts. They each elect a leader, a secretary and a whip.

- The group leader is its chief spokesperson on the council.

- The secretary is responsible for organising meetings of the group and for liaising with the party and other organisations outside the council.

- The whip fulfils the same functions as whip in the parliamentary parties, i.e. communicating group decisions to its members and ensuring that they vote according to these decisions in the council and its committees.

## The Leader of the Council

The leader of the majority group becomes the Leader of the Council – equivalent to the Prime Minister at Westminster. Unlike the Prime Minister, the Leader of the Council does not officially have total discretion in choosing the chairpersons or conveners of the committees of the council – they are elected by the whole council. However, since the majority group will ensure that its candidates fill these positions, the Leader will have great influence in the choice of candidates. So, in effect, it is usually the Leader who decides who will fill these positions.

## The Provost

There is no exact equivalent at national level of the Provost or Convener of the Council. Although this is a civic post and the Provost is usually regarded as the first citizen of the council's area, representing it at official functions and welcoming visitors, this post is also elected by the whole council. This means that it is also a political post, since it will be the majority party which will decide who the Provost will be. The Provost chairs council meetings and, if a vote is drawn, will use that vote to support his/her party's position. The role of the Provost in local politics is, to some extent, a combination of elements of the roles played by the monarch, the Speaker and party politicians in national politics.

## The Group Executive

Groups meet on a regular basis and always before meetings of the whole council to decide the 'party line' on issues which may arise. In many councils, groups also meet before many committee meetings. Most groups have a group executive. This will include the leader, the secretary and the whip and several others elected by the whole group. In many cases, it is the executive which effectively decides how the whole group will vote and this means that, in councils where that group is the majority, it is in a strong position to determine the policies of the council.

## The Committee Structure

Committees play a more significant role in local government than at Westminster. The role of committees may also prove to be important within the Scottish Parliament. There are two types of committee – service committees and resource committees.

- Service committees are responsible for making policy and monitoring the delivery of a specific service within a council department, e.g. education, housing or social work.

- Resource committees deal with matters which are not the responsibility of one specific department, e.g. finance, personnel or information technology.

The most powerful committee is the Policy and Resources Committee which, in most councils, consists of all elected members, unlike other committees which will have a smaller number of councillors. The Council Leader is the chairperson of this committee, and this reflects its importance as the body which decides the overall policy of the council and the allocation of resources to departments.

Detailed discussion of policy is undertaken in the committee which has a specific remit for a service or an area of resources. This allows the full council to 'rubber stamp' the decisions of committees rather than get involved in detailed discussion of all council matters. In reality, on councils where there is a majority political party in control, the real decisions will have been taken beforehand at meetings of the ruling group or its executive.

# Council Officials and Chairpersons/Conveners

The chairpersons or conveners of committees are elected by the full council, but, as already noted, are normally the candidates of the majority party group. They chair the committee meetings and are also expected to act as spokespersons for the particular department or function to which their committee relates, e.g. education. In this regard, they are similar to political heads, i.e. ministers of central government departments. They have the main responsibility of working with the full-time council officials to see that any policy of their party is implemented by the department. Just like parties nationally, those offering themselves for election at a local level have manifestos which they wish to see implemented.

One crucial difference between the chairperson of a council committee and a minister is that a councillor is part-time. Because of this, councillors rely on the director of the department concerned for regular information and advice. However, it should be noted that directors do not have a vote at council meetings and are paid employees of the council, not elected by the public. It is crucial in this situation that a relationship built on respect and trust is built up between the chairperson and director. In this regard, they are similar to top civil servants in central government.

Directors are expected to:

- be responsible for the day-to-day running of their department and the delivery of its service;
- give professional advice to councillors, not just the chairperson, so that they can make informed decisions;
- put into practice the policies decided by councillors;
- be strictly politically neutral and show no favouritism to any political group.

# The Chief Executive

Councils are required to appoint a head of paid service, usually called a chief executive. The chief executive is the head of the management team of directors of departments and has the power to bring matters of importance to the attention of the council, for example, if it is thought that the council is proposing to contravene legislation relating to local government. The chief executive also meets regularly with and advises the Leader of the Council on overall council business. In this, the chief executive has a role similar to that of the Cabinet Secretary working with the Prime Minister.

# Local and Central Government

As stated before, local government is dependent on central government for its very existence and is ultimately responsible to it. In Scotland, the Scottish Office Development Department is responsible for relations between councils and central government. It sets the limits on expenditure by councils, including how much government grant a council will receive and whether to grant it permission to borrow for capital expenditure. It also issues guidelines and circulars to councils for implementation. The role of the Development Department will be taken over by the Scottish Parliament in the year 2000.

# Control by Central Government

Central government's ultimate control of local government has led to Parliament setting up several institutions which monitor the performance of councils. The Accounts Commission is responsible for ensuring that council expenditure is properly accounted for. If it finds that there has been unlawful expenditure, fraud, negligence or misconduct, the Secretary of State may impose a surcharge (effectively a

**DIAGRAM 10**

## Control of Local Government

### By Central Government

- The Authority of Parliament
- The Accounts Commission
- The Commissioner for Local Administration or 'Ombudsman'

### By Others

- Voters
- Taken to Court by Members of the Public
- Peer Pressure from Colleagues in COSLA
- The Media

fine) on councillors or officials. The Commission also produces 'performance indicators' designed to establish whether councils are providing high quality services. It publishes how far each council has met these indicators in a way which allows the public to compare the performances of different councils – so-called 'league tables'.

The Commissioner for Local Administration or 'Ombudsman' can investigate complaints from the public over injustice brought about by 'maladministration' by a council. This can mean neglect, bias, unfairness or excessive delay by a council. The reports of these investigations are published and councils normally accept the Ombudsman's verdict, even if it is not in their favour, and agree to pay compensation although there is no requirement for them to do so.

Since so many of a council's functions are defined by law, it can be taken to court by members of the public who feel that it has acted outwith its powers – 'ultra vires'. Again, councillors and officials can be surcharged if the court finds against them.

Although not an organ of control on councils, the Convention of Scottish Local Authorities (COSLA) was established by Act of Parliament. All Scottish councils are members. It acts as a collective voice for local authorities in their dealings with central government and has often acted as a forum for developing alternative views about issues affecting local government, particularly when the government is proposing actions with which councils disagree. It became a focus of opposition to the Conservative Government in Scotland from 1979 to 1997 and was a major partner in the Scottish Constitutional Convention.

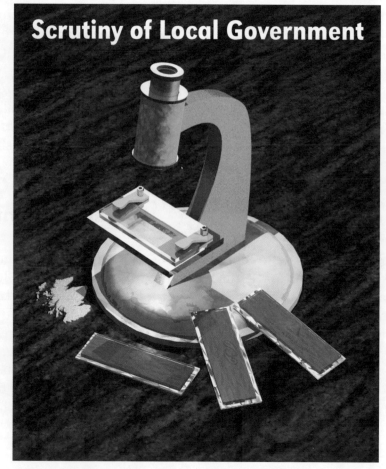

**Scrutiny of Local Government**

# Conflict between Local and Central Government

## Finance – Rates, the Community Charge and the Council Tax

One major issue relating to local government finance in the 1980s was the Community Charge or Poll Tax. This replaced domestic rates in 1989 as a means of raising income locally.

Under rates, a house was given a rateable value, based on the notional rent it might receive, e.g. £300. The council would be aware of the total rateable value of all property in its area. It would also be aware of its total proposed expenditure for the following year and the amount of government grant it was to receive. The council could then calculate how much money it needed to raise from rates, this being the difference between its proposed expenditure and the amount of government grant. It would set a 'rate per pound' for that year. If the rate per pound was 75p, then the occupier of the house with a rateable value of £300 would pay 300 x 75p = £225 in rates.

Many of those who favoured rates recognised the disadvantages but argued that all other European countries had some form of domestic property tax and that the system was based roughly on the ability to pay, the presumption being that people living in a large house could afford higher rates than those living in smaller

DIAGRAM 11

## Moving Towards the Council Tax

### Arguments against Rates

- Not based on ability to pay. An elderly retired widow could be living next door to a wealthy individual still in employment in a similar house and would pay the same rates.
- Not everyone contributed. Only the occupier – the head of the household – of a house paid rates, not all those resident in the house. A household with two adults would pay the same rates as a similar house with four or more adults.
- All registered voters could vote in council elections. So, many could be voting for a council to spend money and they would not be contributing to this expenditure.
- Many people would be using council services, e.g. street lighting, roads, libraries and social work and yet would be contributing nothing.

### Arguments against the Community Charge

- It was not based on ability to pay. The owner of a huge estate with a very large house would pay exactly the same as a tenant on the estate living in a small farmhouse.
- It was a regressive tax. The less income a person had, the greater the proportion of it that the Community Charge would absorb.
- It redistributed wealth from the poor to the affluent. A large family of adults living in a small house would have a substantial bill to pay.
- Everyone had to pay something, even those on Income Support, e.g. pensioners. Even students with no grant or guaranteed income had to pay 25 per cent of the full tax.

properties. In any case, central government grant was still the largest source of council income and everyone paid taxes, whether in income tax, VAT, petrol duty or taxes on tobacco and alcohol.

Those who favoured the Community Charge argued that it removed the unfairness of rates and made the local electorate more responsible, since everyone who voted in elections would be aware that their vote could result in a higher Poll Tax.

Scottish Councils were split on party lines over the Poll Tax – only Conservative controlled councils fully supported it. Labour, Liberal and SNP councils were opposed. Some members of the Labour Party and most of the SNP encouraged people not to pay, hoping that non-payment would cause a crisis in local government finance and force the Government to abandon the Poll Tax. The Liberal Party, although opposed, urged people not to break the law.

In any case, all Labour councils and the one SNP council at the time, Angus District, who had responsibility to collect the Poll Tax agreed to do so and issued bills and reminders to non-payers. It should be noted that most councils opposed to the Poll Tax were sympathetic to those who had genuine difficulty in paying. This has left a legacy of unpaid debt to many of these councils, running into hundreds of millions of pounds across Scotland. Such a situation has added to the difficulties faced by councils in delivering their services to the standard desired.

Other unfortunate legacies of the Poll Tax were the development of a culture of non-payment, which has carried over into the Council Tax system, and a deliberate decision by many not to register to vote. The information used to compile electoral rolls was employed to construct Council Tax registers and some people took the decision not to register to vote in order to avoid paying.

The Poll Tax era was relatively short and effectively ended with the resignation of Margaret Thatcher. However, during the period of its implementation, it soured relations between many councils and central government. The Council Tax was introduced in 1991 and it is similar to rates in being a tax on property rather than on individuals.

## Controlling Council Spending

Other sources of friction between central government and councils in the 1980s also concerned finance. In its desire to control all public expenditure, the Conservative Government gave itself powers to control council spending. These included:

- the power to 'rate cap', i.e., intervene to lower the level of rates, Poll Tax or Council Tax set by a council and to 'clawback' some government grant when expenditure limits had been breached;

- a cut in Housing Support Grant to 2 per cent and in the amount which councils could allocate to council housing from their general budgets, the Revenue Fund Contribution – now at nil. This forced up the rents of council houses and made the buying of these more attractive to their tenants;

- stricter controls over capital spending;

- the introduction of the Private Finance Initiative (PFI). Under the PFI, a private company might build and manage a facility, e.g. a school or leisure centre and the council would pay that company for the delivery of the service. By early 1997, no such agreements had been made by Scottish councils. However, later in the year, some councils were beginning to consider proposals to fund new schools under this initiative which has now been re-named Public-Private Partnerships by the Labour Government.

The Labour Party has stated its decision to remove rate capping, but it may allow this to wait until a Scottish Parliament can examine the issue.

# Education

## Proposing School Closures

In the 1980s, there did not exist in Scotland the same ideological split between the parties about the way local authority schools are organised as there was in England and Wales. There was a consensus that comprehensive education in secondary schools was here to stay and that there would be no return to the selection of pupils for secondary education. It was also thought that primary schools were performing much better than their counterparts in England and Wales. There were, however, several issues which caused conflict between councils and central government.

The Conservative Government was determined to reduce public expenditure or, at least, get the best value for money already being spent. One way it saw of achieving this in local government was to force the closure of schools whose rolls were falling and where there were many fewer pupils than places. They argued that, if these were closed, the savings made could be used to improve or repair other schools or even build new ones. Councils wanted to resist this, since they knew that any proposal to close a school would be met with opposition from parents and the larger community, leading to unpopularity for councillors. However, as the central government grant for schools was cut, they agreed reluctantly to look at candidates for closure.

The strategy which most authorities applied was not simply to close a school with few pupils, since these might be relatively new, with buildings in better condition than more popular ones which would require major refurbishment. Instead they drew up proposals to close older schools, regardless of their roll, redraw the boundaries of catchment areas and reallocate pupils to the newer, emptier schools.

This might have made financial sense, but, because the schools which were older tended to be the more popular ones, it caused unrest among many parents. The situation had been brought

*Paisley Grammar School, Paisley*

about by another change which the government had introduced early in the 1980s – that which allowed parents to make placing requests for their children to attend a school which was not the designated one for their area. This led to many schools, which were perceived as being 'good' academically, becoming very full, and other schools, who were losing their potential pupils, to have falling rolls. The councils were seen as taking decisions which would deny these parents their choice and force their children to attend schools which they had declined to send them to in the first place.

The situation was seen in microcosm in Paisley in Strathclyde, where the Regional Council in 1987 had drawn up a strategy which would have seen the closure of the popular Paisley Grammar, whose buildings were over 100 years old, and the reallocation of its pupils to other secondaries which were newer, but less popular. There was a great deal of protest by parents and even the intervention, by means of a letter of support from Prime Minister Thatcher to the Head Teacher of Paisley Grammar.

In the end, the Regional Council abandoned this strategy, as it met similar opposition throughout Strathclyde. Most popular schools, including Paisley Grammar, remained open. However, it did leave a feeling of injustice within Strathclyde, since they were being blamed for carrying out a policy which had been urged on them by the Conservative Government.

# School Boards and 'Opting Out'

Related to this controversy, although not obviously directly, were another two innovations which the Government introduced through legislation. One was the decision to allow, by law, every school in Scotland to have its own school board. A majority of its members were parents with representation for teachers and other co-opted members. Boards would have the right to approve the spending of the head teacher, to receive information about the school from the council and to have a say in the appointment of senior staff, including the head teacher.

However, the most important power which a board might use would be to initiate a ballot among parents to ascertain whether the school wished to become self-governing, another right given by legislation at the same time. This would have meant that a school threatened by closure, which still had a healthy roll, like Paisley Grammar, could free itself from council control and survive as an independent entity, though still funded by public money. These two measures gave parents the opportunity, if they wished, to break the hold of councils on schools which might be targets for closure and was a threat to the overall power of councils which, in Scotland, were overwhelmingly Labour.

As it turned out, by 1997, only two schools in Scotland had become self-governing. The new Labour Government returned them to local council control and stated that no others would be allowed to 'opt-out' of council control. They also promised to reform, though not abolish school boards. As for closures of schools with falling rolls, by 1997, even Labour councils, burdened with the responsibilities of power, had accepted the arguments for this and the idea was not as controversial as it was when first raised.

# Housing

## Sale of Council Houses

Before 1979, there was consensus among all parties that councils should provide cheap housing for rent. This changed in the 1980s, in the first few years of the 'Thatcher Revolution'.

One of the first things which the Conservative Government did was to make it mandatory on councils to sell houses to sitting tenants of over three years tenure. This was controversial enough, since most councils in Scotland argued that the waiting list for council houses was long and growing and that selling some would lengthen these queues. Also, those tenants who wanted to buy were those who lived in houses which were considered 'good', either because of the social conditions of the area, the type of house or the state of repair of the house. The council would be left with the 'worst' houses. Also, once the tenants decided to sell their houses, they would go on the open market to the highest bidder and would not be allocated, as before, when they were council-owned, to local people in need of a home.

In addition, the Government also required councils to sell these houses at a discount of up to 75 per cent on their market value. Councils were still having to repay charges for loans which built the houses, had also probably spent many thousands on renovating each house and discovered that they were to receive only a fraction of their value. This all added to a drain on the budget which each council had for housing. Added to the changes in the Housing Revenue Account, it amounted to an attack on the concept of cheap council housing for those who could not afford a mortgage.

The Conservative Government argued that their plans would decrease the reliance of people on the state, part of their ideology. They also argued that selling council houses at a discount would give people, who would not otherwise have it, an entry point to the housing market – they would buy their first home cheaply, sell it at a profit and then buy a larger house. This would all contribute to the creation of a 'property-owning democracy', in which people, because they possess property, will feel they have a stake in society and become responsible citizens – another traditional Conservative ideological strand.

## Housing Associations

Another development in public housing which the Conservatives introduced was to encourage housing associations to take over the task of building homes for rents from councils. An agency, Scottish Homes, was set up, funded by public money. It had the task of allocating grants to these associations, which the Government felt would be more responsive to the needs of communities and special groups, e.g. particular areas of towns and cities and

*Partick Housing Association, Glasgow*

disabled people. Many Labour councils, which were hostile to this development at first, eventually saw them as a means to form partnerships to improve their housing stock and, in some cases add to it. In terms of this partnership, councils might donate land for building in return for the right to allocate some of the houses. On other occasions, large areas of housing stock were handed over to housing associations to renovate and let to local people.

The new Labour Government might be more sympathetic to allowing councils to build and let housing. However, the acceptance of much of the Conservative changes by councils themselves probably means there will be no return to the large-scale building of new council homes of the 1950s and 1960s.

# Allegations of Corruption

## Glasgow and Paisley

Labour's stewardship of local government in Scotland in the 1990s was called into question by three affairs which developed in councils within the West of Scotland, which were Labour controlled.

In Glasgow, there were allegations that councillors had offered their votes to candidates for the group leadership in return for attendance at conferences or for trips abroad to represent the Council.

In Paisley, there were allegations of corruption and even criminal activity by councillors and by directors of a council-owned company. This matter was brought into focus when the MP for Paisley South committed suicide and blamed fellow

*John Smith, former Leader of the Labour Party*

party members for conducting a smear campaign against him.

The Labour Party set up inquiries into the conduct of the Labour Groups and the party organisation in Glasgow and Renfrewshire. By late 1997, the inquiry into Renfrewshire had still to publish its report. The inquiry into Glasgow recommended the suspension of nine Labour councillors, including the Leader and the Lord Provost and there was the possibility of legal action following the inquiry and the recommended disciplinary action.

## Monklands

One other affair which had run its course by 1997 (and which had made national headlines) concerned Monklands District Council, on the eastern border of the City of Glasgow.

Monklands District consisted of two large towns, Coatbridge and Airdrie and several former mining and steel villages, together with some small rural communities. What made Monklands of interest to people, not only in Scotland, but throughout the UK was the fact that one of its MPs, Tom Clarke, for Monklands West, had become the Shadow Secretary of State for Scotland, after being elected to the Shadow Cabinet in 1992, and the other, John Smith, for Monklands East, had been elected the Leader of the Labour Party after the General Election of the same year.

## Allegations

If it had not been for this fact, the situation, which began in 1992, would scarcely have made much impact, either in Scotland or at UK level. The District Council was Labour controlled, with eighteen Labour and two SNP councillors. After the 1992 District elections, the Labour Group chose its candidates for leader, provost and the conveners of committees. Four Labour councillors from Airdrie went public to complain that far too many positions of power in the council – including the Leader and Provost – were being given to councillors from Coatbridge, to the detriment of the rest of the district – although, some convenerships had been given to councillors from the villages and other minor positions to Airdrie councillors.

## 'Jobs for the Boys'

At the same time, the letters column of the local newspaper, the Airdrie and Coatbridge Advertiser, published correspondence which alleged that the council practised a sectarian employment policy, preferring to employ Catholics to other religions or none. This was a controversial issue in Monklands, since Coatbridge had always been regarded as a Catholic town and Airdrie a Protestant one, although there were sizable minorities of both religions in the town where the other was the majority. Also, in the area of employment, it was alleged by some of the four Airdrie councillors and others that 'nepotism' was being practised in the council, with many councillors' relatives being employed. There were other claims by Labour's opponents, the SNP and the Conservatives, that membership of the Labour Party was an advantage in gaining employment with the council or in acquiring a council house.

The four Airdrie councillors also raised an old issue – that spending on major projects favoured Coatbridge to the detriment of other areas of the district. They cited three major projects – the Time Capsule leisure centre, Drumpellier Country Park and the Summerlee Heritage Museum – all in Coatbridge. It is interesting to note that all three projects received approval from the full council, including councillors from Airdrie and the other areas, before they went ahead. The land on which Drumpellier Country Park was developed was bequeathed in the Nineteenth Century to the people of Coatbridge and was the property of the District Council, as was the land on which the Time Capsule was built. All three were developed as part of a strategy to attract tourism to the whole district and were the result of collaboration by the District Council and other agencies such as the Countryside Commission, the European Union, the Scottish Office and the Lanarkshire Development Agency.

## Headline News

The affair had a mixture which made it attractive to the media – sectarianism, nepotism, public disagreements between councillors in the same group and ancient rivalry between two towns. What made it irresistible was that the district lay within the parliamentary constituencies of two senior Labour politicians, including the Leader of the Party himself. Monklands was rarely out of the headlines and was clearly an embarrassment to the Labour Party.

In late 1992, the Scottish Labour Party Executive set up its own inquiry into the running of the Labour group, of the district party and of the two constituency parties. The 1993 inquiry report made recommendations, which were actually instructions, on how to improve the running of these bodies, such as a wider representation on council committees and new standing orders for the three party units concerned. It stated that its remit did not cover the allegations about employment and the spending imbalance between the two towns, since it had no locus in these matters and suggested that the Scottish Office should initiate its own inquiry into these.

This did not satisfy the Airdrie councillors and their supporters in the party, nor Labour's opponents. If anything, things became more bitter. The Airdrie councillors, now known popularly as 'the rebels', voted against group decisions in the council and there were several suspensions. The local paper published continually the comments of the rebels and their supporters and national TV took an interest. Even an Australian newspaper published several stories about the affair.

## 'Monklandsgate'

In May 1994, John Smith died and a by-election was held the next month. The campaign was dominated by what had become known popularly as 'Monklandsgate'. The Labour candidate, Helen Liddell, was under fire from all sides, particularly in the Airdrie part of the constituency – about one-tenth of the constituency lay in Coatbridge. A serious blunder was made in the campaign when a decision was made by the campaign leaders to change the agreed line which Tom Clarke and John Smith had followed for years – that the allegations were untrue and had no foundation. The campaign announced that the spending patterns by the council were "unacceptable". This was done while Tom Clarke was on a flight from London and due to be interviewed at Glasgow Airport about urban aid projects in his constituency unaware of the development in the campaign. He repeated the assertion he and Smith had made since 1992. There was an image of the campaign being split. As it turned out, Labour won the by-election with a very much decreased majority – it was calculated that it was the Coatbridge part of the constituency which swung the vote for Labour, with Airdrie voting for the SNP in great numbers.

## The Black Report

The following year the District Council was persuaded to initiate its own inquiry into the whole affair. This was carried out by Professor Black of Edinburgh University and became known as the 'Black Report'. It seemed to agree with all the allegations made against the council and was used by the council leadership's opponents as justification for their criticisms. All former Monklands councillors were debarred by the Labour Party from holding office in the Party or on the new North Lanarkshire Council.

# The Nimmo Smith Report

Following this, the Secretary of State established the Scottish Office's own statutory inquiry, headed by William Nimmo Smith QC. Meanwhile, the Labour Party inquiry continued. The Nimmo Smith Report, in December 1995, was very critical of the Black Report which, it said, only repeated allegations and did not investigate them. It also criticised the local paper for not checking some of the stories it had published about the affair. It found no evidence of nepotism nor sectarianism in the practices of the council, nor any other wrongdoing in the discharging of the council's duties, nor any favouritism to party members. It did concede that the Labour Group leadership was a strong one, which could make some members feel that their views were not being considered. It did not examine the issue of the alleged spending imbalance between Coatbridge and Airdrie.

The Labour leadership of the council felt exonerated by what had been the only official report into the workings of the council and, by far, the most thorough. It came as a shock, therefore, when the Labour Party inquiry recommended that the debarring of former Monklands councillors from party positions and from convenerships in North Lanarkshire Council should remain in place until the next council elections. This was later dropped and several councillors from the former Monklands had, by 1997, posts of varying responsibility in North Lanarkshire. By this time, 'Monklandsgate' as an issue of public interest had faded from memory.

If one lesson can be gleaned from the Monklands affair, it is how, whenever a party has almost total control for a long period of time, the main opposition to its leadership emerges usually from within its own ranks. This kind of opposition is often treated as such and becomes a faction, with its members considered last for posts of responsibility. When ambitions are thwarted, disagreements within the ruling party can become public.